BANGLADESH AND PAKISTAN

ADST-DACOR Diplomats and Diplomacy Series

Since 1776, extraordinary men and women have represented the United States abroad under all sorts of circumstances. What they did and how and why they did it remain little known to their compatriots. In 1995 the Association for Diplomatic Studies and Training (ADST) and Diplomatic and Consular Officers, Retired, Inc. (DACOR) created the Diplomats and Diplomacy book series to increase public knowledge and appreciation of the professionalism of American diplomats and their involvement in world history. Former U.S. ambassador William Milam's *Bangladesh and Pakistan: Flirting with Failure in South Asia* is the 34th volume in the series.

OTHER TITLES IN THE SERIES

Brown, Gordon, *Toussaint's Clause: The Founding Fathers and the Haitian Revolution*

Cohen, Herman J., *Intervening in Africa: Superpower Peacemaking in a Troubled Continent*

Cross, Charles T., *Born a Foreigner: A Memoir of the American Presence in Asia*

Grove, Brandon, *Behind Embassy Walls: The Life and Times of an American Diplomat*

Hart, Parker T., *Saudi Arabia and the United States: Birth of a Security Partnership*

Hoyt, Michael P. E., *Captive in the Congo: A Consul's Return to the Heart of Darkness*

Hume, Cameron R., *Mission to Algiers: Diplomacy by Engagement*

Kux, Dennis, *The United States and Pakistan, 1947–2000: Disenchanted Allies*

Lidegaard, Bo, *Defiant Diplomacy: Henrik Kauffmann, Denmark, and the United States in World War II and the Cold War 1939–1958*

Loeffler, Jane C., *The Architecture of Diplomacy: Building America's Embassies*

Miller, Robert H., *Vietnam and Beyond: A Diplomat's Cold War Education*

Parker, Richard B., *Uncle Sam in Barbary: A Diplomatic History*

Pezzullo, Ralph, *Plunging into Haiti: Clinton, Aristide, and the Defeat of Diplomacy*

Schaffer, Howard B., *Ellsworth Bunker: Global Troubleshooter, Vietnam Hawk*

Straus, Ulrich, *The Anguish of Surrender: Japanese POWs of World War II*

Stephenson, James, *Losing the Golden Hour: An Insider's View of Iraq's Reconstruction*

WILLIAM B. MILAM

Bangladesh and Pakistan
Flirting with Failure in South Asia

Columbia University Press
New York

An ADST-DACOR Diplomats and Diplomacy Book

Columbia University Press
Publishers Since 1893
New York

Library of Congress Cataloging-in-Publication Data

Milam, William B.
Bangladesh and Pakistan : flirting with failure in South Asia / William B. Milam.
    p. cm. — (ADST-DACOR diplomats and diplomacy series)
Includes bibliographical references and index.
ISBN 978-0-231-70066-5 (cloth : alk. paper)
  1. Pakistan—Politics and government. 2. Bangladesh—Politics and government. 3. Islam and politics—Pakistan. 4. Islam and politics—Bangladesh. 5. Pakistan—Civilization. 6. Pangladesh—Civilization. I. Title.
DS384.M38 2008
954.9105--dc22
                                        2008037416

References to Internet Web sites (URLs) were accurate at the time of writing. Neither the author nor Columbia University Press is responsible for URLs that may have expired or changed since the manuscript was prepared.

The views and opinions in this book are solely those of the author and do not necessarily reflect those of the Association for Diplomatic Studies and Training, Diplomatic and Consular Officers, Retired, Inc., or the Government of the United States.

CONTENTS

ACKNOWLEDGMENTS

There is a long list of friends and colleagues whose comments, criticism, ideas, and encouragement helped shape this book and make it better than it otherwise would have been. Its remaining imperfections are, of course, my responsibility alone.

First, I will always be grateful for the place, space, and welcome at the Woodrow Wilson International Center for Scholars that Lee Hamilton and his colleagues have accorded me. I can't think of a more congenial and supportive atmosphere in which to turn out a first book, or any book. Lee Hamilton has been gracious, warm, and always interested in and supportive of my work. In addition, he oversees what must be the most stimulating lunch conversations in Washington. Bob Hathaway, the Chief of the Center's Asia Department, read the manuscript early on and provided extremely trenchant ideas on how to improve it. Dennis Kux, my colleague in the seventh-floor bullpen of Senior Scholars, also read it early and provided many useful suggestions on organization, style, and substance. The good humor and moral support of the other Senior Scholars there, John Sewell, Bill Krist, Zed David, and David Birenbaum kept me going through some down periods.

The book benefited greatly from the insightful comments of several helpful reviewers. The late Craig Baxter, who sadly passed away early in 2008, and did not see the final version, was very supportive. His advice about the book as well as about the ways of the publishing world was instrumental in bringing it to this point. Dr. Mathew J. Nelson, whom I have not met, but hope to soon, provided a review that guided me through the last phases of writing and revision that, I believe, made a manuscript into a real book. The anonymous reviewer of an early draft helped set it on a much clearer course, convincing me that it lacked a clear focus at that early stage.

Michael Dwyer, who not only is Managing Director of Hurst Publishers but also served as copyeditor for this volume, deserves much credit for its pace and readability. His colleague at Hurst, Maria Petalidou, battled the many technical glitches that plagued the back and forth transmissions of the edited versions of the manuscript, and though these slowed the process down a bit, she won the battle. I am very grateful. Thanks also to Margery Thompson, Publishing Director of the Association for Diplomatic Studies and Training, for her excellent advice and assistance, and to the Association itself, for adding the book to the Diplomats and Diplomacy Series.

A number of research assistants helped with different phases of the book, and I owe them all much gratitude. I want especially to mention Sam Franz, who helped with the early chapters, Samier Mansur, who helped accumulate much of the data in chapter 9, especially on social development, and Prashina Gogomal, who helped much with the data collection of the middle chapters.

Finally, I cannot end this without a special acknowledgment to the man I have considered my mentor and model for almost 40 years: Sidney Weintraub, has always given me the encouragement and inspiration of his own example. It was on Sid, who has published many fine books on Latin America, that I first tried out the idea of a book like this, as well as the idea of my taking up writing after a life in the Foreign Service. His positive reaction to the concept of the book (which remains as I envisioned it at the beginning) and his confidence in my ability to write it is what launched this project.

Erika and Fred suffered through their dad's ups and downs while writing the book and—either at a distance or close up—have been constant in their encouragement and understanding. My gratitude and love to them.

Thanks again to all.

PREFACE

This is an interpretive book about Bangladesh and Pakistan since they separated in 1971 based on my first-hand experience as US Ambassador to each country, my close monitoring of their evolution in subsequent years, and my research into their histories and cultures. I hope that *Bangladesh and Pakistan* will prove useful to many different readers who are interested in South Asia. While it makes no claim to be an academic treatise, scholars and students may benefit from the personal experiences it offers and the analytical insights it develops.

The text is arranged thematically so that the democratic episodes in both countries are treated together even though they were separated by periods of military intervention, and military interventions are also treated in a similar fashion even though they were interspersed by years of democratic, or semi-democratic, rule. It seems to me that the democratic episodes are more like each other than they are like the military episodes, and deserve to be treated as such. The same goes for the military episodes.

Economic and social development features only briefly in this book. Its less thematic and more episodic treatment is because it appears to be characterized by long-term behavioral trends. Since social development is, in large part, a function of attitudes toward, and the role of, Non-Governmental Organizations (NGOs), at least in Bangladesh, I have included a section in the economic/social chapter on how NGOs operate in both countries. Opinions of, and behaviour toward, NGOs also are good barometers of social change in both countries.

The book has several recurring motifs. Religion is one—the role and impact of Islam on political, economic and social development. Islam has played a very important role in both the eastern and western peripheries of the Indian subcontinent, being the religion of the majority of the population of the two regions—in contrast to the rest of India, which is, and always was, predominantly Hindu, albeit with a substantial Muslim minority (151 million people) of its own.

I include this discussion of religion because of the irony that the public rationale which induced a majority of Muslims in Punjab, Sindh, NWFP, Balochistan, and Bengal to opt for the Partition of India was that Islam in the subcontinent was under threat, and that Muslims needed a "homeland" in South Asia. Yet religious ties could not hold West and East Pakistan together in the face of large cultural differences and gross political incompetence. It was this conundrum that in some senses prompted me to write *Bangladesh and Pakistan*.

And no wonder. As the historian Ayesha Jalal persuasively argues, Muslim concerns, until late in the game, were mainly about minority rights— the rights of the Muslim minority and how power would be shared—in a Hindu-majority independent India.[1] This sprang from a fear of Hindu majoritarianism. The movement for a separate Pakistan took shape and cloaked itself in communal language only when its political prospects appeared to be very dim, after an especially dismal showing in the election of 1937. Donning such a cloak has distorted and diverted both countries from healthier, perhaps more democratic, development.

I have run into some trouble with religious scholars who are experts in Islam because one of the themes of this book is that both the Muslim states of South Asia are threatened by extremists who profess "political Islam," i.e. Islamism. In several chapters, I use the word "Jihadists," to denote those Islamists who in the name of "political Islam" threaten the very existence of the state we know as Pakistan and, to a lesser extent, of Bangladesh.

The words "Islamist" and "Jihadist" often elicit more heat than light, so a clarification is in order. In this book, "Islamist' and "Jihadist" are not interchangeable. That they are often used as synonyms in Western public discourse is not only misleading, but also unfair.

I believe that the threat posed by Jihadists to both Bangladesh and Pakistan will become clearer as readers persevere with this book, but it is not intended to be taken as an extrapolation to other parts of the Islamic world or to all groups that call themselves Islamist in Muslim South Asia. There are Islamist political parties, NGOs, charities, and other groups throughout that world that do not threaten the state. Many Islamist political parties assert that they are not only democratic in nature but wish only to come to power

---

1   Ayesha Jalal, *The Sole Spokesman – Jinnah, the Muslim League and the Demand for Pakistan* (Cambridge: Cambridge University Press, 1985), p. xvii, see also pp. 7-34.

under democratic procedures. Turkey is the only Muslim country in which an Islamist party has both been elected and had a chance to govern (the FIS Islamist election victory in Algeria in 1991 was annulled by the army).

Experts point out that there is a long history of efforts by Islamic religious groups to make the language of Islam politically meaningful, and this has been true in South Asia as well as the rest of the Muslim world. This would be, I suppose, the short description of Islamism. A longer description of Islamism that I have found comes from a March 2005 publication of the International Crisis Group, whose report defines Islamism as "synonymous with 'Islamic activism', the active assertion and promotion of beliefs, prescriptions, laws or policies that are held to be Islamic in character. There are numerous currents ... [but] what they hold in common is that they found their activism on traditions and teachings of Islam as contained in scripture and authoritative commentaries."[2]

This is not what I am talking about when I describe "Jihadist" groups that threaten the Muslim states of South Asia. The former are extremist in nature and accept, indeed often advocate, the use of violence as a means of gaining political power. There are distinctions between their views of the perfect state, but very little difference among the methods they would employ to achieve one.

Throughout the Islamic world, Jihadists can be divided into three groups: those who defend what they regard as encroachments by non-Muslims on Muslim homelands (called Irredentists); those who use violence to topple regimes in Muslim countries they consider apostate, i.e. "the near enemy;" and those who use violence against "the far enemy," non Islamic countries they consider their implacable enemies—Western countries, in particular the United States—which they believe are eternally hostile to Islam and to their goal of forcing Islamism on the Islamic world.[3] In general, Jihadists consider themselves the armed vanguard of Islamism.

Pakistani and Bangladeshi Jihadists are of all three varieties, but this book concentrates on those that are a particular danger to the two states themselves. Many analysts suspect that these South Asian Jihadists are driven by

---

2   ICG, *Understanding Islamism, Middle East/North Africa Report no. 37* (International Crisis Group [hereafter ICG], March 2, 2005).

3   Fawaz Gerges, *The Far Enemy: Why Jihad Went Global* (New York, Cambridge University Press, 2005). Irredentist Jihadis, according to Gerges, are those who struggle to defend or redeem land they consider to be part of *dar al-islam* (the House of Islam). But is the house of Islam that territory that is now majority Muslim in population, or is it territory that the Ottoman and Mughal Empires controlled 400 years ago, or that the Islamic Caliphate controlled 1250 years ago? A lot depends on that definition.

a Leninist mindset. Their objective is to subvert the state and take it over in any way possible in order to impose their social and political agenda. Thus the word Islamist, as used here, is not a pejorative; but the word Jihadist is.

The great majority of Muslims in Bangladesh, Pakistan, and all of South Asia, I believe, do not accept the larger part of the Islamist retrogressive agenda, and most certainly reject Jihadists who wish to achieve it by revolutionary, Leninist methods. Most South Asian Muslims seek to live in prosperous, democratic, and modern Islamic countries. And, by the way, there are many Islamic politicians and Islamic political parties that are not Islamist and certainly not Jihadist.

Islam in South Asia cannot be understood without reference to Sufism. It was the Sufi mystics and missionaries that converted most Bangladeshi and Pakistani Muslims to that faith, in a long and complicated process, and the legacy of that Sufi conversion remains a strong influence in the political and social development of both countries.

Another motif in this book is culture. The interaction of culture with religion has been very important, especially in the growth of Islam, in South Asia. Culture has been influenced by Islam, and has influenced the tone and expression of Islam. This has affected development across the spectrum, including the role and impact of NGO operations in each country as well as the psychology—the mindset—of Bangladeshis and Pakistanis. History is yet a third important motif, especially the historical legacy of two bloody partitions.

One cannot write a book about Bangladesh and Pakistan and ignore their often antagonistic relationship with India. This is another of the volume's recurring motifs. The behemoth next door has been an important factor in the politics of both countries. The almost six-decade long fear and hostility of Pakistan toward India, that precipitated three wars and at least one mini-war, is what feeds the security paranoia that has driven Pakistani political development toward the praetorian state that it seems to have become.

INTRODUCTION

THE TURNING POINTS

Dhaka, December 6, 1990

The call came from my Deputy while I was dining with some friends. After months of increasingly violent demonstrations against him, President Hussain Muhammed Ershad had suddenly appeared on state television and announced his resignation. It was news that most of the nation had waited for during those turbulent months, but news that many believed they would never hear. For eight years, after the military coup he led, Ershad had ruled arbitrarily and fended off all attempts to unseat him, the army his power base and ultimate protector.

Over those eight years, he had spent much political capital seeking to legitimize his government, attempting to obscure its military core with civilian camouflage. This included his leaving the Army and becoming a civilian President, building his own political party, recreating a subservient parliament, and running elections—which he made sure would come out his way. (In one way or another, he imitated Ziaur Rahman's earlier pattern—which his Pakistani counterpart, Zia ul Haq also copied.) But Ershad's power base remained the military.

In the turbulent months that led to his resignation, the President had run through all the options. He tried to divide the opposition, a tactic that he had used successfully many times before, and which usually had proved feasible because of the contempt with which the leaders of the Bangladesh National Party (BNP) and the Awami League (AL), the two main political parties, held each other. In late November he tried to use force by declaring an emergency and a curfew in Dhaka. This didn't work either. In early

1

December, he finally had been forced to call on the ultimate option—the army, which had stood stolidly aside.

Most observers expected the army to intervene on his side. After all, with its history and tradition of intervention in politics, both as part of the Army of United Pakistan which had ruled during most of that country's history as well as having intervened twice since Bangladesh's independence, was it not likely the Army would step in again to save one of its own? Ershad asked a trusted intermediary, a serving general, to enlist the Army's support, in effect a request that it assume the role of the police and quell the civil unrest which was paralysing Bangladesh and pushing his Presidency to the brink.

In a departure rarely seen until then in South Asia—or, for that matter in much of the developing world—the Bangladesh Army drew back from politics and refused to intervene. In what must have been one of the most interesting meetings in South Asian political history, army leaders told Ershad's envoy that the President was on his own in this crisis—the army would not fire on Bangladeshi citizens to keep him in power. Ershad had run out of time and of options.

"Bliss was it that dawn to be alive, but to be young was very heaven."[1]

In 1990, world politics were rapidly changing. The Berlin Wall had been dismantled, and the Soviet Union had lost control of much of its eastern and central European empire. A year later the Soviet Union itself would come tumbling down. A wave of democracy seemed to be sweeping the world—in Eastern and Central Europe, in the Philippines, and even (ostensibly) in Pakistan; why not in Bangladesh?

Perhaps Begum Khaleda Zia and Sheikh Hasina, the leaders of the BNP and of the AL, and their parties, as well as the Bangladeshi people, were swept up in the euphoria for democracy and freedom that was circling the globe. For whatever reason, the two major parties and most of the minor ones (except Ershad's own party) had put aside their usual hostility and created a true peoples' movement that overthrew a military government.

The next day, crowds numbering in the hundreds of thousands thronged the streets of Dhaka in a joyous and festive mood. I had been called, along with all the other ambassadors, to see the new President. As my car snaked its way slowly through the massive, euphoric, but peaceful, crowds I noticed that almost everyone looked very young—in their teens or twenties. Those

---

1   William Wordsworth, "The Prelude, XI, 1, 108," *Complete Poetical Works* (London: Macmillan, 1888).

following events in Dhaka in the West may have been reminded of the euphoria of Wordsworth's encomium to the French Revolution.

That may have been the high point of modern Bangladeshi politics. The feeling of pride and of a united national resolve, the almost palpable sense of optimism, which may have peaked that afternoon, remained strong and tangible for several months. But the signs of venality and partisanship, often the most common characteristics of Bangladesh's poisonous political culture, soon reappeared and the approaching election increasingly corroded the short era of good will that Ershad's collapse had precipitated.

The pandemic of euphoria that swept the world in those turbulent years made us all feverish with hope and optimism that democracy was here to stay. One of the most notable expressions of this fervor was Francis Fukuyama's book, *The End of History* which, whether the author intended it or not, led to a widespread belief that democracy was an automatic outcome of the dynamic forces of history that were coming together in the late twentieth century.[2]

As it turned out, Bangladesh is a good example that real sustainable democracy requires more than hope—and an Army which eschews political intervention. It requires history—a history of strong and deep institutions, such as a judiciary, that protect and enhance democratic structures, and a culture of openness and tolerance that promotes democratic give and take. Pakistan of 1988 was, perhaps, a better example, with equally weak institutions and a culture no more supportive of democracy, but burdened also with a military which views itself as the national savior and is inclined to intervene in politics at the slightest real or imagined threat to its interests.

Islamabad, October 12, 1999

Once again it was a call from my deputy that announced a change in government. This time I was just awakening from slumber in Sacramento where I had traveled the day before for a family reunion. "Pack your bags," she said, "you have to come back; there's been an Army coup in the last hour." I got up, dutifully packed my bags and left for Islamabad, via Washington. We anticipated that President Clinton, who announced while I was on the plane that he was sending his Ambassador back to Islamabad, would want me to deliver a message to the new military leader, General Pervez Musharraf.

In the early evening of October 12, troops from the 10th Corps, based in nearby Rawalpindi, had arrested Prime Minister Sharif and most of his

---

2   Francis Fukuyama, *The End of History and the Last Man* (New York: Penguin, 1992).

cabinet. After eleven years of hovering in the background, indirectly manipulating government policy, the Pakistan Army was back in full power—in direct charge of the government. Problems between the Army and the Sharif government had been brewing since almost the beginning of Prime Minister Sharif's second term, which began in early 1997, when he and his party, the Pakistan Muslim League, had swept the election and won a huge majority in the National Assembly and the Senate. Journalist wags referred to the PML government as the "empire of the heavy mandate."[3] The PM immediately began using his so-called "mandate" to whittle away at the power of the Army and increase that of his office. This was not well received by the Army and led to a series of problems between it and the Sharif government.

These problems (including a serious political misjudgment by the Prime Minister) coalesced in October and brought the Pakistan Army back to a position with which it was very familiar: direct political ruler of the state. After the fiasco of the short and bloody Kargil war with India, an Army coup looked increasingly likely to many and the US government had even warned publicly against such a move in late September. Three weeks before the coup, an insightful journalist chose a stud farm as a metaphor, writing that the opposition alliance "played the role of testing ponies [to put the mares in the 'right frame of mind'] to the Bonapartist stallions" waiting in the barn.[4]

Musharraf—Coup Maker or National Savior?

I arrived back in Islamabad early in the morning of October 15 and met with the country's new leader, Chief of Army Staff (COAS) Pervez Musharraf, in the late morning. I handed him a letter from President Clinton that called for a swift restoration of democracy and a "road map" and timetable on how and when that restoration would take place. I also used the occasion to question General Musharraf on his intentions regarding foreign as well as domestic policy.

Musharraf had decided to call himself the "Chief Executive" and was striving to maintain a semblance of legitimacy by having the President, Rafiq Tarrar, stay on despite the latter's close personal relationship to the deposed Prime Minister, Nawaz Sharif. In that initial meeting, Musharraf cited the economic and political problems that the elected governments couldn't solve as the reasons for the army's resumption of power. He spoke

---

3   See Ayaz Amir, "Testing Ponies and Waiting Stallions," *Dawn*, September 17, 1999.

4   Amir, "Testing Ponies" *Dawn*, September 17, 1999.

with feeling of replacing "sham" democracy with "real" democracy, explaining that the elected leaders and their parties had continually given short shrift to vital Pakistani national interests. He claimed that the politicians had thought mainly about how to remain in power and reap the benefits of office.

Two things quickly became clear: Musharraf intended to ensure that the military, especially the Army, would have an institutionalized say in government policy. Ultimately he changed the constitution to create a military-dominated National Security Council (NSC) which would control national security policy. He also intended to root out corruption among politicians and established the National Accountability Bureau (NAB) to pursue corruption cases.[5] This soon ran out of steam, but its probes became highly selective as the political season of the 2002 elections approached.

Most important was the fragile health of the economy, which was certainly a subtext of Musharraf's decision-making. The Army believed that Pakistani economic strength was attenuating relative to India, which would ultimately mean that Pakistan's conventional military capability would be sapped relative to that of India as it would be unable to maintain its current rate of spending on arms and equipment.

Over the next three years his mantra of "sham" democracy became the key concept used by the new military government to explain its action and the changes it proposed. At its core, the concept reflected the traditional Army view that civilian politicians could not be trusted to defend the vital national security interests of Pakistan. That elected governments had been undermined by the previous military regime under Zia ul Huq as well as the armed forces' behind-the-scenes veto, were ignored.

The Chief Executive set out in that meeting about as clear an outline of his thinking on the "roadmap" as we would obtain.[6] Direct military rule would last three years. (He kept his promise on this—sort of.) Much political authority and responsibility would be devolved to the local level, bringing on "grass roots" democracy. He even hinted at the constitutional

---

5   This led immediately to the punsters labeling those who were pursued, and sometimes caught, by the NAB as being "nabbed."

6   The US and its Western European allies constantly harassed Musharraf to flesh out this "road map" but details were never forthcoming until the changes were actually announced. In part, this was because the Army seemed to be making it up as it went along. A new planning organization called the National Reconstruction Bureau (NRB) was at the center of efforts to reshape the Pakistani political system, and its work proceeded slowly as it carefully drew up detailed plans for such changes as devolution, and the creation of the NSC.

changes he later made which created an NSC and strengthened the Presidency at the expense of the national and provincial parliaments. In Chapter 8, I will describe, in some detail, the evolution of the various segments of this "road map."

He did not dwell on the attempt to unseat him as Chief of Army Staff, or on Nawaz Sharif's decision to forbid his plane from landing, as important parts of the Army's calculus in resuming power. He was surrounded by army acolytes, a distinct change from our numerous meetings when he was COAS in which, after the first few, he was comfortable meeting with me on a one-on-one basis.

I had come to think of our relationship before the coup as an evolving friendship, and realized with some regret that, with his move to the zenith of the political leadership of Pakistan, that might not go much further. Among other things, I suspected then, and believe now, that the officers with him at that meeting symbolized how he would approach his objectives—as a leader who would reflect Army dogma on domestic and foreign affairs and, where necessary, try to change the Army's mindset before he changed policy.[7]

The Musharraf I had come to know over the previous year was a moderate, cosmopolitan individual, as Army officers go. He seemed open-minded and quite progressive on most social issues. Our discussions had been spirited and free-flowing, though I found him frustratingly rigid in some of his political views, particularly about Pakistani policy in Afghanistan, on which he reflected the Army position completely. Nonetheless, I had enjoyed these discussions, and realized that both of us would have to be much more constrained now that he was now running the country.

---

7   Our meetings after the coup resumed and, in a few months, as he became more confident in his new position, regained their formerly relaxed and friendly atmosphere. But they were more formal, given his position of chief of state and government. I think both of us preferred to have note-takers present. We did have occasional one-on-one meetings among many others after he took power, but those were usually at my request when I had something sensitive to convey that I wished his aides not to hear. At one meeting I had information about a well-known Al-Qaeda second level leader who we believed was transiting Pakistan. I stressed the sensitivity of the information, and when the meeting ended the Chief Executive rose, took the paper I had handed him, folded it, and stuffed it deep into his trouser pocket, so his immediate aides would not know it had been passed. (I hasten to add that we got little help on apprehending this individual until after 9/11.) In fact, 9/11 provoked a difficult situation for Musharraf as he had to make a quick decision to join the US without having built a consensus over the issue with the Army high command. In that case, he did run into opposition from a couple of senior generals, but had by then moved officers who generally were sympathetic to him into command positions. He sidelined the two dissenters without much ado.

That very afternoon I held a large and well-attended press conference at which I tried to perform a delicate balancing act. I condemned the coup on the one hand as a retrogressive and egregious act of military intervention in a country that, after eleven years of civilian rule, seemed to be working its way to real democracy. As the American Ambassador, I could do nothing less and, in truth, I was very disappointed that the Army had chosen to intervene again. On the other hand, I felt it necessary to defend Musharraf's personal beliefs and his character by insisting that he was a moderate and enlightened individual, partly because sections of the Western press had mistakenly picked up the idea that he was an Islamist.

Two Armies Marching in the Same Direction?

After opting out in 1990, the Bangladesh Army opted back into politics in January 2007. The circumstances of this intervention, after seventeen years of eschewing politics, are described in Chapter 6. Suffice to say that the temptation to intervene must have been strong for most of those seventeen years as Army leaders watched the politicians of both major parties fritter away opportunity after opportunity to set the country on a healthier course. That the army turned over the government to civilian technocrats suggests that there remains a strong feeling in the Bangladesh military that politics is best left to civilians.

In Pakistan, the opposite situation obtained until early 2008. It is not clear yet whether the election of February 18, 2008 will alter the Army's credo—that civilians cannot be trusted to safeguard broader national interests and that the military must share power to ensure that these are protected. Moreover the Pakistani Army showed no interest in relinquishing its hold on office until just before the February election. Its steady accumulation of economic and political power over the past twenty-five years suggests that it will have a strong motivation in maintaining its grip on the country, and that it will prove exceedingly difficult for civilians to unravel Pakistan's thirty-year evolution towards a praetorian state.

Bangladesh

The Bangladeshi Army had, until January 2007, substituted international peacekeeping for any involvement in domestic politics. It is deployed frequently on UN missions and has often more peacekeepers in the field at one time than any other force. It had been called out by civilian governments on several occasions for domestic peacekeeping in the past seventeen years but had returned to barracks as soon as possible.

While the Army's mindset on the virtues of military involvement in governing changed radically in the 1980s, civilian politicians and political parties remain fixed in their old attitudes. Political leaders showed little interest in moving beyond the poisonous, zero-sum, political culture that has characterized Bangladesh politics for the last twenty-five years.

There are various explanations of why Bangladeshi democratic development stalled but most close observers agree that certain fundamental features rendered its political culture dysfunctional:

- There was little interest or ability, notwithstanding the homogenous nature of Bangladedshi society, in reaching a consensus from different points of view and less experience with compromise—an essential feature of a working democracy.

- Bangladeshi political leaders assumed that they embodied the national interest and, when in office, had the right to regulate all aspects of society in the greater "national interest"—as they defined it.

- The only politics was redistributive politics. The political leader controlled access to most economic benefits, hence people devoted much time and effort trying to approach him or her in order to obtain their share of those benefits. Success depended on whom they knew. Neither the political leader nor the recipients had the slightest interest in changing this culture.[8]

Despite dysfunctional governance and a poisonous political culture, life for the average Bangladeshi improved during the period of electoral democracy. Economic and (especially) social progress has been widespread and rapid. Ironically, while parties fought over the spoils of the political process, the NGOs have been relatively unfettered in their efforts to improve the lives of the poor. Social development in Bangladesh has been a remarkable contrast to political development, as we shall see in Chapter 9. NGOs dominate the landscape and provide a wealth of social services to this largely rural society while government interventions are hopelessly ineffectual (which even it acknowledges).

---

8   I draw heavily on Hernando De Soto's analysis of the social and cultural reasons which affect developing countries' attempts to modernize for this synthesis (which is entirely mine, however) of the fundamental cultural bases for Bangladesh's poisonous political culture. Hernando de Soto, *The Other Path: The Invisible Revolution in the Third World* (New York: Harper & Row, 1989).

Pakistan

Pakistan has been ruled by its military, either directly or indirectly, for over half of its existence since it emerged in its present form in 1971. In pre-1971 "United Pakistan," military governments ruled for the last twelve of its twenty-three years. The tradition and habits of military rule are well established.

The belief that only the military can be trusted to protect Pakistani national interests has strong roots in society. The chances of this mindset suddenly changing seem remote: it is one example of the confusion of identity that besets Pakistan—the military's interests are taken by a large proportion of the officer corps and enlisted ranks to be synonymous with those of the state. Many in civil society have accepted this rationale for military rule, in part because what constitutes Pakistan's national identity has never been satisfactorily resolved.

Another factor that has led to an often passive acceptance of military rule and to the internal struggle over national identity is the dominant role that India plays in the Pakistani mindset. India itself encouraged this way of thinking with its bellicose statements in the early days, and it is not surprising that there developed in Pakistan a strong perception of India's perfidy and hegemonic intent. The insecurity and mistrust this has bred has, in a sense, "demonized" India in the Pakistani mind, and has led to a reliance on and belief in the military as the ultimate guarantor of national sovereignty.

Many civilian politicians have only been too happy to help the military perpetuate this worldview by allying with the military for personal political gain. A few politicians have endeavored to subordinate the military to civilian political authority, but most of their attempts have been feckless or limited to rhetoric.

An important fact of the Musharraf era is that the Pakistani military has been able to entrench itself further into the political and social fabric through the appointment of many retired military officers to positions in parastatal business or social organizations as well as in the government itself. It has sunk such roots in the political structure, and has such formidable power and experience in governing, that it is able to dominate even when it works through a civilian façade.

The military and its supporters have justified each intervention in Pakistani politics with the same reasoning: it was "necessary" to stop a spiral of chaos and irresponsible, fissiparous behavior. The necessary corollary in the justification is the almost-unquestioned assertion that civilian politicians in Pakistan cannot be trusted with the country's national security. However, the intervention led by Zia ul Huq in 1977, and that led by Musharraf in 1999, appear to have been motivated as much by the Army's desire to restore its former political power and control of government policy as by its vision of itself as national savior.

Political Islam Marching in One Direction in Both Countries —Toward Power

In one sense, however, the two former wings of United Pakistan are converging. Bangladesh is coming more under the influence of the Islamists, growing less tolerant and protective of human rights, and more discriminatory. Since the army intervention in January 2007, the government has taken a stronger stand against Islamist extremism, but whether that will continue when civilian government returns is yet to be seen.

The Musharraf–led military/civilian hybrid government promoted (rhetorically, at least) policies of "enlightened moderation" but was unable or unwilling to push back the growing Islamist influence in Pakistan, or the civilizational agenda of Islamism. The traditional alliance and interdependence of the military and the Islamists remained unbroken. The newly elected civilian government has yet to sort out its policies regarding the Islamist extremist encroachment on the writ of the state, and there is much concern that strong public identification of counter-terrorism with the very unpopular US-led "war on terror" may force it to ease off the military aspects of such policy.

It is unlikely however that either country will become an Islamist state. Although Islamism and extremism are far more deeply rooted in Pakistan, there is little desire on the part of most Pakistanis to see the Islamists running their country and transforming their society. This was demonstrated in the February election. Only if the army leadership decided that its interests would be served by supporting an Islamist state would that option become viable. This is not now the case. While the army maintains its ties with Islamist groups, it would not derive any particular benefit from the establishment of an Islamist state that it does not already enjoy.

In Bangladesh the state is so weak that the Islamist option cannot be ruled out, despite the fact that the country's culture, religious heritage, and open political system would seem to militate against such a transformation. The weakness of the Bangladeshi state and the proclivity of its political parties to ally with Islamists for their own short term political gain are key factors in judging whether the Islamists will ever seize control of it.

It is ironic that both Bangladesh and Pakistan began in 1972 as secular democracies, and had been the two wings of a United Pakistan that, in 1947, was inaugurated with the secular words of its founder, Jinnah, as its inspiration. The two countries have diverged in many respects since that break. Yet, while religion could not hold them together when they were united, it is the only aspect of their separate existence in which they now appear to be converging—in their shift from the secular values of their founders, and vulnerability to Islamism.

Two Countries Separated by a Common History

In order to go forward and see how Bangladesh and Pakistan arrived at the situation that I have described above, one has to reexamine the history of both countries. Thus I look briefly look at their involvement as Muslim majority regions of British India in the independence struggle as well as a cursory description of why Islam became their dominant religion rather than Hinduism, which captured the affiliation of most Indians. This initial historical chapter also explains the relationship between the kind of society that was to emerge in both countries and the languages spoken therein. The language question became a major divisive issue between the two wings of United Pakistan.

Several chapters follow that cover their early and turbulent histories as separate and independent countries. While their political profiles looked somewhat similar in the early years, deep differences were already apparent. Chapter three, for example, describes the political evolution of Ziaur Rahman, who became first the military leader of a Bangladesh which had practically dissolved into chaos, yet led the country away from praetorianism into a civilian-dominated near-democracy before his untimely demise. Chapter four makes clear the contrast between the Bangladesh experience under early military rule and the Pakistani experience under that of Zia ul Huq, which changed the country for the worse in many ways.

These early chapters are based on the author's research. Beginning with chapter five, he was a first-hand observer of many of the events described. The research is occasionally illlustrated, therefore, with pertinent personal experiences, where this adds to the understanding of events or behavior. The author has tried to avoid inserting himself into the narrative; his personal experiences are drawn on only to illustrate or clarify an analytic point.

1

THE LEGACY OF TWO BLOODY PARTITIONS

The Identity Confusion of Muslim South Asia

Bangladesh and Pakistan are similar in several ways. They are both primarily rural, agricultural peasant societies, based on the two great river systems of South Asia. They are both on the periphery of the South Asian subcontinent, and their histories reflect the traditional separation from the center of such regions. The majority of the populations of both regions were converted to Islam slowly over centuries by the Sufis who fused local custom and shrines with Islam.

The two countries are dissimilar in other ways too. Pakistan was a transit area for much of its ancient history and remains today a jumble of many ethnicities and sects—a virtual patchwork of heterogeneity. Bangladesh (or East Bengal) was a backwater until the Ganges river changed course, bringing with it irrigated agriculture and many agricultural entrepreneurs. These were mostly Sufis, who also brought their religion with them. Through a long process of assimilation, even invaders and foreign rulers became "Bengali." Bangladesh is thus among the most homogeneous of developing countries. There is, despite their quarrels, a feeling of "nation" among Bangladeshis that eludes Pakistanis.

In one important respect, Bangladesh and Pakistan share a fundamental problem: both are schizophrenic about their national identity. There is in each country, as one high-ranking official of the Pakistani government once said to the author, a struggle for its soul.[1] Neither country has been able to choose

---

1   The two national identity struggles may be converging, in the sense that: 1) the vision of an Islamic identity for the Pakistani state that connotes being a part of a transnational (worldwide Umma) Islamic polity is similar conceptually to the vision of a pan-Bengali identity or transnational (Bengali) polity; and 2) the Bangladeshi nationalists appear to be more and more closely aligned with the conservative Islamic elements in Bangladesh who want to make it an Islamic state and the Bengali nationalists seem increasingly willing to eschew their former emphasis on secularism to gain political allies and secure political power.

between competing versions of nationalism that accompanied their political struggles for freedom.

Nationalities in Search of Nationhood

Is there a real distinction between nationalism and nation? According to Christophe Jaffrelot, "...Nationalism is an ideology, be it based on territorial or ethnic notions...[but] a nation is a social construction ..."[2] United Pakistan in 1947 would not have come close to fitting this definition of a nation. It was a witches' brew of different ethnic groups with their own identities, languages, and cultures. The early leaders of United Pakistan, in desperation, sought nationhood by adopting a nationalist ideology. Thus it became an ideological state, predicated on being the homeland of South Asian Muslims, animated by fear of, and hostility toward, India.

East Pakistan (East Bengal before partition) came closest to fitting the definition of a nation. Barbara Metcalf notes that Bengal "had long been known as an area marked by regional consciousness and common language, a region whose (sic) Hindu and Muslim population both seemed to have the potential hallmarks of a modern nation."[3] But, in United Pakistan, Bengal was just one more nationality to add to the brew—one whose population outnumbered all the other nationalities combined.

Throughout its twenty-four years there was no overarching national identity in United Pakistan which would have helped to bind together its disparate nationalities, and particularly the two main competing ones, the Punjabis of West Pakistan and the Bengalis of East Pakistan, in order to give them an incentive, the intellectual and emotional basis, from which to work out their profound differences. Separation did not solve the identity crisis of either. Both remain states with at least two competing national identities.

Bengali Nationalism vs. Bangladeshi Nationalism

The national identity conundrum in Bangladesh comes down to whether it is a part of a larger Bengali nation, united by language and culture, comprising several religions, or a Muslim nation of Bengali-speakers, confined

---

2   Cristophe Jaffrelot, "Nationalism Without a Nation: Pakistan Searching for Its Identity," in Cristophe Jaffrelot (ed.), *Pakistan—Nationalism Without a Nation* (London: Zed Books Ltd., 2002), p. 7.

3   Barbara Metcalf, "The Case of Pakistan," in Barbara Metcalfe (ed.), *Islamic Contestations: Essays on Muslims in India and Pakistan* (Karachi: Oxford University Press, 2004), p. 217.

within the borders of what was East Bengal, then East Pakistan, and now Bangladesh. This has been a fundamental political division in Bangladesh since independence.

Pan-Bengali nationalists take a primordial view of the nation—it is based on language and culture. The Bengali nation, then, is the polity, and the geographic area is that in which people are bonded together by the Bengali language and Bengali culture. Muslim majority East Bengal (with a large minority of Hindus), and Hindu majority West Bengal (with a large minority of Muslims) are one nation. Religion, in this view, is not a binding factor. Many Bangladeshis remain attached to this concept of nationhood. Though it has been toned down and modified over the past thirty years, it remains a core principle of the Awami League.

The military government that took power in mid-1975 found a competing national identity to legitimize the party it created, the BNP (Bangladesh Nationalist Party), and to delegitimize the Awami League. As M.A. Hakim and A.S. Huque note in their 1994 study of changes in the Bangladesh constitution, "The existing 'ethnic' identity of the people…was replaced by a territorial identity…Supporters of the [new] regime viewed it as an attempt to draw a line of distinction between the people of Bangladesh and the ethnic Bengalees (*sic*) of West Bengal, and to project the image of Bangladesh as a distinctive Muslim nation."[4]

From 1975 to 1996, military and civilian governments worked to inculcate this competing national identity—elevating religion to a primary element in nationhood—as the main characteristic of national identity. The BNP has consistently reached out to religious elements in society to bolster its political legitimacy.

Pakistan-Islamic State or Homeland for Muslims?

Perhaps, at the very beginning, in 1947, a secular national identity—a refuge for Muslims and other minorities of South Asia—was one of the options for Pakistan. This seems to be what Jinnah had in mind in his famous speech of August 11, 1947, in which he said,

…the first duty of a [g]overnment is to maintain law and order, so that the life, property, and religious beliefs of its subjects are fully protected by the [s]tate… .

---

4   Mahfuzul H. Chowdhury, Mohammed A. Hakim, and Habib Zafarullah, "Politics and Government: The Search for Legitimacy, in Habib Zafarullah (ed.), "*The Zia Episode in Bangladesh Politics* (Denver, CO: International Academic Publishers, Ltd., 1996), p. 26. Quoted in M.A. Hakim and A. S. Huque, "Constitutional Amendments in Bangladesh," *Regional Studies*, vol. 12, no. 2, (1994), pp. 73-90.

We should begin to work in that spirit and in course of time all these angularities of the majority and minority communities...will vanish.... You are free to go to your temples, you are free to go to your mosques or to any other place of worship in this State of Pakistan.... You may belong to any religion or caste or creed—that has nothing to do with the business of the [s]tate.... We are starting in the days when there is no discrimination, no distinction between one community and another, no discrimination between one caste or creed and another. We are starting with this fundamental principle that we are all citizens and equal citizens of one [s]tate.[5]

The apparent secular vision outlined in this speech soon dissipated in the heat of early Pakistani political struggles, and was lost completely after Jinnah died only thirteen months later.[6] The search for a national identity for the new state quickly developed into a contest between two visions, both of which give a prominent role to religion: Pakistan as an Islamic state; and Pakistan as the homeland for Muslims in South Asia. These may seem quite similar, but in their implications for state policy, they are very different. Briefly, the latter would imply a tolerant, inclusive social and political policy; the former a society administered, in some fashion, in accordance with Islamic law, which is generally exclusive though not necessarily rigidly so.

Pakistan's identity crisis is complicated because the essential religious dichotomy is overlaid with crosscutting regional and ethnic tensions that have not abated in the sixty years of its existence. Punjab remains the majority province, with the preponderance of economic power, which dominates the military and the bureaucracy.

---

5   Stanley Wolpert, *Jinnah of Pakistan* (New York: Oxford University Press, 1984), pp. 337-9.

6   The formal acknowledgement of its end, many scholars believe, came when the Objectives Resolution was introduced by the then Prime Minister, Liaquat Ali Khan, in 1949 as a preamble to the draft constitution that the Constituent Assembly was debating. This famous resolution had three basic provisions that must have seemed benign at the time but began the slide away from any pretense at secularism: it indicated that sovereignty over the universe belonged to Allah Almighty and that the authority delegated to the State of Pakistan through its people was a sacred trust; that the principles of democracy, freedom, equality, tolerance, and social justice *as enunciated by Islam* (emphasis mine) should be fully observed; and that Muslims [in Pakistan] would be able to order their lives *in accordance with the teachings and requirements of Islam as set out in the Holy Koran and the Sunnah* (emphasis mine). As benign as this seems now, it effectively began the slow but inexorable insertion of Islamic principles and the notion of an Islamic state into political consciousness as well as the continuing iterations of a constitution. The reference to the Sunnah is, of course, divisive in itself as there is no universally accepted version of the Sunnah. Nonetheless, the religious parties, having got only a small part of the loaf in the Objectives Resolution, eschewed any concerns about its impact and intensified their campaign for Islamization, and politicians slowly and erratically gave way.

A "Mutilated and Moth-Eaten" Pakistan[7]

Why did the Pakistan Muslim League (PML), which led the movement for a separate Pakistan, end up with a country that, to quote Jalal, "...failed to satisfy the interests of the very Muslims who are supposed to have demanded its creation?"[8] Why was it that, at partition, the two largest Muslim majority provinces were cut in half physically and emotionally? East Pakistan lost the economic heart of Bengal, Calcutta, and the proud identity of a unified Bengali nation with its distinctive culture, language, and tradition. Punjab lost the rich farmlands of its eastern part and a history of effective inter-communal government. Both lost the autonomy they had progressively gained under the British Raj, as did Sindh, Balochistan and the NWFP. And the Muslims left behind in India who resided in the Muslim minority provinces? If they had hoped for a Pakistan to protect them against Hindu majoritarianism, they were sorely disappointed.

The Muslim League's original aim was to protect the interests of all Muslims in India, those in the provinces in which they were a majority, and those in the more numerous provinces in which they were a minority. But this would have been possible only in an independent India with a strong central government and guaranteed autonomy for the Muslim minority. This did not appear politically possible given the attitude of the Hindu majority. In the alternative, a confederal setup with physically separate autonomous Muslim and Hindu provinces, it seemed unlikely that Muslim majority provinces could protect the Muslims left behind in Muslim minority provinces.[9] Confronted by this dilemma, Mohammed Ali Jinnah reluctantly concluded that the only solution was a separate Muslim state of Pakistan.

His strategy became clear after the elections of 1937, in which the PML did poorly. He had to fashion the League so that the British would regard

---

7   Mohammed Ali Jinnah as quoted by Jalal, *The Sole Spokesman*, p. 187.

8   Ibid., p. 2.

9   Jalal, *The Sole Spokesman*, pp. 7-15. Jinnah only slowly came to abandon the idea of Muslim/Hindu unity of which he had been the greatest and most steadfast advocate when he first joined the Muslim League in 1913. As this vision receded in the face of his failure to foster it within the Congress, he increasingly turned to separatism to protect Muslim interests in British India and developed the concept of separate nations. He declared that South Asian Islam was "...a distinctive culture and civilization, language and literature, art and architecture, names and nomenclature, sense of values and proportion, legal laws and moral codes, customs and calendar, history and tradition, aptitude and ambitions." Quoted in Lawrence Ziring, *Pakistan in the Twentieth Century—A Political History* (Karachi: Oxford University Press, 1997), p. 21.

it as the sole representative of all the Muslims in British India—in effect, give it the same status as the Congress, which was deemed to speak for the Hindus. This meant that he had to broaden significantly the League's appeal to the political leaders and the Muslim masses in Muslim majority provinces. Yet he had also to maintain the traditional adherence to the League of Muslims in minority provinces. This would involve, as he knew, a delicate balance between the interests of the majority and the minority Muslims and a studied and creative ambiguity about the objectives of the League and the nature of a Pakistani state. Until 1946, the effort teetered on the edge of failure.

Most critical to his strategy, the League would have to win the majority of Muslims in Bengal and Punjab, the key Muslim majority provinces because of their large populations and wealth. Those two provinces had very different but problematic histories with the League. Each had a significant number of non-Muslims and some tradition of inter-communal political cooperation. More importantly, each had competing Muslim political parties with different political outlooks and political leaders whose interests were not at all in concert with those of the League.

Bengal—The More Fertile Ground

Bengal had a proud history of Muslim separatism. The Muslim League began there in 1905, and its headquarters was in Dhaka until 1911. Perhaps its long support of separatism reflected Bengal's distinctive culture and language, and its history of being, in effect, an outsider in South Asia (witness the long period of self-enforced isolation before the Mughal conquest in the 16th century and its reputation, especially of East Bengal, under both the Mughals and the British, as being cut off from the mainstream). But with one-third of the Muslims of South Asia within its borders, and a politically dominant Muslim League after the elections of 1946, Bengal seems, in retrospect, to have been the "…indispensable" province in the Pakistan movement.

In contrast to its weak showing in the other Muslim majority provinces, the Muslim League performed well in the 1937 provincial elections in Bengal. During the Second World War, the League increased its efforts and appeal in the rural areas and began a campaign which was to culminate in its becoming the majority party by the 1946 elections.

By the elections of 1946, the League in Bengal had the look of a mass movement with a rural membership of over one million. In those elections, it won 115 of 121 seats reserved for Muslims—95 percent of the urban Muslim vote and 85 percent of the rural Muslim vote. With this overwhelming victory, the League clearly would lead the next provincial government.

The victory pointed up another League contradiction. The Bengali-speaking leaders of the League were less than enthusiastic about Jinnah's drive for a separate Pakistan, realizing that it might mean the dismemberment of greater Bengal, and hence began discussions with the Bengal Congress Party to see if a coalition could be worked out. Jalal notes that "a League-Congress Ministry in Bengal would have seriously jeopardized Jinnah's all-India strategy." [10] Jinnah was saved, in this instance, by the Congress' national leaders, who called off the negotiations.

Punjab—A Far Less Fertile Patch

The League came late to Punjab and never held power there before Partition. The Unionist Party, an intercommunal party, had effectively exercised power since 1922. It represented the interests of the cross-communal landowning classes of Punjab. The Unionists drew the support of most Punjabis through the influence feudal landowners had over their tenants and workers, the influence of the clan (biraderi) networks that prevail in Punjab and are often controlled by the feudals, and the influence of the Sufi pirs (holy men who are usually also landowners) over their followers. The Muslim League, on the other hand, had a very narrow base of support—primarily among students—and was badly organized. Until the war years, the League ceded leadership on Muslim issues to the Unionist Party and in the elections of 1937 won only one seat in the provincial assembly.

In the mid-1940s the Muslim League moved to challenge the Unionists politically. This had become necessary if the League were to back up its assertion to speak for the Muslims of South Asia. Its Pakistan platform offered a stark alternative to the Unionists' official commitment to the "...integrity and unity of Punjab." [11]

As the League stepped up its communal appeal in the mid-1940s, rural Muslims responded; landowners, pirs and the biraderi networks hopped on the League bandwagon, and brought their followers with them. In other words, the ties of economic interest that had held the Unionist Party together for over twenty years eroded in the face of communally charged claims. With the students again in the vanguard, the League won over 85 percent of Muslim votes in Punjab in the 1946 election, though this was

---

10   Ibid., p. 162.
11   Ibid., p. 103.

not enough to win the right to form a majority government in the province.

The Muslim League's cry of "Islam under attack" had reached the rural Muslim masses and taken effect. It is probably more accurate to say that the rural Muslims of Punjab had decided in favor of the Muslim League because of their rising fear that a Hindu-dominated United India would threaten their beliefs and practices, and had dragged their leaders along with them.[12]

Sindh and NWFP

Even in those provinces with overwhelming majorities of Muslims, the League had great difficulty, and some good luck, in capturing the adherence of political leaders and their followers. Its efforts to give substance to its claim to speak for most Muslims in the subcontinent continued to be undercut by the messy, self-serving politics of the provinces. The introverted provincial approach to politics diverted attention from the goals of the Pakistan movement and undercut its efforts to focus politics on the larger issues of a separate Muslim state. Both Sindh and NWFP, moreover, had strong contrarian streaks which manifested themselves in a desire for autonomy and a rejection of the idea of control from a remote national center—a mindset contrary to that of the League's national leadership.

Sindh's population was 70 percent Muslim at the time of partition. However, its Muslim politicians were very fragmented. Rural Muslims and their pirs and landowners were not easily won over to support the League until the mid-1940s. The Frontier Province had a significantly higher percentage of Muslims than any of the other Muslim majority provinces—almost 92 percent—yet the League lost every election there until the June 1947 referendum in favor of joining Pakistan at Partition. The province with the greatest preponderance of Muslims entered into an independent, separate Pakistan with some hesitation.

The Inherited Disunity of United Pakistan—An Inevitable Separation?

United Pakistan began its existence with the seeds of discord between provinces and regions, and particularly between its East and West wings, sewn into its political fabric. The aspirations and motivations of the leaders and

---

12   Ian Talbot, *Pakistan, A Modern History*, (London: C. Hurst, 1998), pp. 73-4.

peoples of the Muslim majority provinces of British India, which became the new state, were often at cross-purposes with those of Jinnah's Muslim League. Despite the electoral support the League received, which allowed it to speak for a separate Pakistan, politics in the provinces centered essentially around a multitude of local and communal issues more than on any unquenchable desire for a separate Muslim homeland.

It is important to note that the military was in charge of United Pakistan after 1958. The Pakistan military (dominated by Punjabis) felt threatened by the possibility that East Pakistan—which at that time was Pakistan's most populous province—would have an equal say in the affairs of state. But there is more to it than that. The West Pakistani establishment (the oligarchy of feudal landowners, the bureaucracy, and the military) obviously felt that a decentralized Pakistan, which would give fuller vent to East Pakistan's democratic aspirations, was not in its interests. In essence, West Pakistan's political and social leaders preferred a truncated Pakistan to giving the East the right to run its own affairs, and an equal voice in the national affairs of a United Pakistan.[13]

The Intersection of Religion, Language, and Nationalism in the Politics of Separation

Neither Islamic parties nor Islamic schools of thought played a direct political role in the separation of Bangladesh from United Pakistan. In fact, the Jamat-i-Islami, the strongest and most coherent Islamic party in both wings strenuously opposed separation—which proved deleterious to its political fortunes in Bangladesh after separation. But, indirectly, the Islamic mindset favored by the government and the West Pakistani elite exacerbated the drift of the two wings toward civil war and separation. This combined with the language issue (which embodies national identity), and the form of nationalism that had grown up in Pakistan between 1947 and 1970, to create a political dynamic pointing toward separation of the two wings. The miscalculated, and misguided policies of the military government were the added ingredient that made separation inevitable.

In its early years, the nationalist rhetoric of United Pakistan governments was communal. It focused on Pakistan's role as the homeland and refuge of Muslims in South Asia with the implied assertion that it was the guarantor

---

13   There is also anecdotal evidence that raises the question of whether out-and-out racism did not also play a part.

of rights for the Muslims of India. It projected past Muslim glories into the present, and was uniformly and categorically anti-Indian.

The state, especially after the military had taken it over in 1958, imparted a modernist orientation to the Islam it espoused. This was, in fact, to ensure a religious quality to its very secular nationalistic theme of rapid economic growth and technological advancement. It was an emphasis on modernism and progress that harked back to the Aligarh movement of the late nineteenth and early twentieth centuries.[14]

The modernist Islam promoted by the Ayub Khan government had a second aspect—a "contempt for regional expressions of Islam."[15] This modernist religious theme was picked up by the West Pakistani elite which was also committed to rapid economic growth and technological progress. The elite came to view religious expression as personal piety which should conform to modern (read Western) standards and interpretations when dealing with socio-economic issues, and it attached a pejorative connotation to the Islam practiced in Bengal.

The synchretic, inclusive Islam of Bengal as it had evolved under Sufi influence was considered by the military and the West Pakistani elite as "religiously suspect," and certainly not in conformity with the modernist Islam they advocated.[16] It must be noted, however, that the modernist Islam espoused by the government and the elite did not have, generally, popular support. In Punjab, with its own Sufi tradition, the rural masses gave little credence to modernist Islam. Ironically, the Jamat-i-Islami, the major Islamic political party, took a very dim view of both Bengali Islam and modernist Islam. The JI wanted only complete Islamization based on the sacred texts of Islam.

The early governments also promoted the use of Urdu as the national language. Jinnah began the dispute with a famous speech in Dhaka in January 1948 in which he said that Urdu would be the national language of United Pakistan. This was culturally offensive to the Bengalis.[17] In 1951, there were

14 The Aligarh movement begun by Sir Sayed Ahmed Khan was the modernist alternative in the competing schools of Islamic reform. Sir Sayed founded Aligarh University to train young Muslim men in the modern sciences and technology in the belief that Muslims could regain the influence and authority they had once had in India through becoming more western in their education.

15 Metcalf, "The Case of Pakistan," *Islamic Contestations*, p. 224.

16 Ibid., p. 226. Metcalf notes that "Bengal, with a population almost one-fourth Hindu, and with a tradition of openness to Bengali literature and folkways, was deemed...[far away from] the scriptualist and legalist Islam current in ... the West."

17 For probably the first time in many years he was booed by the Bengali crowd.

severe riots in East Pakistan over the language issue which led to a political solution that allowed use of Bengali as a second national language. This political accommodation never really gained political acceptance among the West Pakistani elite. Urdu had become, and remained, for them a symbol of national loyalty and national culture.

It was natural that Urdu became a religious symbol. The Aligarh movement to modernize Islam began where Urdu was the language of choice. To convey the modernistic view of Islam, what better language than Urdu? It became favored by political leaders as enhancing their modernist, secularist, policies emphasizing economic growth and technological progress. As Metcalf notes, "Knowledge of Urdu defined one as a person worthy of respect and ... increasingly defined one as a Muslim."[18]

Urdu had become an important definer of national and religious identity in Punjab, in effect the language of the educated elite in that dominant province. It was the language of education, and had become that of Punjabi culture. Thus the bulk of the military and bureaucracy, as well as the civilian politicians, preferred to use it.

While Bengali was acknowledged to be also a language of great sophistication and long literary tradition, its claim to share equal status as a national language was discounted in the eyes of the West Pakistani elite by its Hindi-like script and by the fact that the great writers in Bengali (Tagore, for example, who was the first non-western writer to win the Nobel Prize for Literature) were almost all Hindu. Worse, the cultural affinity of Bengalis meant that they all, be they Muslim or Hindu, drew no communal distinction and valued their Bengali writers above all others.

The nationalistic theme of rapid economic growth and technological progress also contributed to the strains between the East and West wings that led to their separation. The development strategy of the military government worked, but differentially. This caused growing grievances in the East which saw itself slipping further behind economically and socially because of policies that favored the West—particularly its elite.[19] The perception of accelerating disparity grew in the East, and though the Ayub Khan government understood this, it underestimated its impact.

These perverse forces and symbols might possibly have been muted by rational and wise government policy, especially in the late 1960s when

---

18   Metcalf, "The Case of Pakistan," *Islamic Contestations*, p. 227.

19   Especially the so-called twenty-two families of the West who reputedly controlled most industry and banking in United Pakistan.

things began to fall apart. Whether that would have prevented the separation, or just made it a peaceful and bloodless one, is in the "what if" category of history. Suffice to say, there was precious little wisdom or rationality in the policy followed by the military government, or the political leaders of West Pakistan.

The Military As State Savior or As State Usurper

Another of Jinnah's visions was that Pakistan would be firmly under the control of civilian leaders, and that the military would serve civilian governments.[20] After his death, military intervention became a self-fulfilling prophecy. As the self-proclaimed guarantor of the state of Pakistan's survival—accepted by a large part of the public and civilian politicians—the military won a disproportionate share of the available resources.[21] Access to these made it into an effective and efficient institution at the expense of civilian institutions that would have been, in many other countries, competing or dominant. When in office, civilian governments often sought military support because weak and under-funded civilian institutions could not function effectively.

Because the Pakistan military came to believe that it is the only national institution that understands, and can be trusted to defend, national interests, it it has historically believed that it must always control government policy, either behind the scenes of a civilian façade, or directly. A praetorian state evolved, and military government has been the rule not the exception. Thus another kind of identity confusion arose in Pakistan—the military has come to believe it is synonymous with the state.[22]

In Pakistan, "[O]nly a stable civil government enjoying popular support and legitimacy can restrain the military to its professional domain and deal

---

20 Hasan-Askari Rizvi, *Military, State, and Society in Pakistan* (London: Macmillan, 2000), pp. 6-7. See also the very interesting story on p. 118 of Stephen Cohen's *The Pakistan Army* (Oxford: Oxford University Press, 1998).

21 Jean-luc Racine, "Pakistan and the 'India Syndrome': Between Kashmir and the Nuclear Predicament," in Christophe Jaffrelot (ed.), *Pakistan—Nationalism Without a Nation*, p. 198.

22 This is not a recent phenomenon. The mind set was evident as far back as the late 1960s. See Brigadier A. R. Siddiqi, *East Pakistan—The Endgame: An Onlookers Journal, 1949-1971* (Karachi: Oxford University Press, 2004), pp. 1-32 and pp. 81-96. Siddiqi gives a chilling description of the Army's attitude that it was the national savior when Ayub Khan was toppled from power in early 1969 and its self-identification as the state when the Bengalis were "disrespectful" of the army in the abortive negotiations before the war of separation began on March 26, 1971.

with it from a position of strength."[23] This is, perhaps, becoming less and less likely as the vicious circle becomes stronger and as the military sinks deeper roots into civil institutions and the economy.[24]

The Eastern wing of United Pakistan seemed less inclined to emulate this pattern but after the first experiment with democracy, under the Awami League government of Sheik Mujib, ended in chaos and near anarchy, the Bangladesh military took power and followed till 1990, with one brief interlude of "almost-democracy", the same trajectory as the Pakistani military.[25]

The India Overhang—The Legacy of Two Bloody Partitions

Beyond his unfulfilled vision that Pakistan would be a secular democratic homeland for minorities in South Asia with the military firmly under civilian control, Jinnah also believed that, "once established, [it] would be on good terms with India."[26] It has been just the opposite—an "armed peace," Jean-Luc Racine has called it—since the August 1947 Partition. In fact, as Racine notes, "Pakistan has lived not only next door to India, but in opposition to India."[27]

The hostility and insecurity that characterized the relationship have also influenced Pakistan's internal struggle over its own identity. Moreover contentious relations with India may have accelerated Pakistan's drift toward an ideological Islamic state, and they have certainly been a major factor in the incremental entrenchment of the military in political and economic power and the growth of praetorianism.

The Pakistan Movement, itself, as well as the phenomenon of Partition, contributed to this India-centric outlook. As Pakistan drifted away from Jinnah's vision of a homeland for minorities and more toward an ideological Islamic state, his successors, civilian or military, returned increasingly

---

23   Rizvi, *Military, State, and Society in Pakistan*, p. 3.

24   Hasan Askari-Rizvi, "Dimensions of the Military's Role," *Daily Times of Pakistan*, April 5, 2005, accessed on April 5, 2005 at http://www.dailytimes.com.pk

25   Chapters 3, 4, and 6 cover this period in Bangladesh. The reader will note that in Chapter 4, I point out that under Ziaur Rahman's leadership, Bangladesh seemed headed back toward a democracy in which elected civilian politicians controlled policy and the military served the civilian government. This progress was interrupted by the assassination of Zia Raman in 1981 and the Ershad military coup of 1982. However, democracy was restored in 1991, and the Bangladesh military retired from politics ... for the time being at least.

26   Jean-Luc Racine, "Living With India," *A History of Pakistan and Its Origins* (London: Wimbledon Publishing Company, 2002), p. 113.

27   Racine, "Pakistan and the 'India Syndrome'" in *Pakistan—Nationalism Without a Nation*, op. cit., p. 196.

to the arguments that the Muslim League had used to justify Partition to the Muslim masses: the separate nation theory that emphasized differences between Muslims and Hindus.

Several other factors contributed to the "India Syndrome." India's behavior after Partition, such as its refusal in 1947 to turn over Pakistan's share of the military and financial assets inherited from British India, exacerbated the distrust and ill will. Indian actions in Kashmir to block access to the waters of the Indus in early 1948, forcing Pakistan to sign an agreement it felt unjust, heightened such fears. The image of an India that did not accept its neighbour's existence and which intended through bullying tactics to drive it to collapse quickly became widely accepted in Pakistan.

Above all, the unresolved issue of Kashmir, the first "*causus belli*" between the two new countries, has continued to inflame passions in both and festers as an open wound that affects their relationship. The subject has engendered a wealth of scholarly and popular publications over the fifty-eight years that it has been at the center of Indo/Pak relations and there is no need to rehash those debates here. What has to be grasped about the Kashmir issue is that not only is it dizzyingly complicated and maddingly difficult, but that until it is solved Pakistan and India will not be able to normalize their relations.

Kashmir controls the waters of the Indus that Pakistan needs to irrigate the fields of Punjab and Sindh as well as for energy. This would be enough, in itself, to ensure a quarrel over its possession. But Kashmir is even more important psychologically to both Pakistan and India. To the former, it is the Muslim majority province that got away—it was rightfully theirs most Pakistanis think, and it was stolen by the Indians. In a sense, this is true: the loss of Muslim majority Kashmir undercuts the rationale for a separate Muslim state in South Asia and, thus, Pakistani identity. (This ignores, of course, the fact of Bangladesh—the creation of which should have helped to mitigate that concern.)

Kashmir is important to India's identity also—as a secular, multi-religious state, which protects and cares for minorities. Moreover, the Indian government is determined that Kashmir should not serve as an inspirational model for similar insurgencies and autonomy/independence movements in India's other rebellious states, particularly those in the north-east.

As mentioned above, the "India Syndrome" fostered a sense of insecurity that has led, almost inexorably, to the role the military has assumed for itself in Pakistan—the sole guarantor of state survival.[28] Many factors explain

---

28   Rizvi, *Military, State, and Society*, p. 6.

this insidious evolution. Forces of history, culture, and geography unique, in part, to Pakistan have come together in a perverse way, enabling the military assume this role and bringing most of the population to accept that assertion.

There is now hope that, after sixty years of bellicosity over Kashmir, the two countries have finally chosen to put the issue behind them. Since 2004, the two governments have very gingerly, and with many false starts, begun a dialogue that seeks over time to find a workable solution to Kashmir and to the other bilateral issues that have plagued their relations. It will be a slow and sometimes erratic process as each feels its way into a very new mode of thinking about the subcontinent.

The Two Muslim Homelands of South Asia

This narrative, therefore, really begins on December 16, 1971, when Bangladesh and Pakistan became independent of each other. They began their independent, separate existences as democracies, led by charismatic but flawed leaders, but in both, these stumbling phases of democracy were turbulent, and the leadership of Zulfikar Ali Bhutto in Pakistan and Sheikh Mujibur Rahman in Bangladesh proved inadequate in dealing with the challenges each country faced. Both governments were much alike in their embrace of "populist" and "statist" ideology coupled with widespread nationalization of industry and central planning of the economy. The legacy of these poor choices still troubles the economies of both countries.

The other common element is the military's proclivity to intervene in politics. Military governments replaced the initial democratic dispensations in both countries. In Pakistan, the military took over in 1977 declaring that it had to restore stability and protect security. It has stayed in power, behind the scenes when not in direct charge, until the present. In Bangladesh, the military intervened in 1975 to restore stability to a political/economic situation that was truly chaotic. Though a civilian democratic structure was restored, the military soon intervened again and ruled throughout the 1980s. Electoral politics were restored in 1990 and, for seventeen years, despite miserably poor civilian governance, the Army refrained from intervening. However, when chaos again threatened, in January 2007, the Army again took power and remains in control behind the scenes. Whether its stated objective of reforming political structures and returning power to civilians by the end of 2008 will happen has yet to be seen.

The greatest difference between Bangladesh and Pakistan has been in their social development. Social development indicators tracked by the UN and the World Bank show that, since at least the mid-1980s, when NGO delivery of social services hit full stride, Bangladesh's social development has been on a far steeper upward curve than Pakistan's. Some social indicators—family size and gender equality—have clearly diverged since the separation. Interestingly enough, though the NGOs really took the helm of development initiatives in Bangladesh in the 1980s under a military government, their expansion began in the positive environment of the late 1970s, a period when the political profiles of the two countries looked almost identical—both were under military control, and both were ruled by a general named Zia.

2

FLAWED LEADERS AND FAILED
DEMOCRACIES

Bangladesh and Pakistan began their separate lives in very different circumstances. In Bangladesh, much blood had been spilled, great sections of the population dislocated, and much infrastructure destroyed in the nine-month civil war. Pakistan was virtually untouched—at least physically. But, despite these different initial circumstances, each began its separate existence as a democracy trying to move on from fourteen years of military rule in United Pakistan.

Neither democracy lasted, and both countries—though having experienced intermittent democratic episodes in subsequent decades—have yet to build sufficiently strong and well implanted democratic institutions or achieve the level of governance needed if democracy is to be sustainable. As separate and independent countries, Bangladesh and Pakistan both got off to bad starts under leaders whose enormous charisma was matched only by their flawed vision.

And that is the tale of this chapter—how two leaders, because of their limitations of intellect or inability to anticipate possible future events, and the weaknesses of their character, failed to build upon promising democratic beginnings that characterized the early years of both countries. Sheikh Mujibur Rahman in Bangladesh and Zulfikar Ali Bhutto in Pakistan assumed leadership in a burst of expectation and optimism, but were unable to cash in on the strong mandate they had to nurture and establish viable democracies. History is no kinder to them thirty years after their tragic ends than were their contemporaries, and they must be judged as historical failures because their own flaws were important contributing factors to the demise of democracy on their watch.

Bangladesh

Bangladesh declared its independence on December 16, 1971. It began its separate and independent life with much less in the way of natural, human, and financial resources, as well as management and other skills, than did the new state of Pakistan. What Bangladesh did have in abundance from the outset was enthusiasm. Bangladeshis set out on their national journey with a surfeit of good feeling, and sense of euphoria that allowed their leaders to organize government and write a constitution in what was, starting from scratch, a remarkably short time frame. Despite its extreme poverty and illiteracy, the dislocation caused by the war, and the total absence of traditions of democratic governance, Bangladesh was relatively fertile soil for democracy. Its homogenous population, and a culture that was relatively open to innovation and change, as well as its tradition of grass-roots mobilization, were conducive to democratic growth—bestowing on Bangladesh a more advantageous beginning than many newly independent, developing countries.[1]

There was, however, also a surfeit of corruption, venality, self-aggrandizement, not to mention radical left-wing ideology. The large stock of weapons abandoned after the civil war added to this combustible brew. This combination meant that law and order was a problem from the birth of the new nation, one that was exacerbated as the new government mismanaged economic recovery and demonstrated overt favoritism toward its own partisans. The civilian regime took office with overwhelming support, but its hold on the loyalties of most Bangladeshis was dissipated after three years to a point that undemocratic alternatives became attractive as early as 1975.[2]

---

1   In addition to its homogenous population, openness to new ways of doing things, and experience with grass roots politics, East Pakistan/East Bengal had been home to several mass movements over the first half of the twentieth century protesting and seeking political, economic, or social change. From the peasant movements of the 1920s, 1930s, and 1940s demanding economic justice from landlords (which slowly transformed from a class problem to a communal problem), to the language movements of the 1950s, to the separation movement of the 1960s, Bengalis were much more used to the idea of trying to attain more say in their own lives. See, for example, Taj-ul-Islam Hashmi, "Peasant Nationalism and the Politics of Partition: The Class Communal Symbiosis in East Bengal, 1940-1947," in Ian Talbot and Gurharpal Singh (eds), *Region & Partition—Bengal, Punjab, and the Partition of the Subcontinent* (Karachi, Oxford University Press, 1999), p. 105.

2   The low esteem to which Mujib and his regime had fallen in only three and one half years—from the euphoria of early 1972 to his assassination in August 1975—is demonstrated by the lack of any widespread remorse or sympathy for him and the family, despite the bloody circumstances surrounding the way in which the government fell.

Pakistan

The pattern of military rule that had characterized the "old" (United) Pakistan had been shattered by the traumatic and humiliating events of 1971. In the "new" Pakistan that emerged on December 16 that year, there was the potential to institutionalize democracy. But there were also serious societal, cultural, and institutional barriers which made democratization a formidable task—feudalism, regional and ethnic tensions, a noxious political culture, great poverty and illiteracy, and a tradition of military rule.

The stupendous defeat that the army had suffered in the brief 1971 war with India, and the traumatic loss of the eastern half of United Pakistan had completely undermined the Army's reputation and influence. It might have been accustomed to ruling the nation, but its claim to remain a legitimate player in governance was torpedoed by the unadulterated bungling which led to the disaster, and the military regime's outright prevarication to the Pakistani public before and during the war.

The new civilian government dominated the military.[3] The problem Bhutto faced was to consolidate this state of affairs by effective institutionalization of democratic reforms and the inclusive governance needed by Pakistan's divided ethnic polity to build national feeling. Instead his government fomented political and social dislocation and exacerbated regional tensions which allowed the army to reassert its "right" to intervene in political life. Bhutto's use of the army to settle political problems restored its reputation and, thus, public support for its claim to be the only political actor in Pakistan with the national interest at heart.[4]

MUJIB

From Euphoria to Neuralgia

Sheikh Mujibur Rahman returned to a newly independent Bangladesh from a Pakistani jail on January 10, 1972 to assume leadership of the provisional government.[5] He entered office with overwhelming public sympathy and

---

3   Ian Talbot, *Pakistan: A Modern History*, p. 244. A clear insight and illustration of the power that Bhutto held over the prostrate military (and why the military itched to get back at him) is described in Stanley Wolpert, *Zulfi Bhutto—His Life and Times*, (New York, Karachi, Oxford, Oxford University Press, 1993), pp.171-2.

4   Ibid., p. 245.

5   On December 16, 1971, Dhaka fell to the Indian Army, and the provisional government of Bangladesh, which had been formed in April and was resident in Calcutta, proclaimed its independence. I refer to what had officially been East Pakistan until that date as Ban-

support for the role he had played in gaining Bangladeshi independence. As the undisputed leader of a new Bangladesh, Mujib faced a much more daunting task than just defining his new country through a new constitution. That was the easy part. He faced the prospect of rebuilding a country shattered physically by the civil war, with a dysfunctional economy and crippled transportation system, severe law and order problems, and a population displaced far and wide.

Two days after his return, Mujib relinquished the office of President to become the Prime Minister. This signaled his preference, and that of his party, the Awami League, for a parliamentary system of government. Putting together a constitution was not a serious problem. The vexatious issues that had plagued the framers of the first constitution of United Pakistan—centralization vs. decentralization, federalism vs. unitary state, ethnic and regional equity and balance—did not obtain in Bangladesh.[6]

Under the new constitution, adopted in November 1972, the President appointed the Prime Minister, but only with the approval of Parliament. The PM would choose his ministers from among elected Parliamentarians. There would be direct universal suffrage to elect members of Parliament, but seats were set aside for women, who were to be elected indirectly. Basic political and civil rights were guaranteed by the constitution.

In another important departure from the British/Indian model, the Awami League inserted in the constitution its own political principles— four tenets known as 'Mujibism'—as those principles under which Bangladesh would be governed. The four principles—nationalism, socialism, secularism, and democracy—were the controversial buoys by which the Awami League government intended to steer the ship of state.[7]

The new Bangladesh constitution was firm and precise in making the superior judiciary independent.[8] Two articles (95 and 96) prescribed how judges were to be appointed and removed. Article 22 required that the state ensure the separation of the judiciary from its executive organs.[9] A

---

gladesh in what follows, and to what had been officially West Pakistan before that date as Pakistan.

6   Bangladesh was, perhaps, the only South Asian state for which a unitary structure made sense because of the homogeneity of its people and culture and its language.

7   Craig Baxter, *Bangladesh—From a Nation to a State* (Boulder, CO, Westview Press, 1997), pp. 87-8. The following sections draw heavily on Baxter.

8   In the section of this chapter on Bhutto there will be a fuller explanation of the background on the continual erosion of judicial independence and authority in United Pakistan.

9   Awal Hossain Mollah, *Separation of Judiciary and Judicial Independence in Bangladesh*

fourth, article 7, strongly implied that "there should an impartial, independent, and neutral organ (sic) to see that the executive is not overstepping its limit and parliament is not transgressing any provision of the constitution."[10] The lower judiciary was left under the executive; this was supposed to be temporary.[11]

As the Mujib government came under increasing political and economic pressure, this adherence to liberal constitutionalism and judicial independence broke down. In December, 1974, he declared a state of emergency citing the national security powers of Article 2 of the constitution which he used to abridge civil rights and drastically curtail the judiciary's authority and scope to check and review executive actions. This action began a 15-year process of reducing the independence and limiting the authority of the judiciary which has only been partially restored even though elected, civilian governments have been in power since 1991.[12]

Relations with India: The Beginning of the Roller-Coaster

Unlike Pakistan, in which relations with India have always been problematic, in Bangladesh, they have been hot, cold, or lukewarm, depending on the government in power in each country. In the beginning they were hot. The euphoria that characterized the beginnings of the new state spilled over to India, which was, for a while, looked upon as a close friend and valuable ally. After all, India had helped considerably in securing the separation of Bangladesh from United Pakistan.

The Indians had provided critical help during the war of separation, absorbing about 10 million refugees, and supplying arms and other assistance to the Bengali insurgent forces, and, finally, going to war with Pakistan. On December 6, 1971, three days after India invaded East Pakistan in order to end the conflict and ensure its separation from its Western sibling (surely one of its primary goals), it formally recognized the new state of Bangladesh.[13]

(New York: United Nations), pp. 4-5, accessed 2-14-06 at http://unpan1.un.org/intra-doc/groups/public/documents/APCITY/UNPAN020065.pdf .

10   Sheikh Hafizur Rahman, "Convention of Consultation with Chief Justice Should Be Maintained," *The Daily Star*, Dhaka, April 13, 2003, accessed on January 2, 2006 at http://www.thedaily star.net/law20030/02/.

11   Ibid.

12   Asian Development Bank (ADB), *Judicial Independence Overview and Country-level Summaries--Bangladesh 2003*, (Manila: ADB, 2003), pp. 43-7.

13   Kathryn Jacques, *Bangladesh, India, and Pakistan--International Relations and Regional Tensions in South Asia* (New York: St. Martin's Press, Inc., 2000), p. 101.

In time this heady feeling of closeness to India began to sour into resentment when the Indians took an extraordinarily long time to withdraw their troops (well into 1972), making off with most of the Pakistani military equipment, as well as over 90,000 Pakistani POWs.[14]

The new Bangladeshi state signed a treaty of Friendship, Peace, and Cooperation with India in March 1972 delineating several pivotal bilateral issues that needed to be solved urgently to stabilize political security relations between the two countries.[15]

In subsequent negotiations on these issues, the Indians played hardball .[16] The only issue that was fully resolved during Sheikh Mujib's time in office was on the land borders; the two governments signed a treaty settling that question in May 1974 (which India has not yet ratified). Included in this treaty was a provisional arrangement on access to Bangladeshi enclaves, which sat dormant for about twenty years.[17]

Successor governments backed away from the embrace of India (and, in those days, its Soviet ally) and turned more to the West and to China. These governments, concomitantly, eschewed the India-like secularism of the Awami League and reached out to the Islamic parties, which began the drift toward Islamism which continues to this day. In other words, the consequences of the cooling of the initial warm India-Bangladesh relationship have been profound for the later direction of Bangladesh politics.

Mujib Sinks in a Bog of Corruption and Ineptitude

One axiom of politics is that charismatic leaders of independence movements do not always possess the organizational skills, inclusivist tendencies, or intellectual flexibility needed to lead successfully the country that their charisma has brought about. Mujib, the epitome of charisma, was a good example. It would not have been an easy task, in any case. But Mujib's personal skill set seemed woefully short of the essential mental agility and toughness needed by a leader to mold a new country—called by some "a basket case"—into a viable nation.[18]

---

14   And an even longer time to get out of the Chitagong Hill Tracts.

15   Jacques, *Bangladesh, India, and Pakistan*, p. 198, n 3.

16   Ibid., p. 101.

17   Haaran Ur Rashid, *Foreign Relations of Bangladesh* (Varanasi: Rishi Publications, 2001), pp. 61-73.

18   Stanley Kochanek, *Patron-Client Politics and Business in Bangladesh* (New Delhi: Sage Publications India Pvt Ltd, 1993), p. 83.

On his return, Mujib faced a broken down and dysfunctional economy: a severely damaged transportation infrastructure that, had it had not been for the available water routes and boats, would have resulted in serious food shortages. The major port of Chittagong was completely blocked by sunken ships. Most serious, though, was the almost-complete breakdown of law and order. Armed gangs roamed the countryside. The chaotic economic situation drove many otherwise law-abiding citizens to desperate measures to feed and clothe themselves and their families. The easy availability of weapons fueled the violence.[19]

Internal divisions in the army reduced its effectiveness while the police had virtually collapsed. Thoroughly politicized by the civil war, and traditionally badly paid, the latter often became gangs loyal to a political master who supplemented their meager, and often unpaid, salaries from the proceeds of corruption.

The army is a special story, an example of the fractious character of Bangladeshi politics, and of the unforseen consequences of Mujib's lack of political foresight. At the end of the war, the army was split between two hostile groups, "freedom fighters" and "repatriates". Freedom fighters had fought with the separatist armed forces against the West Pakistanis; repatriates had been interned in Pakistan. But the freedom fighter ranks were also split between those who had not served in the pre-war professional army and those soldiers who had escaped (deserted?) the Pakistan army to join the separatist forces. Mujib favored the former over the latter in promotions and plum assignments.[20]

For example, he refused to name General Ziaur Rahman, a very successful professional soldier before the war and a freedom fighter, as Chief of Army Staff. Ziaur Rahman was a national hero and had been a key officer in the separatist forces. He was the first to announce the formation of a provisional government of Bangladesh from a radio station in Chittagong in March 1971. Despite being subordinated during the war, and shunted aside after it, he remained loyal to the provisional and the Mujib government.

Mujib especially distrusted the "repatriates," who were professional soldiers who had not been able to escape the Pakistani army and were interned in West Pakistan until 1973 (though he, himself, most resembled them in his experience during the war). This group was especially discriminated against in promotions and positions during the Mujib period. To some

---

19   Baxter, *Bangladesh*, pp. 88-9.
20   Ibid., pp. 89-90. This section draws mainly on Baxter.

extent, the division between the "freedom fighters" and the "repatriates" went further than just promotions and positions. It often involved opposing philosophies. The freedom fighters, especially those who had been guerilla fighters during the war, were frequently advocates of very radical political and economic policies, including army organization. Some wanted a "peoples' army," and a few went even further and advocated that officers should be elected by the enlisted men.

Repatriates, on the other hand, were molded in the tradition of the United Pakistan army, which in turn had been shaped in the tradition of the British Indian army. They saw the army as a highly trained and selective organization which served the government in power, and did not take a political role. This latter view, of course, had already been attenuated by the actions of the Pakistan army since it seized power in 1958, and it was progressively battered by the series of army coups which followed Mujib's demise, though it retained a core of adherents whose views came to the fore in the 1990s.

As did Bhutto in Pakistan, Mujib established a paramilitary guard of 10,000 loyal only to him. It was called the National Security Force, and received priority in supplies and equipment as well as general privileges. As its counterpart in Pakistan, this force became a bone in the throat of the regular army, especially the repatriate elements, and was an important factor in Mujib's downfall.

Mujib exacerbated matters by differentiating among the civil service in pretty much the same way as he differentiated among army personnel. He rejected those who had remained at their posts in East Pakistan during the war. Most of these were denied positions even if they had remained with the idea of alleviating the suffering of the people or providing vital services that might help feed them or relocate them. Others were caught in West Pakistan with no escape possible. Only those civil servants who had escaped from East Pakistan, or left their posts in West Pakistan or overseas, were trusted with responsible positions—or, in most cases, any position at all. These were not necessarily the cream of the civil service, and they were supplemented by many political appointees, without skills or ethics, who were moved into civil service jobs, often to pay off a political or financial debt.

In what was probably the most deleterious policy of all, Mujib and his Awami League carried out the "socialism" promise in the constitution blindly and without any second thoughts. Nationalization of industrial units and banks was widespread and indiscriminate. The state would have been stretched beyond its capacity if the government had limited itself to taking over property and assets abandoned by West Pakistanis. But in casting the nationalization net so wide, it increased the administrative burden impossibly on an already weak government.[21]

The elections of March 1973 were the beginning of the end. Mujib and his party were still popular two years after the birth of the country but the accumulating problems were beginning to reduce his appeal. The Awami League won the election, though with a majority significantly reduced from the landslide of 1970. Regrettably, Awami League leaders couldn't resist padding the result by blatantly and unnecessarily rigging the polls. This exacerbated what would become, in a few months, widespread and growing popular discontent with Mujib and the League.

Mujib's Fall

Things deteriorated rapidly after the election. The security problem, already bad before the election, became worse. The perception of the government and its ministers as lawbreakers—the ministers' overt corruption, and the government's overt poll rigging—served to bring the situation into stark relief. The economy, which had been buoyed by foreign assistance, began to crumble. This was made much worse by severe flooding in 1974, and food shortages caused by bad planning, the still devastated transportation infrastructure, and the lack of income for the very poor (who always are the most vulnerable to food shortages). The economic disaster, of course, made the security situation even worse.[22]

In the year after the elections, from mid-1973 to mid-1974, the feeling grew that neither Mujib nor the Awami League were up to the job they had been given. Mujib's reaction was to seek more personal power (as if lack of power were at the root of his problems, rather than bad policies combined with almost overt corruption and incompetence). In December 1974, he declared a state of emergency, which, under the constitution, gave him the power to order arrests, reduce the independence of the judiciary, and limit the freedom of the press. He nationalized a major Bengali-language newspaper and threatened others that might have the temerity to criticize him or his government.

---

21   See especially Kochanek, *Patron-Client Politics*, pp. 74-88. This will be elaborated in Chapter 9.

22   Baxter p. 90-1.

In January 1975, Mujib used his leverage and influence with his party to amend the constitution and further increase his personal power. The amendment created a presidential system and made Mujib President for five years. It gave him full executive power and authorized the formation of a single party to which all government employees were required to belong. Other parties were banned. The courts were enjoined to quit enforcing the fundamental rights enumerated in the constitution. Bangladesh had been transformed from a democracy into a personal dictatorship by the man who led its independence movement. A number of political leaders opposed the move away from democracy, but very few objected in public.

Primary among those who took offense were a number of mid-level military officers who already felt aggrieved by Mujib's actions toward the army, especially his creation of the National Security Force, and his elevation of that force to a status superior to the army. They also objected to his interference in police and army affairs to extricate family members and party friends from arrest for smuggling. They saw his moves towards personal dictatorship as additionally harmful to their interests and the pretext for action to force a change.

On August 15, 1975, a group of mid-level army officers, mostly majors, assassinated Mujib, and in the process killed several members of his family, including his wife and young son. Popular esteem for Mujib had fallen so low by then that few lamented this brutal act, but its legacy continues to haunt Bangladeshi politics.

BHUTTO

Last Chance for Real Democracy in Pakistan?

The best chance that Pakistan has had until now to institutionalize democratic structures and change the pattern of military interventions and involvement in political life was the period between 1972 and 1977 under the charismatic Zulfikar Ali Bhutto.[23] That it did not happen is, perhaps, one

---

23   Hasan-Askari Rizvi, *Military, State, and Society in* Pakistan (New York: St Martin's Press Inc., 2000), pp. 142-3. See also Ian Talbot, *Pakistan*, p. 245. The February 18, 2008 election in Pakistan, in which the party connected with the military government was voted out of office and a "grand coalition" of the two major political parties that opposed the government of former General Pervez Musharraf have a large majority in the National Assembly, as well as the apparent decisions of the newly appointed Chief of Army Staff to distance the Army from political involvement, offer another good chance to establish civilian dominance. Whether it will happen this time is still uncertain, and skeptics abound.

of the great "what ifs" of the history of South Asia—perhaps of the Islamic world. A vibrant and modern democratic Pakistan might have taken South Asia in different and more productive directions in the last thirty-five years, and an Islamic democracy of its size and strength (70 million in 1972, 160 million today) might have played an important role in leading Islamic countries to a more comfortable accommodation with modernism.

In any case, the "new" Pakistan recovered its equilibrium surprisingly quickly after the shattering experience of the separation. In Bhutto's early months, high expectations for its future emerged—from its own people as well as the international community.[24] Bhutto retained the support of most Pakistanis during his time in office, but failed to capitalize on that support to consolidate political institutions that maintained civilian political superiority over the military. Within six years of its new beginning, Pakistan fell back into the political patterns of the "old" United Pakistan.

A New Constitution but the Same Old Divisive Issues —Regionalism and Religion

The Bhutto government's most immediate need was to draw up a new constitution under which Pakistan could be governed. Without the two equal-sized east and west wings, as in United Pakistan, a new formula would have to be found for the new Pakistan that now came in four very unequal political parts with a patchwork of languages, ethnicities, religions, and cultures.

Agreeing on a new formula to share power between the regions and the center, and drafting a constitution to spell it out, proved easier than expected—perhaps too easy.

Consensus was reached surprisingly swiftly on the two historically difficult political questions: how to share power between the federal and the provincial authorities; and how to divide power at federal level between the President and the Prime Minister. For these questions, the 1973 constitution was a serious departure from the constitutions that had been drawn up in 1956 and 1962.[25]

In the constitution, federal/provincial tensions were dealt with by providing for a bicameral legislature—an Assembly elected by popular vote in which legislation would be initiated, and a Senate with equal representation

---

24   Unlike Bangladesh, in which Mujib may have begun his rule with the high hopes of his countrymen, but in the eyes of the rest of the world was in charge of a "basket case."

25   Shahid Javed Burki, *Pakistan, Fifty Years of Nationhood* (Boulder, CO, Westview Press, 1991), p. 47.

from each province. In addition, President Bhutto (who was soon to choose to become Prime Minister in the new Parliamentary system) gave his "solemn word" that he would not interfere in the business of those provincial governments in which his party did not have a majority.[26]

The framers agreed on a parliamentary system, not unlike that of the United Kingdom, in which power was given to the Prime Minister. The President became, in this constitution, a head of state without power. A new article required the President to act only with the Prime Minister's "advice," and that all Presidential ordinances must be countersigned by the Prime Minister.

At Bhutto's instigation, provisions were added aiming to circumscribe formally the Army's power and role, and make it subordinate to the civilian government. Among these were: a "loyalty oath" that required Army officers to swear not to engage in political activity; and a provision that defined "high treason" as any attempt to abrogate or subvert the constitution "by use …or show of force or by other unconstitutional means." The Supreme Court lent its weight to the institutionalization of civilian authority over the military by declaring the 1969 military takeover by Yahya Khan illegal and unconstitutional.[27]

In addition, Bhutto restructured the Army's high command to curb its power and reduced the tenure of the Chief of Army Staff to three years. While in office he directed a disproportionate share of national resources to the military—for reconstruction and re-equipping after the disastrous defeat by India—but also to curry favor and avoid antagonizing it. Yet, inadvertently, he did alienate it by creating a new paramilitary organization, the Federal Security Force (FSF), ostensibly to assist the police in maintaining law and order, but which was seen by the army (perhaps rightly so) as the vanguard of a parallel force.[28]

A New Constitution—The Use of Religion for Political Ends

The religious question—would Pakistan be an "Islamic state" or a homeland for Muslims of South Asia—had troubled Pakistan's constitution making since 1947. The proponents of the "Islamic State" had made steady progress in inserting Islam into the constitution since the Objectives Resolution was approved by the constitutional assembly in 1949.

---

26   Ibid., p. 47.

27   Talbot, *Pakistan--A Modern History,* p. 223.

28   Ibid., p. 222-3.

In a fundamental departure from the two previous constitutions, the framers of the 1973 Constitution agreed that "Islam shall be the State religion of Pakistan." This went far beyond the Constitution of 1956 in attempting to break the impasse over the nature of Pakistan. While seemingly innocuous at the time, this new constitutional principle would come to have a serious effect on Pakistan's future political, economic, and social development.

This constitutional "compromise" was far stronger on the role of religion than the secular approach taken in the constitution of 1962. Yet Bhutto and Ayub Kahn shared the same goals regarding the role of Islam: they both wanted to use it, and Islamic leaders, to build a strong central government. The "modernist Islamic" ideology pushed by the Ayub Khan government was one part of this. The Bhutto government followed the pattern established by Ayub Khan of trying to break the hold of religious leaders (and also, in Bhutto's case, feudal landowners) over the mass of Pakistani citizens.[29]

The Pirs, as descendents of the Sufis, were (and still are) regarded as the mediators between God and their followers, and had significant political influence.[30] Pirs are often linked to powerful landowners, who in Pakistani society also mediate between their powerless minions and government. Bhutto wanted to use the Sufi shrines to weaken the Pirs and the landowners—in other words to eliminate the middlemen and communicate directly with the people.[31] But he also strove, as did Ayub Khan, to identify his party and government with Islam while avoiding the participation in politics of politically active religious leaders.

Both leaders tried to manipulate the Sufis and their shrines as religious symbols they could latch onto to prove their "Islamicness," but at the same time break the power of the pirs over their followers. They considered the pirs to be too closely connected politically to the feudal landowners and resisted the call for a return to literal Islamic law that was unsuitable in the modern world.[32] Bhutto and his party used the Sufi

---

29   Katherine Ewing, "The Politics of Sufism: Redefining the Saints of Pakistan," *Journal of Asian Studies*, 1983, Vol. 42, No. 2, pp. 251-2. This is one of the reasons why the Sultans of Delhi and the Mughals believed that their claim to rule India was enhanced if they were allied with the pirs (see Chapter 1).

30   Ibid., p.252-4. A second set of politically active religious leaders do not accept that spiritual authority and political power are separate; usually called "Islamists," these leaders seek direct political control of Pakistan in order to fashion a "true" Islamic state.

31   Ibid., p.252.

32   Ibid, p. 253.

shrines, through government participation in their rituals, as a symbol of their connection to the common man. The aim was to remove the pir as mediator with the government, but as Katherine Ewing points out, it is difficult to remove the pir's power of mediation unless his religious authority is also removed.[33] Bhutto succeeded in strengthening the authority of the state over pirs' land holdings, but did not touch their religious hold on their followers by banning them or their shrines.

To reduce the power of the landowners, Bhutto and the PPP pushed through a series of land reforms. Caught between his wish to attenuate the power of landowners and his own feudal instincts and fear of losing their political support, Bhutto's land reform programme proved half-hearted and there were enough loopholes to allow landowners to escape any significant redistribution of their holdings.[34]

The Islamists made other inroads as they inched toward the Islamic state they wanted. After resisting for many months in the constitutional debate, Bhutto and the PPP yielded on other demands: that the offices of President and Prime Minister could only be held by Muslims (one of the criteria of an Islamic state); that the state would "provide facilities" so Muslims could fashion their lives to the teachings of Islam; that the state would promote the teaching of the Koran and the Sunnah; and that the government would appoint a Council of Islamic Ideology to ensure that laws were in accordance with the teachings of Islam. The most egregious Islamist-inspired action, which Bhutto supported, was a National Assembly proclamation that the Ahmadiyya sect was not "Muslim."

These concessions were what it cost Bhutto, politically, to wean away the Islamist parties from an alliance with his two major political opponents. The unlikely combination of the secular National Awami Party of the NWFP, which was strongly inclined toward Pashtun nationalism (which sometimes went so far as favoring "Pushtunistan" over Pakistan), and the party of religious leader, Pir Pagaro, Bhutto's main political ri-

---

33 Katherine Ewing, *The Pir or Sufi Saint in Pakistani Islam* (unpublished PhD dissertation, University of Chicago, 1980), p. 219. Also see Ewing, "The Politics of Sufism…," *Journal of Asian Studies*, p. 258. Many of the religious leaders (called ulama) had been seeking political control they argued was required in a true Islamic state. In the days of an Indian Islamic state, during the Delhi Sultanate and the Mughal Empire, there had been an arrangement between the ulama and the Sultans/Emperors that "allowed the government to deviate from Islamic law as long as its supremacy was acknowledged and the potential for the evolution of society toward a more perfect embodiment of Islam was possible."

34 Ewing, "The Politics of Sufism," p. 258. For more detail see Talbot, *Pakistan—A Modern History*, pp. 230-1.

val in Sindh, had tried to link up with the Islamist parties to force him and the PPP from office. Bhutto had incurred their wrath by replacing provincial governments in Sindh and NWFP (forgetting his pledge not to interfere) and raised their fears of domination of provincial affairs by the center. (Bhutto later invoked "Governor's Rule" in NWFP, which exacerbated their fears by putting the province under direction of the central government.)

Judicial Autonomy and Authority: Given by One Hand, Taken by the Other

The 1973 constitution was supposed to rectify the restrictions on the judiciary that had grown during the last twelve years of United Pakistan and restore its autonomy and authority vis à vis the executive. Indeed it went some way toward formally enhanced protection of political rights by emphasizing the jurisdiction of superior courts to hear writs appealing executive actions that abridged such rights and granting these courts the power of interim relief.

Wartime preventive detention laws and other security rules were not, however, rescinded; political dissidents were jailed using these statutes, as the government cited hostile relations with India and domestic terrorism to justify such actions.[35] The conflict between executive authority and political and civil rights remained a sensitive issue during the Bhutto years, particularly as Prime Minister Bhutto continually extended his power and authority, often at the expense of the courts.

The Prime Minister, facing increasing political opposition in many parts of Pakistan, especially in Balochistan and NWFP, used his parliamentary party to amend the constitution (almost before the ink was dry), increasing his power and scope by, inter alia, narrowing the authority of the courts and of the legislatures. These amendments also took away the authority of the Parliament and the judiciary to oversee the Prime Minister's programs as well as those of his party.[36]

After a hopeful start in 1972 and 1973, the judiciary fought a losing battle to maintain the formal autonomy and authority it had gained from the new constitution. There were many conflicting policies and political principles that complicated the judiciary's struggle to maintain its position: Bhutto's drive to centralize the economy vs. the general desire to decentral-

---

35   Paula Newberg, *Judging the State: Courts and Constitutional Politics in Pakistan* (Cambridge: Cambridge University Press, 1995), p. 138.

36   Ibid., p.139.

ize politically; his use of emergency powers to quell unrest and political opposition *vs.* a desire on the part of most of the polity to strengthen constitutional democracy; and the continuing demands for provincial (or communal) autonomy *vs.* the visceral Pakistani leanings of Federal politicians, Punjabis, the bureaucracy, and the military toward a centralized state.

The judiciary's authority was continually diminished by Bhutto's amendments to the constitution and the former sought legal grounds which would enable it to protect some rights. As Paula Newberg describes it, while the judiciary "tried to separate actions taken by or against the government from those taken for political or partisan purposes...the People's Party often did not differentiate between the two, acting as if citizen's rights were no more than another set of obstacles in the path of political power."[37]

Relations with India: A Bad Continuum

While relations with India went from warm cooperation to chilly caution during the Mujib years in Bangladesh, they changed from very bad (how else would one characterize war and crushing defeat?) to peaceful hostility during the Bhutto years in Pakistan. In other words the relationship deteriorated in Bangladesh and improved marginally in Pakistan, but each country ended up in more or less the same position—each feared and seriously distrusted India's designs and ambitions—by the time Mujib and Bhutto left the stage.

In Pakistan, this was an improvement, if only at the margin. Bhutto's strength was in foreign policy, and it turned out that his only lasting achievements (notwithstanding his building of the PPP) were in the foreign affairs of the reborn Pakistan. His ambition was to use foreign as well as domestic policy to rebuild Pakistan, politically, economically, and psychologically after the disaster of the 1971 war and the trauma of separation of over half of its former citizens into another country. In fact, his foreign policy contributed, more or less, to that goal, while his domestic policy undermined it.

His overall foreign policy aim was to recalibrate Pakistan's paranoid relationship with India, reduce political and security dependence on the United States (the US arms embargo, dating from the 1965 war with India, remained in place) and the Western industrial countries by building closer ties with China, the Islamic countries of the Middle East, and the Third World, in general. He cut Pakistan's ties with Western-oriented organizations, including the Commonwealth, and the Southeast Asia Treaty Organiza-

---

37   Ibid., p. 143.

tion (SEATO), but maintained links with the Central Treaty Organization (CENTO) in order to foster good relations with key Islamic countries, especially Iran and Turkey.[38]

Bhutto intended to become a big player among the nations of the Islamic world, and of the developing world too, and thereby project an image of an independent and non-aligned foreign policy. He sought closer relationships with Islamic countries and a larger role in pan-Islamic organizations, which culminated in Pakistan hosting an Islamic summit, which every Islamic leader except the Shah of Iran attended. The summit was, perhaps, the high point of Bhutto's political career, and certainly of his campaign to restore Pakistani prestige. His other major objective of finding a platform for espousing the interests of the developing countries was accomplished when Bhutto led Pakistan into the Non-Aligned Movement (NAM).[39]

To balance and deter India's military superiority, demonstrated and exacerbated by the 1971 war and defeat, Bhutto initiated the clandestine program to build a nuclear weapon. This decision preceded India's first nuclear test by two years but it was a policy that Bhutto had been advocating since 1965. He also hoped, it appears, that possession of nuclear capability would restore some of Pakistan's international prestige, and that it would give him additional leverage over the military.[40]

Many consider that his greatest foreign affairs triumph was the July 1972 Simla Agreement that officially ended the 1971 war with India, yet there was less than met the eye in this accord that overlooked more problems than it solved, Bhutto played it brilliantly to domestic audiences. His ability to explain away the lacunae and magnify the achievements of the agreement went far toward his objective of repairing the psychological wounds left by the war. It also solved some of the immediate post-war bilateral problems with India, and it put others on hold for a while.

These problems included the repatriation of 93,000 Pakistani POWs held by the Indian army and the return of 6,000 square miles of Pakistani territory occupied by India when hostilities ceased. Bhutto had to press these issues on Indira Gandhi, the Indian Prime Minister, while dealing with New Delhi's demands for a "no war" clause and for Pakistani recognition of Bangladesh.[41]

---

38   Lawrence Ziring, *Pakistan in the Twentieth Century—A Political History* (Karachi: Oxford University Press, 1997), p. 385.

39   Ibid., p. 387-8.

40   Talbot, *Pakistan—A Modern History*, p. 238.

41   Ibid., p. 235.

Though negotiating from a much weaker position, Bhutto, known by his friends to be a "great bluffer when he held a poor hand," rebuffed Mrs Gandhi's insistence that he sign on to the "no war" clause and her attempt to bait an agreement to recognize Bangladesh with the return of the Pakistani prisoners. Bhutto appeared to be prepared to let the meeting fail rather than to give in on either point.[42] He did not get the POWs back till a year or so later. India would not agree to that unless Bangladesh was at the negotiating table, which would have required Pakistani recognition of the new state.[43] But he did regain Pakistan's lost territory. In addition, in addressing the Kashmir issue each side agreed "to respect the line of control" that was in effect when hostilities ceased in December 1971. India undoubtedly saw this as tantamount and setting the stage for the line of control to become an international boundary. Bhutto, and probably most Pakistanis saw it as a papering over a fundamental disagreement with India until Pakistan regained the strength to assert its claims again.[44]

Instead of a "no war" clause, Bhutto agreed to a provision that the two countries "had resolved to settle their differences by peaceful means through bilateral negotiations or by any other peaceful means mutually agreed upon between them."[45] Each side has, in subsequent years, interpreted this to suit its own immediate needs—and, to no one's surprise, has done so quite differently.

Simla also promoted the resumption of trade and communication links, including overflights, and scientific and cultural exchanges. Prisoner repatriation was accomplished through bilateral negotiations in August 1973 when India dropped its insistence that their return was linked to recognition of Bangladesh.[46] Bhutto relented on the question of recognizing Bangladesh in February 1974 (and invited Mujib to the Islamic Summit). Mujib then abandoned his plan to try 195 Pakistani military prisoners as war criminals and sent them home.

In essence, Bhutto constructed a foreign policy which seemed to be directed at restoring Pakistani self-esteem and reconstructing its military and diplomatic strength, by turning his attention away from the almost unique

---

42   Wolpert, *Zulfi Bhutto*, p. 190. This was the period of warm relations between Bangladesh and India.

43   Talbot, *Pakistan--A Modern* History, p. 236.

44   Wolpert, *Zulfi Bhutto*, p. 193.

45   Ibid., p. 190.1

46   Ibid., p. 191. By then, Indo/Bangladeshi relations were cooling off rapidly.

focus on India of his predecessors. This was, he believed, critical to his political success in Pakistan, but, in reality, nothing in his policy or in his rhetoric diminished the India-centric concerns of most of the Pakistani polity. Pakistanis seemed to read Bhutto, as do his biographers, as being convinced that the country's inevitable destiny was to "rise again some day to reclaim Kashmir" and assert its leadership of the Islamic world.[47]

Bhutto's Decline

Despite the provisions of the new constitution, the idea of subordinating the army to civilian political control apparently became quickly subordinated itself to the exigencies of politics and remaining in power. Bhutto's use of the army, particularly in Balochistan from 1973 to 1977 returned it to a political role and revived its self esteem.[48]

He eliminated the Civil Service of Pakistan (CSP), the elitist and paternalistic bureaucracy steeped in 200 years of tradition of the British-created Indian Civil Service.[49] This was aimed at weakening the Pakistani (read Punjabi) establishment of which the CSP had been the most enduring component. This demoralized the senior bureaucracy and probably lowered the quality of its services. According to Burki, however, it also broke the bureaucracy's power over the economy, in the long run. He notes, on the other hand, that the paternalistic CSP operated under a commonly understood "rules of the game" which placed important constraints on executive action, and by doing so "removed an important check on politicians' use of discretion."[50]

Bhutto, who hailed from Sindh, probably had another objective in eliminating the CSP. He wanted to meet the demands of the Sindhis, who had become disaffected by the growing power and influence of the immigrant Mohajirs in the major Sindhi cities of Karachi and Hyderabad, as well as the overweening Punjabi presence. His civil service reform turned out to be, also, a preference scheme for Sindhis in the bureaucracy.

Perhaps the failure with the most far-reaching long-term impact was the myopic refusal of Bhutto and the PPP to transform the party from a col-

---

47   Ibid., pp. 191-2

48   Talbot, *Pakistan—A Modern History*, pp. 226-7, 243. See also Newberg, *Judging the State*, p. 141.

49   Stephen Cohen, *The Idea of Pakistan* (Washington: The Brookings Institution, 2004), p. 143.

50   Burki, *Pakistan*, p. 75..

lection of opposition interests centered upon its charismatic leader to an institutionalized party—in other words, into a real political party. The PPP remained undemocratic in its structure, based on patronage, or clientism, rather than merit or distinction. This may have preordained the return of the Army to its self-appointed political role as protector of the state.[51]

There was a growing fear that Bhutto's ultimate aim was a one-party state—with, of course, the PPP as its sole party. This concern took form when Bhutto dismissed the provincial government of Balochistan in February 1974, in obvious violation of his promise not to interfere with provincial governments controlled by other parties. The government of the North West Frontier Province (NWFP), controlled by his major opponent, the National Awami Party (NAP), resigned in protest. Bhutto, and the central government ruled both provinces.[52]

In May 1974, Bhutto pushed an amendment through the national parliament giving the central government authority to ban any political party that was "operating in a manner prejudicial to the sovereignty or integrity of the country." Though the amendment stipulated that the Supreme Court had to approve any such ban, this appears not to have been a hindrance, as the NAP was banned soon after. The worry about whether Bhutto was seeking to form a one-party state spread to the elites and the military after Mujib turned Bangladesh into a one-party state in January 1975.[53]

Bhutto also eroded his popularity with groups that had supported its populist, progressive platform. His land reforms had little impact other than allowing some landlords to increase their holdings at the expense of others who were considered political enemies. This not only alienated the few landlords whose land was taken away, but the left wing of the PPP which advocated, and expected, real land reform. His labor reforms, which pleased the left, alienated a large part of the small trading and merchant class of Punjab, which had lent important support in the 1970 election.

The wholesale nationalization of large and even medium-sized industry failed to win over those segments that were potential PPP supporters. In many instances, Bhutto used nationalization to reward PPP stalwarts or supporters—which strengthened the client-patron nature of the party and made it more resistant to reform. The nationalization of the large banks began the use of large, uncollateralized loans to party favorites; these loans

51   Talbot, *Pakistan—A Modern History*, p. 218.
52   Burki, *Pakistan*, p. 47.
53   Ibid., pp. 47-8.

were not repaid, and in fact were not expected to be repaid. They served as a source of income, and thus of payoffs, for PPP loyalists. This inaugurated a system which continued under future "democratic" dispensations and brought many Pakistani banks to the brink of, if not actual, insolvency, a practice that severely weakened the country's financial system.[54]

The Irony of Bhutto's Fall

Despite the negative reaction to his policies, Bhutto's populist vision still enjoyed the support of a plurality of Pakistanis. The proximate cause of his downfall, the suspected rigging of the election of 1977, need not, therefore, have happened. Bhutto and the PPP probably won the election legitimately, but overzealous PPP local leaders, especially in Punjab, appear to have rigged the polls in their districts—probably to enhance their own standing. These rigged districts served to inflate the PPP national majority, but it is almost certain they did not affect the outcome of the election.

Bhutto had called the election in early January perceiving the opposition to be divided and weak. Surprisingly, within a few days, it had organized itself into a nine-party alliance with a coherent platform. This alliance drew large crowds and expected a reasonable showing, but not a victory. In the event, it won less than 20 percent of the seats, and later claimed that its disappointing showing was due to rigging.

Public feeling against this perceived electoral fraud slowly gathered momentum and mass demonstrations against the Bhutto government began about a month after the election. Desperate to stay in power, Bhutto looked for allies wherever he could find them, sometimes in the most unlikely places. In a move that would have lasting consequences, he reverted to the time honored habit of past (and future) political leaders by trying to buy off Islamist groups. These had been among his fiercest critics throughout his political career because of his "apostate" life style. His government banned alcoholic beverages from being sold or consumed (prohibition obtains to this day, and has been a bonanza for bootleggers ever since); gambling was also banned; and nightclubs and bars were closed. In a little-noticed irony, the weekend holiday moved from Sunday to Friday on July 1—four days before his fall from power.

Bhutto also abandoned his policy of trying to break the power of the feudals and the pirs and institutionalize "Islamic socialism" and democracy. The inroads his government might have made in democratizing society were

---

54   Talbot, *Pakistan—A Modern History*, p. 234.

undone in an instant. He wanted to boost his support in rural areas, and made alliances with the same powerful landowners whose power he had wanted earlier to break.[55]

Bhutto may have over-reacted as the demonstrations spread and became more violent over several weeks. He declared martial law in the major cities, but this proved to no avail and was troubling to the Army, which was expected to enforce it against demonstrators; as these demonstrations centered in Punjab, this required the preponderantly Punjabi army to use force on Punjabi demonstrators. Senior army officers could not tolerate this for very long, primarily because they feared that rank and file soldiers might disobey orders to take punitive action against their own kinsmen.

On July 5, six and one-half years after the debacle of the separation of the two wings of Pakistan, the lowest point in its history, the Army had recovered enough prestige and self-esteem to resume its self-appointed role as "savior of the nation." It removed Bhutto and the PPP government from power, and the recently appointed Chief of Army Staff, General Zia ul Huq, became Chief Martial Law Administrator (CMLA). Zia first announced the army takeover as a 90-day interim measure until new elections could be held. The 90 days turned into 91 months.

Bhutto spent a brief period under house arrest. After his release, he announced publicly that he planned to participate in the new elections, and drew large crowds in several public appearances. He might very well have regained power had the elections been held without interference, and had he been free to run. But the possibility that he would return immediately to power (given his well-known penchant for political hard ball) posed too great a risk for the military leaders of the coup. He was arrested in September 1977, two months after he had been removed by the army, for complicity in a murder. The elections were "postponed"—repeatedly. Convicted of the charge, Bhutto was executed twenty-one months after his fall.

---

55   William Richter, "The Political Dynamics of Islamic Resurgence in Pakistan," *Asia Survey*, 19, No.6, 1979, pp. 547-57.

50

3

FROM MILITARY TO CIVILIAN RULE
IN BANGLADESH

Chaos followed Mujib's demise. The severe instability that followed the assassination brought a second military coup less than three months later, on November 3, 1975, by a radical faction of the Army. A third coup, by the traditional, professional core of the Army, came four days later. The professional army restored stability—an anomaly that Bangladeshis had become familiar with during their twenty-four years as part of United Pakistan—stability through military coup. In keeping with the apparent Bengali urge to sweeten military regimes with a civilian overtone, the leaders of the November 3 coup selected former Chief Justice Abu Sadat Muhammed Sayem as President and as concurrent Chief Martial Law Administrator (CMLA). Sayem remained in both positions after the November 7 coup, and he appointed General Ziaur Rahman as a deputy Martial Law Administrator. The Zia era had begun.[1]

Ziaur Rahman and the Politics of Hope and Transition
—A Short-Lived but Fecund Era

The period of direct military rule lasted until February 1979. It is important to note, at this point, that, despite the seeming parallels, the early years of military rule in Bangladesh differed from the equivalent period in Pakistan. It appears in retrospect that the military officer who became political leader, Ziaur Rahman, grew steadily more disinclined to perpetuate the army in power and was to lead Bangladesh back to a democratic political structure

---

1   Neither in charge nor a figurehead, Sayem was in an unenviable position. The military, and Zia, needed him for the civilian cover he gave, so he had some leverage, but no troops—they were all Zia's. As Zia strengthened his position, so Sayem's weakened.

in which civilian politicians would dominate. As we will see in the next chapter, his Pakistani counterpart, Zia ul Huq was clearly determined to keep the military as the dominant political force in Pakistan. There are some observers, however, who believe that Ziaur Rahman's only real objective was to perpetuate himself in power by any means that could be arranged—preferably, but not necessarily, by ones that appeared democratic.

In the early days of military rule, Ziaur Rahman's policies closely resembled Zia ul Huq's in their Jacobin crushing of political parties and civilian politicians, and their suppression of dissent and protest, as he searched for a way back to stability.[2] In Ziaur Rahman's case these policies may have been necessary to prevent more attempts by the radical military factions (those mentioned in Chapter 2, primarily from the "freedom fighter" elements of the army) to take over the government. He spent much of the first year weeding out unreliable elements in the Army and restoring discipline in the military—in which discontent remained a problem for some time. Ziaur Rahman had the disadvantage of leading a fragmented army, and attempts on the part of military factions to intervene in politics became the rule, rather than the exception.[3]

Zia also reversed Mujib's policy of not utilizing talented civil servants if they had opted to stay at their posts in East Pakistan or been caught in West Pakistan at the beginning of the war of separation. He made full use of those bureaucrats who had been discarded by Mujib and searched for talented Bangladeshis whatever their past might be. As is often the case, many of the senior civil servants teamed up with the military government and improved greatly the efficiency of the senior administration.[4]

While the constitution remained in force (unlike the Ershad military intervention which is covered in Chapter 6), the original independence and authority of the judiciary, considerably reduced by Mujib in 1974, was not fully restored by Zia.[5] For example, the Proclamation Order of 1977, *inter alia*, eliminated the requirement of the original document that two-thirds of Parliament approve the removal by the executive of a Supreme Court

---

2   Baxter, *Bangladesh*, p. 95.

3   Ibid., p. 95.

4   Ibid., p. 94.

5   Nor were, despite the promise of the new leaders to do so, the authoritarian powers that Mujib had created for himself in July 1974 rescinded by the group who took over the government after his assassination. The chaotic, unstable situation that obtained prevented such liberalization. See James Heitzman and Robert Worden, ed., *Bangladesh, a country study*, (Washington: Library of Congress, 1988), p. 36.

judge. Instead a Supreme Judicial Council, comprising the Chief Justice and the next two senior judges, was set up to advise the President that a judge should be removed.

Zia's policies of even-handed enforcement of the law fostered an attitude of trust toward the court system which greatly increased the court's authority in the eyes of Bangladeshis despite the curtailment of rights that came automatically with martial law.[6] As we will see below, Zia used his power as chief martial law administrator to issues a series of proclamations which modified the constitution and, thus, changed the course of Bangladesh politics. His first proclamation rescinded Mujib's one party system, set up in the fourth amendment of January 1975, but he chose not to curtail the powers that amendment had given the President.[7]

After the Parliamentary election of 1979, which fully restored a democratic structure, Zia proposed and his Parliament passed the fifth amendment to the constitution which removed all martial law actions, proclamations, and laws from the review of the judicial branch. Such amendments are common in martial law regimes to indemnify military rulers from retrospective legal action by subsequent civilian governments, primarily for their (usually unconstitutional, and possibly treasonous) seizure of the government.[8] In this respect, Ziaur Rahman, Muhammed Ershad, Zia ul Huq, and Pervez Musharraf have acted exactly alike.

Politics Resumes—Zia Consolidates Power

The leaders of the August 15 coup against Mujib, had promised that political activity would begin in a year, in August 1976, and that national elections would be held in February 1977. This pledge was repeated by the leaders of the two November coups. Much of the army officer corps was skeptical that either date was feasible, given the disorderly conditions that continued to prevail—though at a decreasing level—in the early months of martial law. In the event, political activity commenced again in August 1976, but only in a very circumscribed way. National elections were a more contentious issue, and provoked the first public disagreement between the civilian President, Sayem, and his military deputies. The military won the

---

6   Baxter, *Bangladesh*, p. 94.

7   Mahfuzal H. Chowdhury, Muham A.Hakim, and Habib Zafarullah, "Politics and Government—the Search for Legitimacy," in *The Zia Episode in Bangladesh Politics*, edited by Habib Zafarullah (Denver: Academic Books, International Academic Publishers, Ltd., 2000), p. 25.

8   Ibid., pp. 25-6.

argument, and the martial law government announced in November 1976 that the elections scheduled for February 1977 would be postponed to a later, unspecified, date. Local non-partisan elections were allowed to take place in January 1977, however.[9]

Sayem resigned as CMLA because of this decision, although he remained as President, with Zia assuming this the role too. After Sayem's resignation as CMLA, Zia further consolidated his power, and enhanced his already widespread popularity by his constant travels around the country espousing the politics of hope. He produced, and promoted all over the nation, a political and economic program of nineteen points, designed to exhort the population to pull together in a more strenuous and organized manner for the national good and, at the same time, to offer hope for a better future. It emphasized increasing food production (always popular in a country in which most of the population lived on the margin of hunger). It also set out a plan for integrated rural development which included a variety of social development programs that had modernization of society as one implicit goal. Most important among these was an emphasis on family planning.

Zia had developed political ambitions, and much of the Bangladesh population supported those aspirations as the first ray of optimism in their mostly hard-scrabble lives.[10] In April 1977, Sayem resigned as President citing health reasons. Zia was named President, a reflection of his power over the military and his immense popularity with the public. A few of the old-time politicians objected to his accession to the Presidency, and were widely ignored. Zia promised elections, but still gave no dates. They came sooner than expected.

When he assumed the Presidency, Zia's first and most pressing objective was to establish legitimacy for his government. All military regimes have this problem. In part he attempted to deal with this question through promulgating constitutional amendments that would win the support of certain parts of civil society. But the main thrust of his strategy to establish legitimacy was to enter politics. For that he needed a political party.

His first step was to go to the nation for its verdict in a referendum on whether he should continue in office. Using his nineteen-point program as a basis for the campaign, he blanketed the country promoting his agenda,

---

9   Craig Baxter, *Bangladesh*, p. 96.

10   Most of the available evidence suggests that Zia's concern for the future of his country predated his development of political ambitions. Because of his early and untimely demise, we shall never know if he would have resisted the corruptions of office to which most South Asian leaders have succumbed in one way or another.

asking for peoples' support to continue in the office of President. Unsurprisingly, he won an overwhelming mandate when, according to the official statistics, 98.9 percent of those voting supported his continuing in office.[11] Of more import, perhaps, was that 88.5 percent of the electorate turned out—a far higher percentage than in any previous election in Bangladesh. There were, and still are, of course, a number of politicians and political observers skeptical of these numbers. Zia's willingness to allow such polling figures to be used is, according to some observers, an indication that he "saw democratic processes merely as instruments of political power; paths to be negotiated so that the real work could be done independently of such concerns." Such critics pointed out "that he was a military man intent on using military methods to control the destiny of a nation ...[and] would leave a political legacy able to be exploited by his successor[s]...."[12]

This resounding referendum victory guided Zia's next steps. First he chose a Vice President, an office that had been unoccupied since the coup against the Mujib government, as both Sayem and his predecessor left the office vacant. Having received a huge popular endorsement both of his policies and of the objectives of the martial law government, Zia selected a respected civilian to be the number two. He chose Abdus Sattar, a highly respected East Pakistani jurist, who had been appointed as Justice of the Supreme Court of United Pakistan in 1968, before separation. Sattar had served as chief election commissioner and had run the 1970 election that was widely accepted as free and fair. In November 1975 Sayem had named Sattar as his special assistant, and later as advisor for law and parliamentary affairs. He continued in this latter capacity while he was Vice President.

Zia's Political Aims: The Indian Connection

National elections were the next obvious political step, but those couldn't take place until the political party was constructed. Zia wanted a party to reflect his political thinking and to support the direction in which he would take the country, which was a markedly different direction than the Awami League wanted to take it. He entrusted the task of building

---

11   Denis Wright, "The Rise of Zia: From Soldier to Politician," in *The Zia Episode in Bangladesh Politics*, p.14. The "extravagance" of this figure has been duly noted by most analysts, but Wright notes that " it is even more an expression of a more subtle insecurity by Zia in the world of politics."

12   Wright, "The Rise of Zia...," *The Zia Episode*, 15. This "legacy" refers to the openings Zia left for the authoritarian perversions of the constitution and the political process of the Ershad military regime.

that party to Sattar. The aim was to balance and offer an alternative to the Awami League and its pro-India, socialist, secularist, Bengali nationalist philosophy. Though there were many voices within the new party, as it grew and evolved, as there were in the Awami League, its overall philosophy, formulated by Zia, could be described as much less friendly to and more suspicious of India (though not antagonistic, just as one would not antagonize the 600 pound gorilla next door).[13]

This tied in perfectly with his pro-western and free enterprise economic and industrial policies. India was, at the time, an advocate of the socialist, central planning approach to economic development. It was consistent also with Zia's emphasis on Bangladeshi (as opposed to pan-Bengali) nationalism. Finally, it fitted the on-going efforts of Zia and the military since the November 1975 coup to reach out to conservative and Islamic elements to secure legitimacy. Zia and his team were probably, in any case, more Islamic in outlook than the bulk of the opposition, though they were not, by any means, fundamentalist or even conservative. Relations with India were difficult enough to make his emphasis on a more nationalist identity palatable to many Bangladeshis, and to aid him in his search among the Islamic groups for legitimacy.

The primary bilateral issue with India in the early Zia years was water: sharing of the Ganges River water diverted and stored by the newly constructed Faraka Barrage (Dam). Prior to Mujib's demise, his government and India had reached an agreement on water-sharing that promised Bangladesh a minimum amount of water during the "low-flow" period of April and May. However, in 1976, in a unusually dry period, massive amounts of Ganges water was taken by India. This caused serious navigational and irrigation problems downstream in Bangladesh. Four districts down river were seriously affected, but the Indians steadfastly refused to negotiate a resolution acceptable to Bangladesh.[14]

Bangladesh brought the issue of the unilateral Indian diversion of this water to the United Nations General Assembly. India contended that the matter should be settled bilaterally, but the Assembly supported Bangladesh in saying that the matter should be settled at the ministerial level. This failed when the two sides could not agree on a minimum amount for

---

13   Kathryn Jacques, *Bangladesh, India, and Pakistan: International Relations and Regional Tensions in South Asia* (New York: St Martin's Press, 2000), p. 100.

14   Haran ur Rashid, *Foreign Relations of Bangladesh* (Varenessi, India: Rishi Publications, 2001), p. 75.

Bangladesh during all seasons.[15] The impasse remained until the Indian government changed after a general election in March 1977, when the new government took a more cooperative line toward Bangladesh and reached a provisional agreement acceptable to both sides which cut the previous difference in half. This was supposed to last for five years while a permanent arrangement was negotiated.[16] (This never happened, however, and for twenty years Southeastern Bangladesh suffered from water shortages during the low-water season. It was mostly rectified by the Ganges Water Treaty of 1996, which partitioned the water equally when flow is lower than average, gives Bangladesh a set amount when it is about average, and India a set amount when the flow is high.)

Other bilateral issues remained stubbornly unresolved despite two Zia visits to Delhi in 1980. By then the Congress government of Indira Gandhi had returned to power, and repeated the general tone of its previous post-Mujib hard-edged diplomacy toward Bangladesh.

A Mutinous Interlude

Sattar began to build the party, and a "national front" to support Zia. The elections were widely expected to be held in the spring of the following year, 1978 but preparations were set back by an unexpected and unrelated spontaneous event that shook the government and the country to its foundations. In early October 1977, a large number of air force enlisted men mutinied at the Dhaka air base. They were joined by some enlisted men from other services, but it was primarily an air force affair. The mutiny may have been triggered by a much more minor mutiny at the army base in Bogra, in Northern Bengal, but its origins are unclear. Other minor mutinies had occurred since August 1975, usually pro-Mujib in nature, but they were easily and summarily dealt with. The Dhaka mutiny of October 1977 was far more dangerous and traumatic.

The mutineers attacked Zia's residence, and probably would have killed him, had his guards been less alert and able to drive the mutineers off. The radio station in Dhaka was captured by the mutineers and their message of rebellion was broadcast for a few hours until loyal troops were able to recapture it. The rebels killed a number of air force officers who were at the airport for negotiations with a Japanese Red Army group that had hijacked a Japan Air Lines plane and taken it to Dhaka the previous week.

---

15   Ibid., p. 76.
16   Ibid., p. 77.

The mutiny was quickly, and bloodily, put down by the army. The government described it as a dispute over pay and service conditions, and this was probably the primary driver, but there remains the suspicion that some elements still sympathetic to Mujib and his policies also took part. The fallout of this event affected the senior military leadership, and ultimately the political future of Zia and the nation. The air force chief, Mahmud, who had escaped being killed by the mutineers, was dismissed from both his command and his post as food minister, and sent abroad. The military intelligence chief and his civilian counterpart were also dismissed, as none of the intelligence services had an inkling of the coming mutiny. Three senior army officers who were in line for the position of army chief when Zia decided to step down were sent to other assignments or retired. One of these was a key leader and planner in Zia's assassination four years later.

From Military Government to Elected Civilian Government

If the dangers of a politicized military had not previously been fully visible to Zia, they certainly were after the mutiny. He strengthened his determination to isolate the military from politics and after a few months of minimal political activity to quiet fears and stabilize the country (and the military) proceeded quickly with his strategy to "civilianize" the government more fully. He began to ensure that he was described in the press as "President," never as "General." All the other officers in the cabinet were required either to resign from the military or from the cabinet. Thirteen civilian politicians were appointed to the cabinet, mostly in minor posts. These were mainly associated with his new political party or with its allies from parties that made up the national front, called JAGODAL, which would support Zia's candidacy for President.

The formation of the front was announced in February 1978. It was a mélange of right, left and centrist parties that made strange political bedfellows but all agreed on two things: Zia for President; and a Presidential form of government, as set out in Mujib's 1975 amendments to the 1972 constitution. But they also agreed to strip the constitution of all the restrictive, one-party provisions that Mujib had also sponsored.

The election rules were promulgated in April 1978 and the Presidential election was held on June 3 that year. Zia, the candidate of the JAGODAL front, ran on a Bangladesh nationalist platform, with the nineteen point program still as its central plank. The opposition front, primarily the two parts of the Awami League, put up General Abdul Shani Osmany against

Zia. Osmany, a former Colonel in the army of United Pakistan before separation, was also an icon of the liberation struggle who commanded the freedom fighters during that war (as such, he had been Zia's commanding officer). He was also a political hero, having resigned from the Mujib government in public protest in early 1975 over the constitutional changes and the imposition of one-party rule. Despite his credentials, he was no match for Zia, who received slightly over 75 percent of the vote. The election appears to have been free and fair; thus Zia was now the legitimate freely elected President of Bangladesh.[17]

The election settled the issue of whether Bangladesh would have a presidential or parliamentary form of government for the next fourteen years. Osmany's Awami League platform included a pledge to return to a parliamentary form of government. In the election, the people spoke, freely and fairly, both for Zia and for presidential government. The next step would be the election of a parliament, but one that would function in a presidential system as a check and balance on presidential power and policy.

But first, a cabinet of ministers had to be formed from the council of advisors that had served as a cabinet, in form if not in name, since November 1975. Representatives of the parties in the front that supported Zia were given prominent spots, and there were sixteen holdovers from the council of advisors. JAGODAL was consolidated into one party, which was renamed the Bangladesh Nationalist Party (BNP). Vice President Sattar became the head of the BNP. Some of the left-leaning parties in the front, declined to become part of the BNP, and reformed as independent parties. While the BNP was taking shape, the Awami League split into two parties, with the larger remnant maintaining the positions and philosophies of Mujib, and the smaller remnant disavowing many of the most extreme of those positions.

The government needed to be further civilized to bestow full legitimacy on the parliamentary elections. Zia began that process by resigning as Chief of Staff of the Army, a position he had retained since the initiation of the military government, and had held concurrently with the Presidency. He pledged to withdraw martial law after the elections and "make the new parliament sovereign."[18] The opposition demanded that martial law be rescinded before the elections, but Zia refused to do so.

---

17   Baxter, *Bangladesh*, pp. 98-9, table 8.1.

18   Mahfuzul H. Chowdhury, Muhammed A. Hakim, and Habib Zafarullah, "Politics And Government: The Search for Legitimacy," *The Zia Episode*, p. 31.

The elections for the new kind of parliament were held in February 1979. Zia campaigned strenuously for his new party, and was rewarded with another large vote of confidence by Bangladeshis. Though the BNP received only 41.2 percent of the vote, it swept 207 of 300 seats in the parliament. Votes for the other parties were scattered among a number of smaller parties and the larger rump of the Awami League which took 24.5 percent of the popular vote but won only 39 seats. A coalition of the rump of the old Muslim League and another like-minded party won 8 percent of the vote and 20 seats. Zia kept his word and abolished martial law in April of 1979, three and half years after it had been introduced.[19]

Zia's Fledgling Democracy

Zia lived for two years after the parliamentary election; the second democratic episode in Bangladesh, over which he presided, survived another year. During his brief reign as a democratically elected, civilian president, economic and social programs were promulgated, and a pattern of societal behavior established that laid the basis of a far-reaching social revolution. Though democracy failed after Zia's assassination, one aspect of his legacy, the social revolution, continued to build momentum because Bangladeshi society demanded it during the autocratic interregnum that followed. No government, no matter how autocratic, could have halted this revolution without an extreme popular backlash.

The period after the parliamentary elections until Zia's death was marked by a significant increase in political stability that may be the most important achievement of his time in government. While Bangladesh politics, at the time of his death, would probably not have met the tests of full fledged democracy, the foundations were being laid. The Presidency was strong—more so because Zia remained very popular among the people. The Parliament was weak, in that it was not yet an effective check on the Presidency. It met regularly, however, and debated the policy issues and problems systematically and fully. In effect it was setting the stage for when it would exercise more effectively the checks and balances that the constitution assigned to it. The bureaucracy was working efficiently under the direction of government ministers, the economy was progressing, and social development was approaching "takeoff".[20]

---

19   Baxter, *Bangladesh*, p. 98.

20   Chowdhury, *et. al*, "Politics and Government," *The Zia Episode*, p. 37.

In retrospect, it seems clear that Zia was slowly building a center-right political coalition that would have the support of moderates and conservatives, as well as those elements of society, including Islamic groups, more inclined to support Bangladeshi nationalism, to be skeptical about India's designs and ambitions, and open to an Islamic orientation. This would ensure that there would be a civilian political counterweight to the Awami League and that the military would not be tempted or encouraged to intervene in politics in the future by the lack of such a civilian counterweight.

Whether the latter objective was Zia's design, or not, it is clearly the implication of the direction he had taken as he civilianized and democratized his government.[21] As long as he was the civilian President—he retained authority and links to the military as Commander-in-Chief of the defense forces—the bulk of the army seemed content that its views on policy carried great weight. However, some elements of the latter's freedom fighter faction were suspicious of Zia and skeptical of the direction he was taking.

One manifestation of his close and continuing links to the military, as a civilian, was his periodic conferences with the "formation commanders," which provided the army a way of contributing to the government's policy process. This gave the army confidence that its views were being listened to closely. Zia's early demise reawakened the military to the implication of the political direction he had taken, and to the fact that it no longer had an institutional handle on national policy. This realization led, in a very short time, to the demise of a budding democracy.

Zia Is Killed and Hope for Democracy Dies with Him

On May 29, 1981, Zia came to Chittagong to sort out a dispute between two factions of the BNP. At around 4 am on the morning of May 30, the Circuit House where he was staying overnight was stormed by three

---

21   The more complicated, thus realistic, view is that Zia began as a believer in the benign authoritarian model of government (with the implied use of force to effect compliance by society) in developing countries such as Bangladesh but his thinking evolved over the years of his stewardship away from that model to a more pluralistic one in which civilian politics (implying compromises) is necessary for effective government. Sayed Mahmud Ali, "The Demise of Zia," in *The Zia Episodes*, pp. 162-3, writes, "Although he restored pluralist politics and to some extent, representative electoral processes, [Zia] retained substantial power in his own hands. The façade of democracy was useful but only as a façade...In the late 1970s he seemed to have recognized the need to build alternatives to his military power base, and his shift away from overt dependence on force to pluralist, 'civilian politics,' which necessitated compromises over questions of ideological purity, was apparently a principal cause of resentment in 'nationalist' circles, giving rise to numerous conspiracies which, in the end, cost him his life."

coordinated strike teams of army officers, following a plan worked out and authorized by Major General Muhammed Manzur, commander of the 24th Division, headquartered in Chittagong. Zia was very lightly guarded, given the number of threats that the intelligence services had become aware of, and the bad relations between him and Manzur.[22] In the initial assault, four soldiers, two officers, and a policeman were killed. As the attackers ran through the Circuit House shouting, "where is the President?" Zia emerged from his room in his pajamas and was shot down summarily by Lt Colonel Motiur Rahman with a salvo from an automatic weapon.[23] The Zia era ended, as it had started, in blood.

The assassination might be ascribed to unfinished business—incomplete integration of the army. General Manzur, the army officer who planned the assassination and whose officers carried it out at his command, was a "freedom fighter." Manzur's personal unhappiness over the apparent end of his career does not fully explan his actions. He had, evidently, in a recent meeting of formation commanders accused Zia of "betraying the army and threatening the nationalist cause" by his civilianization of the government.[24] Except for General Manzur's small group of officers in Chittagong, the rest of the military remained loyal to the democratic government. Under the direction of Major General Ershad, a repatriate, who had replaced Zia as Army Chief of Staff when Zia gave up the position, General Manzur and

---

22 Manzur apparently had a personal grudge against Zia, dating from his abrupt transfer to Chittagong after the October 1977 air force mutiny. This took him out of the line to be Army Chief of Staff. Moreover, he had clashed with Zia several times in recent months over the direction that Zia was taking the nation ("delinking the army from national decision making") and had also been insubordinate to the Army Chief of Staff, General Ershad, several times. Manzur learned only a few days before Zia's visit to Chittagong that he was being transferred to command the Defense Services Command and Staff College, essentially a sinecure to get him out of the way and without any command over combat troops.

23 There had been several thwarted threats, and at least one actual attempt, on Zia'a life in the months leading up to the assassination. The intelligence agencies were particularly wary of danger to Zia in Chittagong because of the bad blood between him and Manzur. Why he was so lightly guarded is not clear. The usual conspiracy theories are in evidence, especially those putting General Ershad at the center of the conspiracy. Zia's widow is said to have suspected such a conspiracy; on the other hand, Zia's personality may be an equally reliable explanation. Sayed Mahmud Ali, "The Demise of Zia," in *The Zia Episode*, p. 154, writes, "…supremely confident of himself and his ability to overcome crises, Zia never paid any attention [to intelligence agency warnings]. He had, after all, survived numerous attempts, starting from the early days of the war of independence when…he barely escaped a Pakistani plan to eliminate him. He could not let a group of hot-headed officers disrupt his plans to build a 'new Bangladesh.' "

24 Ali, "The Demise of Zia" *The Zia Episode*, p. 154.

his accomplices were tracked down and either killed on the spot or tried and hanged as traitors.

The democracy survived for almost another year, albeit in a feeble condition. Sattar became Acting President, on Zia's death, as provided in the constitution. He called for new elections within 180 days, as also called for by the constitution, and kept the government pretty much as it had been under Zia. But he lacked the one thing that Zia had, even after he retired from the army and became a civilian President: close ties and great influence with the army.

The various factions of the BNP—formerly the various parties that came together to become the BNP—were unable to agree on a candidate for the election from among several prominent contenders. None of these could capture enough support from other factions to gain the nomination. Though elderly and beginning to show his age, Sattar was the only candidate the factionalized party could agree on.

The opposition was in worse shape. It was badly split, with thirty-eight candidates, but only two of any note. General Osmany ran again, but this time as the candidate of a small splinter party. The major opposition came again from the Awami League, in particular from the larger remnant of the party which had split after the last presidential election. Many thought that Mujib's daughter, Sheikh Hasina, should be the party's candidate. She had been away from home in India at the time of the killing of Mujib and most of the rest of the family, and had returned to Bangladesh from India just before Zia's assassination after being elected head of the Awami League. But she had come back too recently, and the party leaders decided that Kamal Hossain, a distinguished lawyer and internationally well known ally of Mujib, would be a better candidate against Sattar. Hossain had written the 1973 constitution and later been foreign minister.

The election was held in mid-November 1981. Despite worries about his age and health, Sattar won almost two-thirds of the vote, a convincing victory for the BNP. It suggested that the people still supported the policies that Zia had initiated. Kamal Hossain received 26 percent, and the other 37 candidates split the remaining 8 percent.[25]

Sattar certainly had received a mandate to lead the nation. He apparently took his overwhelming victory as a mandate to civilianize the government further. Although Zia had left no serving military officers at high levels in the government, and had taken off his own uniform, he kept in close touch

---

25   Craig Baxter, *Bangladesh*, p. 104.

with his former colleagues from the armed forces; they believed that they still had significant influence through their informal ties with him. Sattar appointed civilian politicians as his Vice President, Prime Minister, and to most of the other cabinet positions. A few retired military officers were appointed to minor cabinet positions, but his government and cabinet was essentially without military influence.

The army, which had thought of itself as being *primus inter pares* in the running of the government, now found itself outside the door looking in through the keyhole. Army chief of staff Ershad, who had kept the army loyal through the crisis of Zia's assassination and the subsequent democratic succession, demanded an institutionalized role for the military in policy making. There is considerable evidence that Ershad was being pressured hard by the officer corps to regain the inside advantage that they thought they had under Zia.

Sattar's initial response was to say publicly that he saw no role for the military except to defend the nation. The army increased the pressure, and threatened to sieze power if their demands were not accommodated. Sattar, now on the defensive, agreed in January 1982 to set up a National Security Council (NSC), which would be the ultimate policy-making body on issues of internal or external security. It would consist of the three service chiefs, from the military side, and the President, Vice President, and Prime Minister from the civilian side.[26] The NSC satisfied neither Ershad nor the army officer corps, who seem to have had more ambitious visions of the army's role in governing Bangladesh. Ershad increased the pressure and Sattar reshuffled his cabinet in February, sacking his Vice President and several other cabinet ministers who the military disliked. He fought back, however, by sending a number of military officers serving in lower levels of the government back to their units—an attempt to curtail the armed forces' influence.

That was the final straw for the army. On March 24, 1982, the army removed Sattar and his new Vice President from office, dissolved the cabinet and the parliament, and declared martial law. Ershad became CMLA with the naval and air chiefs as the deputies. A few days later a relatively unknown jurist was appointed President, and Ershad became President of the Council of Ministers, or prime minister. He announced that the military had been forced to take over because it was the only organized national

---

26   This was another attempt to copy the concept that existed at times in Turkey. Pakistan has also had its flings with the NSC concept. But, except in Turkey, these NSCs do not seem to satisfy either the military or the civilian sides.

institution which could be relied on to defend the national interest, and that it would rule until new elections could be held. It should be noted that the martial law government "suspended" the constitution; it did not abrogate it.

Thus ended the second episode of what might be called a budding democracy in Bangladesh. Though brief, the Zia democratic episode planted the seeds of a social development revolution in very rich soil. Bangladesh now faced nine years of military or quasi-military government in which its leaders were military men in civilian garb behind the façade of a constitution that had no checks and balances on executive power. Yet the memory of Zia's brief democratic flowering remained strong, as did that of Bangladesh's initial days under Mujib, and they contributed to sustained popular resistance to the Ershad regime and a desire to restore democracy.

Zia as President and "Democratic" Leader

Zia's early and untimely demise did not halt the social and economic development he inaugurated (see Chapter 9) which continued with the acquiescence of the succeeding governments, if not always their effective support. While Zia set the stage for an ongoing and accelerating social development program, he neglected to strengthen the institutions that underpin a democratic system—and set in motion some trends that undermined it, especially his acquiescence to corruption as a way to buy off potential enemies and reward supporters. His outreach to Islamic forces and redefinition of the nation more in Islamic terms boosted the Islamists politically, and growing Islamism has become worrisome. He failed also to set up a mechanism for the automatic and peaceful transfer of power, and to pick a viable successor. (Sattar remained his VP, but was unable to control events after Zia's death.) Perhaps Zia thought he had plenty of time to take care of these loose ends.

Zia wanted to change the direction of the country. The basis of his policy remained the nineteen-point program he had used as his platform before the May 1977 referendum. After the referendum, and during the 18-month period leading up to the Presidential and Parliamentary elections, Zia and his government began implementation of the manifesto in concert with multilateral and bilateral donor agencies. In many cases, the agencies and NGOs took over the delivery of social services, with the tacit agreement of the government. This program of integrated rural development combined production-boosting programs—the development of infrastructure through popular food-for-work programs, for example—with social development programs, including primary and secondary education, delivered primarily by NGOs. (Chapter 9 explains these interrrelated issues in much greater detail.)

Zia's radical change in social and economic development policy was consistent with, and accompanied by, a sharp change in philosophical direction. The secularist fundamental principle that Mujib put in the constitution was excised and the overriding principle became trust and faith in Almighty Allah. The principle of Bengali nationalism (which would include Hindu Bengalis in West Bengal) was eschewed, and Bangladeshi nationalism (emphasizing the Islamic nation of Bangladesh) became the watchword. The principle of socialism was redefined. While there was some warming of relations during the government of Morarji Desai in Delhi, Zia distanced Bangladesh from India politically, while seeking closer ties with Islamic nations and the West. Relations with Pakistan improved too. He sought more regional cooperation, proposing in 1980 a conference of the seven nations of South Asia to discuss ideas for collaboration in a number of fields. This initiative bore fruit two years after his death when the South Asian Association for Regional Cooperation (SAARC) was formed.

The Enigma of Ziaur Rahman

Historians and social scientists are confronted with serious contradictions and difficult issues in evaluating Ziaur Rahman. His motivations and objectives are a mystery, in part because he left no written testimony outlining them, and in part because he seemed to be going one way, but may, in fact, have been going another. He was a military leader who returned his country to civilian rule—a rare occurrence in South Asia or indeed the third world—and to civilian-dominated, two-party electoral democracy in particular. But whether that was his intention, or simply an unintended by-product of his drive for power and stability in Bangladesh, may never be known.

It was, perhaps, Ziaur Rahman's hair-raising experience in two military uprisings that took him on a different path from Zia ul Huq in Pakistan. He was nearly killed twice by mutinous soldiers—the first time by those who carried out the November 3, 1975 coup (who, of course, held the government for four days); and the second time by the air force enlisted men who mutinied in October 1977. Denis Wright speculates that "the unleashing of anarchic political and military power" alerted Zia "to the depths of the political bankruptcy into which Bangladesh had fallen, the perilous danger which the politicization (sic) of the military forces posed for both himself and for the security of the country."[27]

His initial accomplishments were to stabilize and revitalize a military that was on the verge, in 1975, of disintegrating into numerous factions. It became again, over the early years of his regime, a coherent force. He restored the chain of command and gradually eliminated a number of officers that had been infected with the revolutionary ardor that emanated from the war of separation and the infusion into the fighting ranks of nonprofessional officers of radical political views. This took time, and the use of some force, yet was not complete after six years. The holdover of factionalism in the military cost him his life.

One thing seems clear: Zia was a pragmatic nationalist and that was his main—maybe his only—principle. This helps to explain the many contradictions. He used democratic processes to wield political power, but it is doubtful that he believed in them, certainly not at the beginning of his tenure. He used corruption to ensure loyalty among his followers and subordinates. Yet, as far as we know, he was uncorrupt and incorruptible himself (except maybe to the corruption of power). He also discarded without a trace of remorse some of the important principles for which he and many other Bangladeshis had fought a bloody war of separation from United Pakistan. For example, he was roundly condemned by his opponents, especially in the military, for reaching out to forces in the polity (especially the Islamists) that had opposed the creation of Bangladesh. His response was a typical combination of pragmatism and political vision—that he wanted to unite and integrate the entire population of Bangladesh into a national identity.

Politically, he left a mixed legacy. Among his most positive bequests to the nation was the reintroduction of the multiparty political system that had withered under Mujib. This ensured that all the political forces in Bangladesh participated in politics, and left only the most extreme outside the system to try to cause trouble. While the creation of the BNP gave the nation a major alternative in philosophy and policy to the Awami League, it was not at first a party with a natural base and wide popular appeal. The BNP was, in a sense, imposed from the top down, by the government, and reflected the same authoritarian style as official machinery under Zia. The BNP won elections handily because Zia was extraordinarily popular.

---

27   Wright, "The Rise of Zia" *The Zia Episode,* p. 12.

The civilian dominated, two-party electoral democracy lasted only a year beyond his assassination. The presidential system, which Ershad clearly preferred to the messiness of parliamentary politics, continued under him but did not feature in the era of elected democracies. Whether, given the poisonous political culture of Bangladesh, governance would be any better than it is under the parliamentary system is doubtful.

Zia restored stability to Bangladesh when it appeared to be on the path towards catastrophic and chaotic failure. He used the methods that he thought necessary, and the only methods he really knew—military ones. More than stability, he seems to have brought hope back to a beleaguered population, as disillusioned as he was by the near anarchy that obtained in the final months of Mujib's democratic experiment. He traveled widely throughout Bangladesh, mingling with the common people in a new and unprecedented form of politicking. But his political legacy involved an authoritarian system of almost-personal rule. While this might be justified because of his success in bringing the country back from the brink, it was liable to misuse by less scrupulous politicians. In fact, Ershad extended this system of personal rule to one of a very different kind—featuring corruption, self-aggrandizement, and cronyism. In some superficial ways, his system was similar to that of Zia. There are two distinct differences: Zia was overwhelmingly popular while he was leading the country and had no need to resort to repression or undemocratic methods to exercise power. He was also honest and trustworthy. Ershad possessed neither of these attributes.

Though it remains controversial, as noted in Chapter 1, Zia's move to recognize and emphasize Bangladeshi rather than Bengali identity had merit. It was intended to bring the entire population—including the minorities as well as Islamic elements—under the rubric of Bangladeshi national identity and for this reason Zia discarded secularism, one of the political principles that Mujib had incorporated in the constitution. His pragmatism extended also to economics. In fact, he seems never to have had a coherent economic program; his main objective was to back away from the nationalization excesses of the Mujib regime. He did this because of the intense pressure on him from many quarters—international donors, some parts of the military, and the business community. His authoritarian style of governance extended to economic policy, and his government continued to see the public sector as "the prime mover of development."[28]

---

28   Stanley A. Kochanak, *Patron-Client Politics and Business in Bangladesh* (New Delhi: Sage Publications, 1994), p. 93.

This dampened the enthusiasm of the Bangladeshi private sector and its investment plans.

According to Habib Zafarullah, Zia saw himself "as a 'benevolent, modernizing' leader, laying emphasis on the *social and economic development of the country, the role of women in public and community service, the cultural development of children and youth,* ... [emphasis added]. He gave a new nationalist identity to the people by fusing historical, cultural, religious, and geographical attitudes."[29]

His emphasis on economic and social development laid the basis for the extensive and innovative economic and social development programs that have characterized Bangladesh in the past twenty years. This has had, and will continue to have, the greatest impact on the overall development of Bangladesh. Again, it is not clear that Zia had any particularly clear or distinct vision about this. He wanted to improve the lot of the people, in part because that would help stability, and it would ensure their support for him. He seemed to welcome all those who had ideas that would promote social development and was particularly concerned about the rapidly expanding population of Bangladesh.

Zia's accomplishments and methods illuminate the serious questions of means and ends in the development of countries. Is democracy always the first principle of political development from which all else flows? Zia, whether he meant to or not, was working toward a real democracy. But his style and his political system led to the perversions of the Ershad regime. Zia also laid the basis for the half-democracy that now obtains in Bangladesh. He created the two-party system that ensures that, even with miserable governance (see Chapter 6), neither party enjoys a monopoly. And, with his emphasis on innovative programs of social development, Zia laid the basis for the durable and robust democracy that must develop if Bangladesh is to continue its progress as a leader in social development among both the Third World and the Muslim world.

It is hard to imagine what would have happened to Bangladesh had Ziaur Rahman been assassinated in 1975 instead of 1981. A failed state on the model of Afghanistan or Liberia might well have resulted. Zia saved Bangladesh from that fate. He did so with methods that were, at first, anything but democratic, though never as harsh as some other authoritarian military regimes. And whether by design or by accident, he guided the country to a position at which it seemed poised to enter the ranks of fledging electoral

---

29   Habib Zafarullah, "The Legacy of Zia," in *The Zia Episode in Bangladesh Politics*, p. 178.

democracies under civilian control. He was that rare apparition—the benign despot. The danger is that for every leader like Zia, there are hundreds like Ershad (or Zia ul Huq) whose motives are (or become so when in power) much more self-serving and pernicious.

4

FROM MILITARY TO SEMI-MILITARY
RULE IN PAKISTAN

Post-separation Pakistan has been governed directly by its army for almost half of the thirty-six years of its existence. Elected governments have been in power, or nominally in power, for the other half. After the military removed the Bhutto government in 1977, General Zia ul Huq and the army ruled directly for eight years. A military/civilian hybrid government (the civilianized version of a military government) took over for three additional years with Zia ul Huq still in charge—and still in uniform. Only Zia's death in a plane crash in 1988 ended this military intervention.

In 1999, the army under General Pervez Musharraf took over again from an elected government. The Musharraf military dispensation ruled directly for three years, until it created its own, perhaps slightly less coherent, hybrid elected government to lend it civilian flavor. Like Zia ul Huq, Musharraf heads this hybrid and remains in uniform.

The parallels between the first military regime of post-separation Pakistan, led by Zia ul Huq, and the second, led by Pervez Musharraf, are striking in several ways. It is almost as if there is a playbook for military intervention that the army follows faithfully without ever updating it. Like the civilian governments that the Musharraf government succeeded, which seemed unable to draw lessons from the past of what not to repeat, the army appears not to have learned from its mistakes.

One subtle—and worrisome—trend, which military governments have perforce fostered is a growing and strengthening symbiotic relationship between the army and the political and economic institutions of the state. This has resulted, *inter alia,* from the embedding of active and retired military personnel in those institutions. The use of such officers for purposes which serve primarily the army's interests is always justified as being in the interests of the state—the civilians can't be trusted to do the job right, or honestly. The inevitable result is that the interests of the state and the army are increasingly seen as identical.

The Zia regime institutionalized this pattern. Though Pakistan had previous military governments, they were much more alliances between a military head of state and the bureaucracy which ran the country. Zia, however, introduced what can only be described as a military "junta" style of leadership—even most of the high-ranking bureaucracy was consigned to the outer reaches of influence on policy.

A more dangerous corollary of this symbiotic relationship is the willingness of the army, during a military regime, to ally with political forces that are malign—whose long-run interests and objectives for the country are inimical to the modernist goals professed by the army. The army fosters these alliances to bolster its position within the state and its control over the state and the society. This began in the Zia regime with a series of alliances with Islamist forces, and appeared to flower for awhile at the political level in the early stages of the military/civilian hybrid government of Musharraf. But this anomalous relationship has wilted of late.

The difference between the two regimes on the religious issues turned out to be more rhetorical than real. Musharraf, an avowed modernist, for example, announced in January 2002 a program for the "transformation" of Pakistan into a modern society. That this objective was contradicted by his government's alliance with the Islamic parties in the National Assembly, seemed not to trouble him. The military/Islamist political alliance broke down at the end of 2004, after which Musharraf became not only the political enemy of the Islamist political parties but the target of several assassination attempts by their jihadi offshoots.

The use of Islamist extremists (called jihadists) by the Pakistan army to fight proxy wars, the first (with U.S. support and encouragement) against the Soviets in Afghanistan, the second to aid the internal insurgency in Kashmir against the Indian government, has had a deleterious effect, domestically, on Pakistani society, and in its relations with India. The mobilisation of the jihadis in this fashion began under Zia, and related to his policy of Islamization. This alliance—directed at Kashmir—has continued under Musharraf, but at lower levels and with much more acrimony. Since 9/11 the jihadists have become alienated from Musharraf both for his moves to restore harmony in the relationship with India (which involves backing away from the proxy war in Kashmir) and for his alliance with the United States against the Taliban and Al Qaeda in Afghanistan.

Zia ul Huq, 1977 to 1988: Militarization and Islamization Gain Momentum and Official Sanction

On July 4, 1977, at the residence of the U.S. Ambassador in Islamabad, during a reception celebrating U.S. Independence Day, the Embassy political counselor asked General Zia ul Huq, the Pakistani Army Chief, if he would be available the next day for a meeting. Zia replied that he was completely tied up the next day. He wasn't kidding: on July 5, he led an army coup d'état which ousted the Prime Minister, Zulfikar Ali Bhutto, and his PPP government.

Zia promised elections and a return to democracy within 90 days, but it took 91 months for the military government he led to hold elections. When they took place in 1985 those elections, non-party polls to choose a civilian government that had, at best, limited power, were a pale imitation of the real thing. In 1988, Zia proved the emptiness of his promise to restore democracy by abruptly firing his hand-picked Prime Minister, Mohammed Khan Junejo, and dismissing the military/civilian hybrid elected government that he had created when they appeared to be carrying out policies that were contrary to those Zia wanted.[1]

The Army as the State—Another Kind of Identity Confusion

In his eleven years in power, Zia fostered a burgeoning growth in the symbiotic relationship between the army and the state which was, in part, an outgrowth of his "junta" structure mentioned above. According to Talbot, Zia envisioned a qualitatively different, and greater, role for the army than any of the previous military leaders of Pakistan. In his view, the army would not only be, as always in the view of his predecessors, the guarantor of Pakistan's territorial integrity and domestic stability, but it would also be central to the extension of Pakistan as an ideological state.[2]

He pushed the army's role far deeper into the polity—into the politics and political institutions of the state. He oversaw a huge increase in the number of active and retired military officers who were placed in state institutions, and the exponential growth of the army's involvement in business—from

---

1   Talbot, *Pakistan—A Modern History*, pp. 263-7.

2   Ibid., p. 255.

the manufacture of military equipment to the participation of the army pension fund in commercial ventures. The tentacles of the army reached deeper and deeper into the fabric of Pakistani society under Zia, and this trend has continued in subsequent governments, and expanded again in the Musharraf regime.

At the outset of his eleven-year tenure as Pakistan's political and military leader, Zia's mindset was not well known, and was probably not fully formed. Certainly, he feared that the political chaos, which obtained in Pakistan in the early months of 1977, endangered the unity and stability of the country. Such fear was perhaps natural only six years after the traumatic loss of the eastern wing of East Pakistan, and must have been widely shared in the army and among the establishment. He also feared the divisive effect this instability seemed to be having on the army itself, not yet fully recovered from the psychological shock or the physical damage of the 1971 political debacle and the crushing military defeat at the hands of its arch-enemy India. Some historians believe that Zia's hand was forced in leading the coup by mid-level army officers who felt the army must stop Bhutto and rectify the situation before it was wrecked by its own internal divisions.[3]

Zia may have truly believed, when he assumed power, that conditions would permit the rapid restoration of civilian government. But he and his team were soon convinced that a return to civilian control must be postponed. The primary consideration appears to have been the enormous popularity that Bhutto demonstrated, his impressive power to draw crowds at political rallies as soon as he was released from detention.

There was no doubt that Bhutto would win the election, and it would chill the hearts of coup-makers anywhere to contemplate the quick return to power of the leader they had just deposed. The certainty that Bhutto would win meant danger to Zia and his advisors personally, but it also meant that their objective of revitalizing Pakistan, of establishing a national identity and making it an ideological state, would certainly not be realized if the election were allowed to take place. And Zia, along perhaps with some of his supporters, must have felt keenly disappointed that his appeals "to chaste Islamic behavior [was not] enough to turn the people against the PPP leader..." whose behavior was well known by the public to be anything but chaste.[4] No doubt, it was these considerations that drove the

---

3   Lawrence Ziring, *Pakistan in the Twentieth Century—A Political History* (Karachi: Oxford University Press, 1997), p. 430.

4   Ibid., 435.

decision to arrest Bhutto a second time, to put him on trial, and ultimately to execute him.

Delaying elections, while transforming Pakistan politically and socially, became the strategy. The political transformation involved formulating a form of government in which democracy would be "strengthened" by the inclusion of authoritarian executive powers, thereby allowing the army to remain in control of policy.

Zia wanted a social transformation that would meld his goal of revitalizing Pakistan with that of building the national identity of an ideological state. He sought to establish a national identity that would reach across social, political, regional, ethnic, and sectarian divisions to form a truly integrated nation, one with—in the words of one well-known thinker on nationhood—"a relative moral, mental, and cultural unity of its inhabitants who consciously adhere to the state and its laws."[5] The process had political and constitutional tracks, which of course, were interrelated.

In the early years of his rule, Zia concentrated on strengthening the authority of his military regime, changing the constitution, undermining political and social elites, and weakening political parties to eliminate the possibility that his hold on power could be challenged by any element of civil society. Perhaps the first act to inaugurate the process was his assumption of the Presidency, upon the expiration in September 1978 of the term of Fazal Elahi Chaudhry, who held the office when the military coup occurred. He remained as Chief of Army Staff, however, until his death.

The first target to bring about this transformation was the political parties. Their tumultuous history gave reasonable cause. They were believed to waste no opportunity to sacrifice the national interest for political power. Much of the military viewed political parties as engines of division and strife, instead of unity and harmony, and to be contradictory to the principles of an Islamic state. These notions drove the regime's view that political parties were one of the root causes of Pakistan's failure to evolve into a true nation.

The military regime banned political activity, and thereby abolished the raison d'etre of parties, when it declared martial law. In 1979, it endeavored to allow parties to operate but to control and limit them by requiring them to register with the Election Commission (which didn't have much else to do in those days), publish formal manifestos, and submit their ac-

---

5   M. Mauss, "La Nation" (1920), *Oeuvre*, Tome 3, Paris: Minuit, 1969, p. 584. Quoted
    in Christophe Jaffrelot (ed., "Nationalism Without a Nation: Pakistan Searching for its
    Identity," *Pakistan—Nationalism Without a Nation* (London: Zed Books, 2002), 7, au-
    thor's translation.

counts for audit. Many civil society organizations—student groups, Islamic organizations, and others—were also neutralized by martial law edicts limiting their activities.

The second major political thrust of the Zia's early years was the insistence that the military—in effect the army—should have a permanent role in the making of state policy, no matter what the political system might be. The argument was that while political parties could not be trusted to elevate national interest over their own parochial concerns on national issues, the army could be. It was claimed by the Zia regime that this idea had to be enshrined in the constitution to ensure its survival.

The fundamental unresolved fissures that had plagued Pakistan since its creation (its identity as a nation and its fissiparous tendencies as a state) were not alleviated under Zia's rule. Punjab remained at the center of Pakistani politics, and its power and influence remained a neuralgic issue. The relationship between the central government and the other provinces, Sindh, Balochistan, and the NWFP continued to rankle. Zia was a Punjabi, and the army was (and still is) mainly a Punjabi organization.

The center/periphery problem was exacerbated by Zia's emphasis on Islamization. The traditional inattention and paucity of resources devoted to the development of social, especially educational, infrastructure continued to affect overall development adversely. Human capital was (and remains) woefully underdeveloped in Pakistan. Related to this is the ever present problem of deficient mobilization of domestic resources for all aspects of development, i.e. a national savings rate well below that necessary for rapid growth and development, and a reliance on foreign savings (borrowing).

There were new elements in the political situation that made life easier for the General during his eleven-year tenure. The political situation in Southwest Asia changed fundamentally in two ways in the first two years of the new military regime, and this diverted the attention of the Western democracies from Zia's repeated failure to keep his word on elections. First, from the early days of the his regime, domestic turbulence grew in Iran until the Shah of Iran was toppled; Iran—the major power just to the west of Pakistan—became engulfed by a fundamentalist revolution, which changed the geo-strategic situation for the Zia regime radically.

Second, at the end of 1979, the Soviet Union invaded Pakistan's other neighbor to the west, Afghanistan. This engendered a massive reaction in the West that resulted in large inflows of foreign funds that helped to mask Pakistan's economic fragility—which the regime had done little to resolve.

The Soviet invasion also brought the regime a semblance of legitimacy in the eyes of the West, especially the US, because of Pakistan's role in the alliance forged against the Soviets.

Unlike the previous military regimes, and the intermittent civilian ones, which relied on, and were ultimately manipulated by, the bureaucracy, Zia controlled the bureaucrats and made them dependent on him and his regime. He did this by using the army to run the state and by surrounding himself at every level with active or retired military officers in high level operational or advisory capacities. Civilians were relegated to receiving and following orders. Despite Pakistan's previous military leaders, this was its first experience of a military "junta." When it came time for his regime to morph into a civilian government, this enabled Zia to retain greater authority—in fact, highly autocratic authority.

It was in the Zia era that the shadowy military intelligence elements began their rapid growth in size and power. They have continued expanding, at least in influence, during both the civilian interludes and the period of direct military rule. The primary agency is the Inter Services Intelligence (ISI), which has both an international role, mainly in the South Asian region, primarily against India, and a domestic role. It has become the military's eyes and ears in domestic politics, and some observers claim that the ISI is also the military's brain on domestic political issues. The ISI is the clandestine operations arm that the military relies on to ensure its domestic political paramountcy, including interfering in elections, monitoring opponents and strongly influencing civil politicians and other prominent members of civil society.

As an intelligence agency, naturally little is known about the ISI's activities, and even less about its domestic, rather than foreign, operations. The main source of information about what it does in Pakistan appears to be the rumor mill, hence it is hard to offer more than speculation as to its role, and influence. However, it is known to be extremely active in domestic politics. Among its domestic tasks are surveillance of foreigners in Pakistan, including foreign diplomats, politically active Pakistanis, and the media.

The ISI's foreign operations are, for some reason, better known and understood. It manages covert operations outside Pakistan. This included its long and complicated relationship with the Afghan mujahideen during the war against the Soviets, and later the jihadists who slipped into Kashmir to help the insurgency against the Indians. It is its domestic operations that are of concern in this book.

The agency has been deeply involved in domestic operations since the 1950s. During the 1965 war with India, the ISI was heavily criticized for not being able to locate the main Indian strike force because it was too busy watching political opponents at home and tapping telephone lines. Its domestic role appears to have expanded well beyond surveillance in recent years, and, *inter alia*, it has almost certainly been involved in rigging elections, at least since 1990. In Chapters 7 and 8, the role of the ISI during the democratic episode of the 1990s and under the military government of Pervez Musharraf, especially in the election of 2002, will be discussed.

The Judiciary Goes Along to Get Along—And Loses Badly

The legal basis of the Zia ul Huq military regime was tested early on in his tenure. Zulfikar Bhutto's wife, Nusrat, petitioned the Supreme Court challenging the validity of the detention order under which her husband had been imprisoned, which was a challenge to the legality of the military regime. Among other allegations of the petition was that the regime had arrested Bhutto to prevent him and his party from participating in the promised elections.[6] Zia undercut the petition's allegation as to the motivation of Bhutto's arrest by postponing (again), as the case was being heard, national elections. Whether this made any difference or not, the court supported the military government's position and, thus effectively legalized the coup. The decision implicitly gave the martial law government a warrant to hold and retain power as it wished.[7]

The decision was based on the "doctrine of necessity," which had been used as far back as 1954 by Pakistan courts to justify interventions into the governance of the country by Governors General, Presidents, and the military. This doctrine essentially raises public order as the paramount task of governing, and justifies interventions which are premised on restoring public order.[8] "Necessity" has provided the Pakistani military with the legal justification for its interventions and its continuing undermining of democracy.

This decision should be seen in the political context of the early Zia years. The military government had a firm hold on power, but the courts wanted to hang on to the jurisdiction and independence that had been theirs, even under Bhutto (slimmer though it was than that granted in the

---

6   Paula Newberg, *Judging the State—Courts and Constitutional Politics in Pakistan* (Cambridge University Press, 1995), p.162.

7   Talbot, *Pakistan—A Modern History*, p. 257.

8   Newberg, *Judging the State*. p. 3

1973 constitution). The court felt the *Nusrat Bhutto* decision gave it the scope to judge the necessity of government actions, and that this would preserve some vestige of its review authority. As Newberg states, "[i]n this limited sense, they could argue that military power had not overruled individual rights and that in the absence of organized political parties (which were soon formally outlawed), individual voices could still be heard."[9]

It may have been a desperate attempt to preserve some judicial check on the executive power of the military government and on violations of civil rights. But it began a long downward slide in public respect for the courts and their authority. The immediate effect was that the case against Bhutto went ahead, seemingly on a fast track and with some disregard to judicial probity.[10] This caused "profound public dismay with the civil courts for years…,"[11] and probably made the frequent use of special and military tribunals more acceptable. In reaction to the precipitous decline in their public respect after Bhutto's execution, judges' rulings became more strident, according to Newberg, in those cases against the government which the courts could hear.[12]

As in the past, the judiciary had assumed that "the absence of constitutional governance…was a temporary phenomenon." Thus, though now working in a much more limited space which it had granted itself, the judiciary remained a problem for the Zia regime and for his drive to consolidate power in the President (he had assumed that office in September 1978). This was a struggle that the judiciary could not win though "its decisions blunted the sharp edge of military oppression…," according to Newberg.[13]

Zia had the last word, as was to be expected. In March 1981, in response to increasingly active political opposition, he issued a Provisional Constitution Order (PCO), which gave almost all power to the executive, in the context of setting up a deliberative body called the Majilis-e-Shura (Federal Council).[14] This order included the power to extend military rule without constraint, and to amend the constitution retrospectively. The PCO also followed the usual form of indemnifying the martial law regime for any

---

9   Ibid., 172

10   Talbot, *Pakistan—A Modern History*, p. 258.

11   Newberg, *Judging the State*, p. 173.

12   Ibid., p.173.

13   Ibid., p.180.

14   Shahid Javed Burki, *Pakistan—Fifty Years of Nationhood* (Boulder, CO: Westview Press,1991), 53

laws or actions it had taken, and it granted immunity from civil prosecution to members of the armed forces.

Most historians skip over that part of the PCO that effectively rendered the superior judiciary impotent juridically. Because of, as the PCO says, "doubts...as regards the powers and jurisdictions of the Superior courts," the order stripped almost all authority from the judiciary at one stroke, canceling judicial review, and leaving the assumption of temporary constitutional suspension in tatters.[15] The superior judiciary was also required to take a new oath to uphold the PCO. Those most hostile were not invited to take this oath, and some who were invited refused to do so.

Thus, four years after the Zia military regime came to power, the judiciary's intention to remain a check, albeit a limited one, on executive power came to naught. No vestige of an independent judiciary remained, and this was to be the case until martial law was lifted in 1985. Civil rights disappeared, and thousands of civilians who opposed the regime were detained. Military courts and special tribunals were used for many cases, and by 1984 the government maintained publicly that military courts could try civilians under military law.

As will be described below, the increasing opposition to martial law finally led Zia to back away from it and, in 1985, set up a hybrid civilian/ military government structure in which the executive (Zia and the military) still retained definitive power over the elected National Assembly and the Prime Minister. To promulgate this, Zia issued another Constitutional Order which revived the 1973 Constitution in emasculated form. Zia's previous PCOs were made into the eighth amendment which carried on the constitutional changes of his PCOs, including those that barred the judiciary from accepting petitions of redress to the actions or laws of the martial law regime. This amendment added a provision that the President could dismiss the Prime Minister or the National and Provincial Assemblies at will. This had serious consequences for future elected regimes, as we will see.

This, as has been noted, converted military martial law to civilian martial law.[16] The public, however, took the lifting of martial law as an opportunity to use the courts to challenge the acts of the regime and to seek to redress grievances, including the judgments of the military courts. Many

---

15   Newberg, *Judging the State*, 181. The quote is from the Preamble of the PCO (Lahore: Civil and Criminal Law Publication, 1983) cited by Newberg.

16   Ibid., 191.

of the regime's detained opponents, or those released from detention, petitioned the courts for compensation. Slowly the superior courts began to chip away at the constitutional provisions which Zia had added to make access to the judiciary very difficult. The superior courts in this period, as Newberg notes, "became the vehicles for altering the relationship between the state and citizen under a constitutional order otherwise inaccessible to challenge."[17] In 1987, the Karachi High Court ruled that the constitutional immunity of the military regime was not complete as some challenges to convictions by military courts could be reviewed by civil courts.

This review power was extended by the Lahore High Court a few weeks later which ruled that military court sentences could be reviewed on the merits of each case. This ruling also trimmed the almost limitless interpretation of "necessity" which the regime had propounded. Though the judiciary downplayed the significance of these rulings, feeling that it might not be wise to move too quickly to challenge Zia, the courts were returning, intentionally or not, to their previous role as independent check on both the executive and the legislative branch. Zia's sudden death in August 1988 opened the gates to accelerating their reassertion of judicial independence and authority.

Islamization: To Find a National Identity or to Identify National Fissures?

There were two major discontinuities that Zia initiated that resulted in political legacies that continue to have profound and deleterious consequences for Pakistan's long run viability, and for the prospects of real democracy there. First, he attempted to turn Pakistan into an "ideological state" by implementing Islamization, which he announced in February 1979.[18] He began in earnest a process which had occurred only in fits and starts in the past, and only when earlier governments—primarily that of Zulfikar Ali Bhutto—had felt impelled to try to mollify the religious parties to shore up their political support or reduce political pressure on some other set of issues. Zia gave real impetus and official sanction to Islamizing society and as

---

17   One important breakthrough case was heard and decided just prior to Zia's death, a
      challenge by Benazir Bhutto and the PPP to Zia's revisions to the 1962 Political Parties
      Act which had effectively stopped parties from organizing and standing in elections. The
      Supreme Court overruled his amendments and left open the question of whether parties
      could organize. This ruling, which might have been considered a great challenge to Zia,
      came too soon before his death to know what his reaction would have been.

18   Talbot, *Pakistan—A Modern History*, p. 245.

a pious individual there is little doubt that he saw nothing invidious in his plan. Zia and the army saw this push for Islamization as a way to establish a constituency for, and the legitimacy of, the military regime. They may have hoped to give the regime a reason to continue to move slowly and deliberately in the promised return to democracy.

Beyond that, it seems Zia envisioned Islamization as the way to solve the age-old fundamental problem of Pakistan: the lack of a coherent national identity. Was it created as a state for Muslims in South Asia, or as an Islamic State?[19] However, Zia's own beliefs undercut this objective, as they were "based on narrow Sunni interpretations of Islamic theology,"[20] which divided religious forces, as well as the secular forces, in the polity.

While apologists argue that Zia's Islamization policies made only limited progress, Islamization imbedded itself deeply enough in the legal, political, and economic system, as well as in the psyche of the polity, so that the more secular minded governments that followed were unable to reverse it. (Not all were equally interested in doing so, and all yielded to the temptation to use the Islamists for their own political purposes.) Thus Islamization has continued to make creeping progress under subsequent governments whether they wanted it or not.

To many of its supporters, Islamization became the Zia regime's main objective.[21] It appealed mainly to the religious parties and the elements in society who supported them, primarily the core of small traders and urban-dwellers who shared his pious mindset. For many of those who opposed the regime, this policy just gave them one more reason to resist it. Despite the resistance, Islamization made serious inroads and has continued to creep further into everyday affairs. Moreover the conditions of Pakistani life—the growing poverty, encroaching "jihadi" culture and rising sympathy for religious activists like the Taliban, and the growing impression that Islam is under attack by the West—seem to increase the attraction of Islamization.

But despite this continued encroachment, Pakistan has not yet become an Islamic state. The secular and modernist forces, which Zia may have underestimated, or simply not understood, continue to oppose Islamization. They resisted when Zia introduced the concept as government policy, and

---

19   Ibid., p. 245.

20   S. V. R. Nasr, "Islam, the State and the Rise of Sectarian Militancy in Pakistan," *Pakistan—Nationalism Without a Nation*, p. 88.

21   Talbot, *Pakistan—A Modern History*, p. 270.

continued resisting each time the government introduced another increment of Islamization.[22]

In part; these forces were successful in stopping various aspects of the Islamization policy because it was opening dangerous rifts even wider. As Zia introduced specific Islamization measures, severe divisions opened up between the sects of Islam represented in Pakistan. These soon led to escalating violence between armed factions of some Sunni and Shia groups This took on an international flavor as the Saudis and the Iranians aided the Sunni and the Shia groups respectively, and soon there developed a low level proxy war between the protagonists of the two major strains of Islam—using Pakistani fighters. The violence became so severe that, in a country with already dangerous fissiparous tendencies, and escalating ethnic tension in Sindh between Mohajirs and Sindhis, even moderate supporters of Islamization backed away, and it surely turned the army against the policy.

A benign Islamization policy, emphasizing the aspects of Islam that the various sects could agree on, might have gained wide acceptance quickly, and served Zia's objective of finding a national identity for Pakistan and more legitimacy for his regime. But his approach seemed ruled by his Sunni upbringing, and his sympathy was with the revivalist Deobandi school of Islam. As one historian wrote, "the emphasis [of the Zia approach] was on the regulative, punitive, and extractive aspects [mandatory taxes] of Islam, rather than on its social and economic egalitarianism."[23] Islamization, whether Zia intended it that way or not, took a rigid approach which made it difficult to find general acceptance, in part because the goal appeared to be to enforce laws and regulations for "moral uplift."[24] There were misguided attempts to symbolize Islamization by imposing a dress code for

---

22   While the four democratically elected governments of the 1990s were both pusillanimous and opportunist in their relation with Islamist parties, as was the Musharraf government, though it espoused loudly "enlightened moderation," formal Islamization has been pretty much on hold since Zia ul Huq. The informal hold of Islamism on society has strengthened, however, because the Islamists continue to advance their civilizational agenda vigorously and governments do not resist it as vigorously, and often make Faustian bargains with the Islamists (which strengthens them) while social and economic conditions in Pakistan do not improve much. In addition, the past 2-3 years have seen the actual takeover of large parts of the Tribal Areas and some "settled areas" west of the Indus River by Taliban/jihadi groups.

23   Talbot, *Pakistan—A Modern History,* p. 271-2, quoting Hasan-Askari Rizvi, quote unreferenced.

24   Talbot, *Pakistan—A Modern History,* p. 272.

women and requiring males to wear beards—both drew strong criticism and were widely resisted.[25]

Zia introduced measures to Islamize four areas of Pakistani society. His earliest proposals, in 1979, involved Islamizing the penal code with a series of rules called the Hudood Ordinances. These called for punishments spelled out in the Qur'an and the Sunnah (a series of writings from oral tradition giving the example of the Prophet Mohammed and of the first two—or four—caliphs). The Hudood Ordinances were the most notorious of the Islamization measures proposed by Zia because of their advocacy of such supposed Qur'an-ordained punishments as severing the hand of thieves, and their highly controversial treatment of sexual crimes (e.g. stoning adulterers—later ruled out by the courts). The discrimination against women that these ordinances engendered evoked great opposition in Pakistan among women's groups and led to several violent demonstrations in which women protestors were hurt or killed.[26] (In addition, in 1984, a set of restrictive laws were passed against the members of the Ahmadiyya sect.) There was also great opposition from the international community. Some of these ordinances were later rolled back by the courts, and in 2006 at Musharraf's behest the National Assembly rescinded the two that were considered most egregious. Many still remain in the penal code, however.

Zia followed the Hudood Ordinances with measures to Islamize the judicial system. The earliest, in 1979, created Sharia courts in each province. That proved unworkable as the courts were too cumbersome and overwhelmed with frivolous cases, so he followed with the creation of a Federal Sharia court. This didn't work either, so Zia added the "ulema" in an advisory role and later created additional Sharia courts. Ultimately, Pakistan had a cumbersome and wildly inefficient mix of overlapping and competing Sharia and traditional courts, none of which seemed able to deliver timely decisions.

The Zia regime approached Islamization on several different levels. In addition to the political and juridical amendments described above and the attempts to change the economy described below, he also altered Bhutto's policy of undermining the pirs. While his government also wanted to reduce the pirs' political influence over their followers, Zia had much less interest in identifying with the Sufis than either Bhutto or Ayub Khan

---

25   Ibid., p. 272. Sufism is the dominant school of Islam in Bangladesh, and is part of the reason why the two former halves of the Muslim homeland of South Asia separated and why their development paths have taken such decidedly different directions.

26   Ibid., p. 275-6.

because the core of his Islamic support came from the leaders and followers of the more scripturalist schools among Islamic reformers, such as the Deobandis. They rejected the traditional Sufi role of mediator between man and God.[27]

The government began to stress that the Sufi saints themselves were highly educated scholars. In other words, they were part of the Ulema. The idea was, evidently, to minimize "the distinction between the saints and the Ulema, Sufism and Shariat...[the] central organizing principle [became] the Muslim community... united by obedience to God and his laws (shariat)."[28] This clearly spoke to the core of Zia's Islamic supporters, who followed the beliefs of the Scripturalist, reformist schools, and who believed that Muslims had lost power in South Asia because they had eschewed the true teaching and example of the Prophet. These schools of thought saw Pakistan as the opportunity to reunify political, spiritual, and scholarly authority in a "pure" Islamic state.[29]

The Islamization of the economy could have had the most severe short-term impact on Pakistan. The regime initially attempted to abolish interest (*riba*), but the application was partial and mixed. In the first place, interest could not be abolished on Pakistan's immense and growing foreign obligations. On domestic debt, several government-owned financial institutions eliminated interest and used profit- or loss-sharing or asset mark up as a basis of attracting customers. Many savings banks began to offer these accounts as alternatives to interest bearing accounts.

The widespread view in the business and financial community was that Pakistan could not hope to compete for foreign resources with an interest-free financial sector. This opinion was shared by a large part of the government's economic team. As a result, there were continuous attempts to overturn the Islamic economic measures in the courts. To this day, the measure which abolishes interest on all financial transactions remains tied up in the courts, with the tacit acquiescence of the government.

The imposition of *zakat*, a compulsory deduction from wages of an Islamic charity tax, only exacerbated the political and sectarian problems that the Islamization policy had created as well as opening serious questions of equity. Its economic impact was negligible compared with its political

---

27 Katherine Ewing, *The Pir or Sufi Saint in Pakistani Islam* (Chicago, unpublished Ph.D. dissertation, University of Chicago, 1980), pp. 193 & 211.

28 Katherine Ewing, "The Politics of Sufism: Redefining the Saints of Pakistan, *The Journal of Asian Studies*, 42, No. 2, 1983, pp. 251-68.

29 Ewing, *The Pir or Sufi Saint...*, p. 217.

one. The mandatory nature of the *zakat* tax, which led to the creation of a large state administration, led to protests and hard feelings against the government, especially in the Shia community, much of which felt it was being forced to follow the Sunni Hanafi code of behavior. Many Sunnis also prefer a voluntary approach to charity. Thus, though Shias were soon exempted from *zakat*, and the later imposition of a tax on farmers' crops, this issue remained a sore point.

In the long run, the largest impact of the Islamization policy may well have been its measures of educational "reform." These were inspired by, and reflected, the Zia government's goal of transforming Pakistan into an ideological state.[30] Study of the Qur'an, Islam, and of Pakistan became compulsory. Textbooks were revised extensively to reflect the government's line, not only on religion, but on most matters including the alleged lack of martial qualities of Hindus and the supposed perfidy of India.

In a move which could have had a very negative impact, the Zia government addressed the great shortfall in elementary schooling, and the resulting widespread illiteracy, especially among the poor, by sanctioning religious schools—known as madrassas—both politically and financially. The impact of the decision is still being debated, and unsurprisingly is the subject of an intense controversy, which we will return to in Chapter 9. In any case, the narrowness of the madrassas' curriculum, and their restricted social views, do little to prepare young Pakistanis for the modern, globalized world.

Another reason to be concerned about madrassas is that some—a small, but nonetheless dangerous, minority—teach a radical Islamist philosophy that inculcates jihadi militancy and serve as recruiting grounds for jihadi "warriors." These radical madrassas have contributed to the growth of "jihadi" culture and the so-called "Talibanization" of Pakistan. Though the vast majority of madrassas are not in this radical category, they contribute little, if anything, to the development of human capital in Pakistan.

The upshot of Zia's Islamization campaign is a country that is more religious, and less tolerant and pluralistic than hitherto. While some apologists claim, for example, that the Hudood ordinances actually improved the status of women by giving the rights accorded by the Quran to women in the tribal areas who had none under tribal law, this is not borne out by empirical studies. These ordinances indubitably made life worse, in reality, for women, by expanding the range of legal discrimination they faced,

---

30 Talbot, *Pakistan—A Modern History,* p. 278.

by imposing dress codes and by the requirement that evidence given by women in courts counted for half of a man's evidence.

But women were only one group that faced higher levels of discrimination. Religious minorities felt the brunt of increased discrimination, which even worked its way into law. The worst affected were the Ahmadiyya, delared apostate in 1974, who the Zia regime specifically targeted in discriminatory laws enacted in1984.[31] The Ahmadiyya have suffered greatly since then, both as the victims of violence and by being brought to court on trumped-up charges. Christians and Hindus suffered also, primarily because the introduction of a law against blasphemy towards the Prophet gave rise to much abuse and false accusations to the courts, motivated primarily by the desire for personal gain.

Ian Talbot summarized neatly this misdirected attempt to find a national identity for Pakistan, which Zia also used to build a political constituency and legitimize his regime:

> Islamization appeared to have reduced a great faith tradition, rich in humanity, culture, and a sense of social justice, to a system of punishments and persecution of minority groups. Zia left behind not only a political process distorted by the eighth amendment, which enabled his successors to dismiss elected Prime Ministers with impunity, but an atmosphere of bigotry, fanaticism, and distorted values.[32]

Saved By The War

The war against the Soviet Union in Afghanistan was of crucial importance in helping Zia remain in power. Pakistan became, in the eyes of the West, in particular the US, a "frontline" state against Soviet expansionism. It received large amounts of military and economic assistance. This brought large inflows of liquidity, which kept the economy growing at a rate that masked its serious structural flaws. It also permitted the army to re-equip, keeping its officer class content and satisfied with its leadership. Equally important, the Afghan war solidified the growing relationship between the army (especially, its main military intelligence agency, Inter Services Intelligence) and militantly radical jihadist groups which became the tool of the state in its proxy wars, first with the Soviets in Afghanistan, later with Indian security forces in Kashmir.

---

31   Ahmadiyyas are a sect that claims a later prophet (Mirza Ghulam Ahmad) than Mohammed. Though they claim to be Islamic, many Muslims reject this.

32   Talbot, *Pakistan—A Modern History*, p. 286.

Negotiations under the United Nations' aegis between the Afghan Marxist government of Najibullah, propped up by the Soviets, and Pakistan's military government had gone on half-heartedly in Geneva for six years, but both sides became serious about them in 1987. In Pakistan the growing refugee problem, escalating domestic violence and turmoil, fueled in part by the spillover of the war across its borders, precipitated this change in course. The Afghan government was under pressure from its Soviet patrons (experiencing the first signs of weakness that ultimately led to the collapse of the Soviet state) who were demanding that Najibullah find a settlement that would get them off the hook.

In April 1988, they came to an agreement that tried to balance the promise of a Soviet termination of support to the Kabul regime and troop withdrawal with a Pakistani pledge to stop funneling US and other outside aid to the mujahiddin against the Kabul regime and its Soviet defenders. The two governments (the Soviets and US were not parties to the agreement, but acted as its guarantors) also promised not to interfere in each other's affairs. The mujahiddin were not party to the agreement either, and unlike the Soviets, who clearly wanted a way out (and probably the US), refused to go along with it because it left in situ the Najibullah government, the overthrow of which had been one of their principal objectives. The Pakistani government was supposed to keep these groups under control, but it did not. Zia, in fact, reversed his previous position and proposed postponing the final accord to keep pressure on the mujahiddin and the Najibullah government to come to some *modus vivendi* in Afghanistan. Both the Soviets and the US rejected Zia's proposal. In a daring act of defiance, Zia's hand-picked Prime Minister, Mohammed Khan Junejo, ordered the Pakistani representative to sign the agreement.

The result was that the war continued—now among the mujahiddin groups, and between them and Najibullah's government. The refugee burden on Pakistan persisted, and its social fabric continued to be undermined by the spillover effects of the war in Afghanistan. In the mean time US assistance declined rapidly because of the Soviet withdrawal, as did its willingness to turn a blind eye to dubious democratization and, more importantly, the rapid progress of Pakistan's nuclear weapons programme.

The success of the mujahiddin against the Soviets in Afghanistan, which coincided with a spectacular political change in Moscow and a serious weakening of Soviet power (later leading to its collapse) was, in fact, probably not the best outcome for Pakistan—though it no doubt appeared that way at the time. Apart from encouraging the jihadists and the army as to the benefits of their alliance and the tactics they had learned, it probably convinced them, and Zia, that they could force through their choice of who would rule the new Afghanistan. They chose not to carry out the role they had agreed to in the Geneva Agreement of 1988, and to promote the most fundamentalist of the many mujahiddin groups vying to lead the country. But the long internecine struggle for power between the latter increasingly destabilized Pakistan as well as Afghanistan.

Civil Society Pushes Back—Zia Beats a Slow Retreat Toward Hybrid Government

After reeling from the martial law crackdowns in the first years of Zia's rule, civil society began to fight back. In early 1981, three and a half years after the General had assumed power, the opposition political parties coalesced into an alliance called the Movement Forthe Restoration of Democracy (MRD). In the following years, despite much pressure and harassment against them and their leaders, the MRD slowly increased the pressure on the Zia regime to return to democratic political structures.

Zia slowly retreated before this pressure, but it was a tactical withdrawal while he tried to put in place the foundations of the new political structure he envisioned. Soon after the formation of the MRD, Zia announced the creation of an appointive Federal Council—called the Majilis-e-Shura—which would have an advisory role, ostensibly on Islamization, and promised expanded political activity in the future, but only to those parties duly registered. Pressure from the MRD increased dramatically in 1983, and Zia responded by publishing a road map to democracy.

The MRD alliance focused in its campaigns on preserving the 1973 constitution, figuring this was the best way to resist Zia's onslaught against the parties, and to ensure an eventual return to democratic politics. It also believed that Zia's Islamization policy was designed to weaken, if not eliminate, political parties, and it continually resisted the policy while trying not to appear anti-Islamic.

The attrition continued, and in 1984 Zia sought to ensure that popular pressure would not derail his elaborate political and social agenda. He held a referendum in December 1984, which was designed to secure popular approval of his Islamization measures, and indirectly to continue his term as President for a further five years.[33] Many experts questioned the constitutionality of this referendum, but it eliminated the constitutional problem he faced, which called for the election of the President after the election of the National Assembly and the Senate. This was a risk that Zia did not want to take.

Following an affirmative vote on this referendum (the size of the turnout was hotly disputed), Zia announced non-party elections for a National Assembly and Provincial Assemblies to take place in March 1985. These elections, the first in Pakistan since 1977, produced a large turnout—a fact not contested by any of the parties—and some surprises for the Zia government. Primary among them was the very poor showing of the religious parties that had been the main political supporters of Zia and of his Islamization policy.

This gave much pause to the newly-elected government, though not so much to Zia, in continuing the drive toward Islamization. A second outcome was a stark division in the poll between rural and urban areas. Zia's supporters—primarily the large landowners and rural elites—won the rural areas. His opponents won the urban areas. This mix did not bode well for an Assembly inclined to enlarge its policy role.

Zia moved quickly after the elections to ensure the continuity of his policies and the dominance of the army in the governing structure. A presidential order changed the constitution radically, shifting power almost completely from the elected Assemblies to the President. In fact, though still called the 1973 Constitution, the document was now so different as to be a completely new constitution. The President served as both head of state and head of government. The Prime Minister—who was picked by the President rather than by the Assembly—was clearly and completely subservient to the President and served at his pleasure. Zia picked an old-line politician from Sindh, Mohammed Khan Junejo, who had served in one of his earlier cabinets, as Prime Minister.

Zia appears to have been trying to meld the Parliamentary system, which is the basis of the 1973 Constitution, with the Presidential system, which he and the army clearly preferred. When martial law was lifted there was

---

33   This maneuver may well have been modeled on the referendum that Ziaur Rahman held in 1978, though that was more straight forward and not, given Ziaur Rahman's enormous popularity at the time, necessitated by fear of what would have happened if a Parliament had been elected first. Moreover, there was no legal need or popular call for a parliamentary election first as the Bangladesh constitution prescribed a presidential system after Mujib changed it in January 1975.

not much noticeable difference in the way the government operated. If it had not been trumpeted so loudly by the government, the lifting of martial law might hardly have been noticed. Whether consciously or otherwise, Zia, by his relationship with the elected part of government, was heading toward one-party rule.

This hybrid constitution was meant to preserve the power and prerogatives of the army under a façade of parliamentary government. Whether it was an instrument that would have met the long-term political needs of Pakistan is unclear, though many analysts thought that this was an unlikely outcome.[34] Pakistan's deep problems seem almost to demand a decentralized political system, in which provinces have the autonomy to meet the needs of their diverse populations.

The "democratic" opposition to Zia kept up their pressure against the regime after the elections so as to avoid marginalization and exclusion, even though its previous coherence broke down. The pressure coincided with a significant increase in domestic turmoil as ethnic and sectarian tensions began to boil over, in part heated up by spillover effects of the war in Afghanistan. Sindh became a virtual war zone again, as violence erupted between ethnic Sindhis and the Mohajirs, who had come as refugees from India in 1947 and gained considerable economic and political influence. (The Sindhi/Mohajir problem has perplexed and challenged all the Pakistani governments of the last 25 years. None of the latter—neither the Zia regime, nor subsequent elected governments, nor indeed Musharraf's government—have been able to solve it, though the most recent military regime has been much less troubled by it than the others.) In addition, Karachi became one of the main battlegrounds between Sunni and Shia terrorist groups. The violence in Sindh proved so unquenchable that Zia was forced to use the army to quell it, and the repercussions were partly responsible for the demise of the elected government in the spring of 1988.

The Sindh problem was very complex, and it was clear the government could not really handle it in a satisfactory way. It fell back repeatedly on putting disturbances down by force because it could not envision a political solution. This would have required the art of democratic compromise, and political trade-offs common in democracy. Mohajirs, Sindhis, and Pathans were at each others' throats. Each needed political space, a cut of the pie, and a share of provincial power. This was not a solution that came easily to a government such as Zia's.

---

34   Including the author.

The legacy of inaction in Sindh is a continual festering political sore that, even when it is not erupting, is always threatening to do so. The worst aspects of the problem were left for later governments, incubating strife for future generations. Organizations devoted to Mohajir and Sindhi nationalism have at times entered national politics and been used cynically by the major political parties with the promise but not the reality of power-sharing. This has spawned militantly violent sub-groups which have proven almost impossible to eliminate.

Zia was under pressure because of the growing violence in Sindh and the continuing problems in Afghanistan, and he was particularly upset by the assertions of authority on the part of Prime Minister Junejo. In May 1988, using the autocratic powers given the President by the eighth amendment, to show that he was boss, he dismissed his hand-picked Prime Minister and the cabinet and dissolved the National Assembly and all the Provincial Assemblies. It was back to direct military rule without the fig leaf of a democracy that he had so laboriously created. One historian believes that Zia was contemplating revising the constitution and establishing an outright and undiluted Presidential system.[35] We shall never know, as he was killed in a plane crash before his next political step was revealed.

India—A Footnote in the Zia ul Huq Story

Relations with India were, more or less, on hold during the Zia years. Histories of the period give little space to India yet, as historian Lawrence Ziring writes, "[t]he problem for Pakistan... remained India."[36] Its huge neighbor remained much in Pakistani minds, but the important issues and problems in foreign and security affairs during Zia's tenure were located to the West, in Afghanistan (described above) and Iran. The usual suspicions and

---

35   Shahid Javed Burki, *Pakistan—Fifty Years of Nationhood,* p. 65.

36   Ziring, *Pakistan,* 491. Even Ziring only devotes 3 ½ pp. of an 80-pp. chapter on Zia ul Huq to relations with India. Other scholars' accounts of the Zia period are equally minimal on Indian relations. Talbot, *Pakistan,* for example, devotes 40 pp. to Zia's rule and legacy without mention of India. Personal reminiscences such as General K. M. Arif, *Khaki Shadows—Pakistan 1947-1997* (Karachi: Oxford University Press, 2001), pp. 176-7, mentions India primarily in the context of the war in Afghanistan and India's collaboration with the Soviet Union, its ally, to try to get Pakistan to back off of its assistance to the Afghan resistance. General Arif, in *Working with Zia, Pakistan's Power Politics 1977-1988,* (Karachi: Oxford University Press, 1995) discusses relations with India only in the context of the competing nuclear programs and non-proliferation issues. Lt. General Faiz Ali Chisti, *Betrayals of Another Kind—Islam, Democracy, and the Army in Pakistan,* (London: Asia Publishing House, 1989), pp. 209-11, covers relations with India not in his chapters on Zia, but in a separate chapter in which he describes the general history of strained relations with India.

distrust of India remained strong, however, and there was no progress in enhancing mutual understanding or reducing tension. Relations between the two countries in this period were characterized by frequent charges of interference or sabotage, and one period of serious tension when both sides massed troops along the border.

Both countries were dealing with insurgencies, and suspected the other side of interfering clandestinely to fuel their respective internal problems. Pakistan accused India of helping to foment the insurgency in Balochistan and the ethnic unrest in Sindh; India accused Pakistan of aiding Sikh insurgents in East Punjab. In the 1986 border confrontation, Zia demonstrated statesmanship by going to Delhi (ostensibly for a cricket match) and agreeing with the Indian leader, Rajiv Gandhi, to a mutual withdrawal of forces and a reduction of the tension. In September 1987, Pakistani troops engaged in a serious skirmish with Indian troops in the remote Siachen Glacier in Kashmir. India announced that this was the most serious conflict between the two parties since the '71 war. Pakistan played down its significance, calling it a minor incident, and obviously wanting to deemphasize its importance and let it drop.

Pakistan wanted only one war at a time. As Ziring writes, "[w]ith the war continuing in Afghanistan, Islamabad wanted no part of a war with India.[37] As on the economy (covered in Chapter 9), Zia wasted an opportunity; his predilections prevented him from using a relatively benign 11-year period when there were almost no major crises with India to try to initiate a process of reconciliation. However, it takes two to tango in diplomacy also, and it seems unlikely that India was ready to dance either.

The Legacy of Zia ul Huq

Unlike Ziaur Rahman in Bangladesh, there is little ambiguity in the record of Zia ul Huq and the impact he had on Pakistan's political, economic and social development. In retrospect, his legacy is unrelievedly negative. Even the army's excuse for taking power in 1977—the usual one of the threat to national security from civil disorder and undisciplined politicians and political parties—is hardly compelling. In comparison to the chaos that Ziaur Rahman faced in Bangladesh, the situation in Pakistan in July 1977 appeared manageable. It is quite likely, however, that influential cadres in the army saw in the street demonstrations against Bhutto the opportunity to retake the power that it had lost through its own mistakes seven years earlier.

---

37   Ziring, *Pakistan*, p. 490.

Zia ul Huq may have begun in office without a clear agenda. However, within months of assuming power, his objectives seem to have narrowed to a couple of points. The first was to ensure that the military remained dominant in politics in Pakistan and retained a firm grip on policy, especially foreign and security affairs. In this he succeeded. The elected governments that followed him did not have full sovereign power over policy. Even after Nawaz Sharif won an enormous mandate in 1997, the army would not give up power. When it looked like Nawaz was building up a coalition to reduce the military's policy leverage, the army removed him from power and ruled directly for three years before reverting to the hybrid, military/ civilian structure that Zia had created in 1985, and in which it holds complete power.

The second objective on Zia ul Huq's agenda was the Islamization of society. Many observers suggest that though it has had a seriously adverse impact on Pakistan, militarization not Islamization is the fundamental problem in the country. That assertion is the subject of a separate book, but the real question is whether the Islamists would have made the inroads they have if the military had not had power in Pakistan for over half of its history.

A few things seem certain. As a result of the growing Islamization of society, Pakistan has become a less tolerant, less inclusive society. Islamic radicalism has grown, and the society has become more "Talibanized." Although the Islamists have established a strong foothold in society, they seem unable to transform this into significant electoral gains. The success they recorded in the 2002 elections (53 seats in the Assembly) turned out to be an anomaly—in 2008 when they won only 5 seats. Nontheless, the growth of Islamism has made Pakistan more difficult to govern, and a more questionable ally.

Pakistan and Bangladesh may both have had military governments, led by two generals named Zia in the late 1970s. The comparison stops there. The balance sheet for Ziaur Rahman, though it shows some minuses, is essentially positive. Bangladesh is better because he was the country's leader. The balance sheet for Zia ul Huq in Pakistan shows a long list of negatives, and one has to peer at the fine print to find anything to feel good about.

5

THE ERSHAD MILITARY INTERVENTION

Four and a Half Years of Martial Law

Most Bangladeshis looked back on the November 7, 1975 coup as justified and, perhaps the only answer, after the serious mismanagement and power-grabbing of the later Mujib years and the violence and severe instability of the three-month period after Mujib's assassination. The Ershad coup could not be justified in the same way because the situation was far different and nowhere near so threatening to public order or stability. Immediate reaction appears to have been muted while the regime was sized up (which some observers call a grace period), but within a year of taking power, Ershad and the military were losing public traction rapidly as it became progressively clearer that they had no intention of being a "temporary" government that turned power back to the civilians after rectifying the problems that led them to seize power.[1]

This became apparent as Ershad proceeded to try to establish legitimacy for his military regime. As the realization set in, Ershad came to be seen by much of the public as an unscrupulous and self-aggrandizing general leading an army which hungered for political power. In the view of their opponents, they were usurpers—having illegally deposed the Sattar government, which the people had freely elected.[2]

---

1   Lawrence Ziring, *Bangladesh—From Mujib to Ershad, An Interpretive Study* (Karachi: Oxford University Press, 1992), p. 158. Ziring appears to believe that Ershad enjoyed a period of grace from the public until he named himself President in 1983, which clinched the impression that he was a usurper, not a saviour. The author is less sure (not having been there), but most politicians that I talked to would not agree with that interpretation in retrospect. Though it was telegraphed, the coup may have caught them by surprise; moreover the leadership of the two major political parties was new and not well organized.

2   Craig Baxter, *Bangladesh, From a Nation to a State* (Boulder, CO: Westview Press, 1997), p. 107.

Ershad used the usual (and careworn) justification: the threat to national security from political and social "indiscipline," corruption, economic hard times, law and order problems, and an insufficiency of food on the markets made military intervention necessary. In a move mimicking Ziaur Rahman, he announced an eighteen-point program to rectify all these problems. He promised elections when the problems were ameliorated, and suspended the constitution.[3] In fact, parliamentary elections (boycotted by one major political party) were not held for four years—until May 1986—and martial law not ended until November of the same year.

To help him govern, and lend a little civilian flavor to the martial law government, Ershad appointed a council of advisors (again mimicking the November 1975 coup). This body included several distinguished civil servants who brought some respect to the government, though it was not clear why they had joined.[4] Ershad also rehabilitated the two military officers who were dismissed after the October 1977 mutiny and added them to the Council. Ershad selected former Supreme Court Justice Abul Muhammed Ahsanuddin Chowdhury as the new President.

This could have been, in fact, a propitious time for an even sharper break with the statist, central planning approach to economic development than Zia was able to effect. The military that had, under Ershad's leadership, taken control of the country was disciplined and no longer riven by factional disagreement. The political left was in retreat, the memory of the economic disaster it had inspired during Mujib's time still fresh and neuralgic.[5] That little was accomplished along the lines of continued reform is due primarily, it would seem, to the way that Ershad and the military took power and to his personal vanities and weaknesses.

In comparison with Bangladesh's previous leaders, Mujib and Zia, Ershad was a bland personality, an Army officer who seemed more at home behind a desk than on the battlefield. His strength seemed to be administration, not military or political combat. In the Army, he had been a low-profile organizer rather than a leader. In politics, he preferred dialogue to confrontation. He lacked both charisma and any overarching vision of the

---

3   Ibid., p. 108.

4   One of these distinguished men, the late Obaidullah Khan, was well known to the author, and a man of strong character and rectitude. We never talked about it, and it remains a mystery why he would have been persuaded to help bring some aura of legitimacy to this regime.

5   Stanley Kochanek, *Patron-Client Politics and Business in Bangladesh* (New Delhi: Sage Publications India Pvt Ltd, 1993, p. 95.

direction in which the nation should proceed. According to one reputable outside observer, his goal was not to create a "politically integrated society, but a relatively unified one…"[6]

The Early Ershad Years—Trying for Legitimacy and a Political Future

Thus began a long period of unrest and hostility toward the military government. Ershad tried to establish his authority and enhance his political prospects with a number of proposed changes to Zia's policies and programs designed to attract additional support from the business community and the conservative elements. He was also desperately seeking ways to gain a shred of legitimacy and cloak his regime in a civilian dress. Most of his proposals met with stiff resistance, and evoked public demonstrations that varied in strength and violence depending on whether they involved the major political parties or only smaller groups defending some special interest.

Ershad took particular aim at the system of local government—a form of devolution of power to the local level—that Zia had set up.[7] Zia had intended the new dispensation to put local bodies in charge of their own development, both the planning and the implementation. That this new arrangement also helped Zia politically was probably what disturbed Ershad about it. He replaced Zia's system—which was not in effect long enough to become really operative, and therefore had not become so imbedded in the political structure that the people understood what the loss meant—and replaced it with one that served better his political needs.

The new system increased the number of districts from twenty to sixty and divided them into 460 sub-districts, called upazillas. The sub-districts replaced what had been the police stations, called thanas, which had been

---

6   Ziring, *Bangladesh—From Mujib to Ershad*, pp. 153-4.

7   The system of local government has been a favorite "plaything" of Bangladeshi political leaders since independence, and has been changed many times primarily to give leaders control of politics in the countryside and allow them to establish systems of patronage which would ensure such control. For a concise history of local government evolution see Chapter 5, "Decentralizing To Improve Service Delivery," of the World Bank's report, *Taming Leviathan: Reforming Governance in Bangladesh* (Washington: World Bank, 2005), pp. 56-8. The structure of local government was organized as follows: There is a basic structure of four tiers. The smallest unit is the "gram" (village), of which there are about 40,000. The next size unit is the "union" (collection of villages). There are some 4,500 of these. The "upazila" (sub district) is the next size, and there are 469 of these. Finally, there is the "zila" (district), of which there are sixty-four. Various governments have changed which units have elected councils, and which councils are in charge of funds allocated to them. But this basic four-tier structure has altered little since British colonial times.

around since the British Raj. Each upazilla had about 9 to 10 union councils which became the main local government to which people took their problems and from which they expected services. The military government explained this change as directed at bringing development planning to the people, but clearly it would support better Ershad's intention to form his own political party, and through that party, to rule Bangladesh in the future.

Ershad almost completely eliminated judicial independence and reduced its authority substantially under a 1982 martial law regulation that took away the Supreme Court's jurisdiction to protect fundamental civil rights and required all courts to operate under the law provided by and the proclamations of the chief martial law administrator. Special and summary martial law courts were established whose judgments were not subject to review by the Supreme Court or other courts. Later on the seventh amendment was passed which indemnified Ershad and his fellow coup-makers from any judicial scrutiny of their proclamations, judgments, and actions during the martial law period.[8]

He also tried to change the judicial system (perhaps weaken it) by dispersing judicial power geographically, which would also help him entrench his position politically. He proposed that the High Court of the Supreme Court have benches in cities outside Dhaka. This created a great stir and one of the first of a constant series of demonstrations—this one involving a strike by lawyers, always a potent influence in the litigious Bengali culture. Ultimately, this dispersion plan was declared unconstitutional by the Supreme Court.[9]

To curry favour with the religious parties, Ershad announced in December 1982 that he wanted the constitution to be based on Sharia, Islamic law, and that Arabic be a part of the primary school curriculum. While Zia had pulled the Constitution back from the strict and unalloyed secular document that it had been at first under Mujib, the leap from Islam as the official religion to Sharia as the only law was far too great for the Bangladesh polity. There were intense demonstrations in early 1983 during which many arrests of students and political leaders took place, including the leaders of both major political parties, Begum Khaleda Zia, new head of the BNP,

---

8   www.geographic.org, *Bangladesh Judiciary* (www.theodora.com, 1988), retrieved January 2, 2006 from http://www.photius.com/countries/bangladesh/government/bangladesh_government_judiciary.

9   Mahmudul Islam, *Constitutional Law of Bangladesh* (Dhaka: Bangladesh Institute of Law and International Affairs, 1995), pp. 366-7.

and widow of Ziaur Rahman, and Sheikh Hasina, new leader of the Awami League, and daughter of Mujib.[10]

An important component of Ershad's search for legitimacy and a political future was his program of economic liberalization, especially relating to industrial policy. There was great pressure from industrialists, who he sought as the core of a constituency, to free up the rules for ownership of industry—much of which was still owned by the state—and for investment, including foreign investment. A series of incremental steps to liberalize the economy became a central part of the ongoing confrontation between Ershad and his vocal opposition.[11]

The effort was, in fact, an attempt to reverse the economic philosophy of "Mujibism," thus a frontal assault on the Awami League. Ershad might have imagined that the AL's bitter enemy, the BNP would have rushed to his support, but this did not occur. The BNP leader, Begum Zia, remained steadfast in her opposition to Ershad, partly because she believed that he was mixed up somehow in the assassination of her husband.[12]

The most daring step was his decision to denationalize the jute mills and privatize other state-owned industrial assets, the details of which and his other industrial policies will be covered in Chapter 9. The effort came to nothing, mainly because it was supported by few Bangladeshis, apart from the industrialists who had pressed for it (and outsiders like the World Bank). Because of this dearth of popular support, and because they were politically painful, Ershad implemented his new policies timidly and erratically. They more or less came to a halt by 1985.[13]

Tumultuous Politics and No Progress

Ershad's government began 1983 with plans to stabilize the political situation and legitimize his rule. These started with his partial and slightly absurd lifting of the ban on political activity—parties could hold meetings, but only indoors.[14] The opposition balked and agreed on a five-point program to pressure the government, demanding an end to the partial ban on political activity; the release of political prisoners, an end to press censorship,

---

10   Baxter, *Bangladesh,* p. 110.

11   Kochanek, *Patron-Client Politics,* pp. 95-6.

12   Ziring, *Bangladesh—From Mujib to Ershad,* p. 157.

13   Ibid., p. 99.

14   Outdoor political rallies with attendance numbering in the tens of thousands are a staple of Bangladeshi politics. Thus limiting political meetings to indoor sites is a significant restraint on political activity.

an end to martial law, and a parliamentary election before one was held for President.

Following the script used by both Ziaur Rahman (who meant it) and Zia ul Huq (who didn't) Ershad sought to civilianize the military government. In November 1983, he announced presidential elections for May of the following year, and hard on the heels of that, the formation of a new political party, the People's Party, which was intended to provide him with organized support in his effort to legitimize his regime. President Chowdhury suddenly resigned (probably under pressure) and Ershad nominated himself to be President. He thought he stood a better chance of election as an incumbent. If there was a grace period, it ended with this decision to become President.[15]

The decision to have a Presidential election first was directly contrary to the most important point in the combined opposition's five-point program. The two major parties frimly believed that their strength at the grass roots level would ensure that one or both would end up controlling parliament and, through that, the Presidency. (Despite the common objective that parliamentary elections be held first, the two parties fundamentally disagreed on the role of Parliament, with the BNP holding fast to the subordinated parliament of the Presidential system created by Ziaur Rahman, and the Awami League determined to revert to a parliamentary system with a ceremonial President.)[16]

Ershad's November announcement set off a chain of violent demonstrations that returned the situation to the status quo ante. The May 1984 election was called off, and both the BNP and the Awami League leaders ended up eventually in jail, where they remained for about a month, though doubtless not in the same cell. The political situation in Bangladesh at the end of 1983 was thus exactly the same as at the beginning of the year—no elections scheduled, martial law still in effect, the opposition still determined to force Ershad from office. He had to go back to square one in his campaign to legitimize the regime and hold an election that would pass muster with the international community (and forget the opposition).

Trying to begin 1984 on a more positive and constructive note, Ershad agreed that presidential and parliamentary elections would be held at the same time, in May. Demonstrations continued and so kept up the pressure on the regime while the two opposition leaders, Begum Zia and Sheikh

---

15 Baxter, *Bangladesh*, p. 111. See endnote 1.

16 Ibid., p. 111.

Hasina engaged in talks to try to resolve the impasse. In early May, in an attempt to compromise, Ershad gave way and announced that the Presidential election would be held after the parliamentary election, but put off the latter until the end of 1984. The opposition demurred and demonstrations continued. In October, Ershad postponed the parliamentary elections indefinitely.

In most respects, then, 1984 ended as it began, with the same conditions obtaining as the year before. One difference, however, was the creeping civilianization of the martial law government. Several prominent politicians who had joined the People's Party also accepted ministerial positions, and Ataur Rahman Khan, a very respected figure from the days of United Pakistan, became Prime Minister in March. Also, to put a more benign face on the military government, ministers from Sattar's cabinet who had been jailed on corruption charges were released.

There was little change or forward motion in 1985, though Ershad continued to try to enhance his legitimacy. At about this point, he seemed to give up on trying to co-opt the opposition through dialogue.[17] Borrowing an idea from his Pakistani analog, Zia ul Huq, he held a referendum which posed the question of whether he should continue as President. Unsurprisingly, he claimed that he received a large affirmative vote, but few believed that the poll had been free or fair. Legitimacy remained elusive. Local elections, which the opposition boycotted, were held in May, while the two major party leaders enjoyed once again the comforts of jail.

Politics Begins—After a Fashion

Both the opposition and Ershad tired of marking time, and politics heated up again in 1986. Parties and trade unions were allowed to function again, and Ershad tried once more to schedule a parliamentary election—this time for April. He also took the opportunity to turn his People's Party into a new party called Jatiya—the National Party. Ershad also relaxed several martial law provisions, but his price was that the major parties agree to participate in the election he had scheduled. Again they thought better of the suggestion, and the deal was off.

But then it was on again, or partially. There was great pressure within the Awami League, and from its allied parties, to participate in the election. Sheikh Hasina waffled, and finally agreed that her party and its allies would participate. The BNP remained adamant that it would make no deal with

---

17   Ziring, *Bangladesh—From Mujib to Ershad*, p. 168.

Ershad, and remained on the sidelines.[18] (This was held to be much to its credit a few years later when Ershad actually fell from power.)

To accommodate Sheikh Hasina's late entry, the election was delayed until early May. The outcome was closer than one would have predicted given that the Jatiya Party was in power. There was extensive rigging by both the government and the Awami League in the districts they controlled. However, the government did win 153 seats in the Assembly, an outright majority, almost twice as many seats as the Awami League's 76. All the other parties (except the boycotting BNP) won the remaining 71 seats.[19]

Getting Parliament to meet with all its members present was almost as difficult as getting to the election itself. The Awami League and it partners staged a boycott until Ershad rescinded martial law. Ershad would not end martial law until the Parliament indemnified all the actions taken by the martial law government as legal and regular, which, *inter alia*, would ensure that Ershad and his cronies could not be prosecuted for the coup and the application of martial law. Eventually, Parliament minus the Awami League members passed the indemnification as the seventh amendment to the constitution. Ershad then ended martial law on November 10 and put a new cabinet in office.

In the meantime, there was movement on the Presidential front. After the May Parliamentary election Ershad set October for a Presidential election. Following the example of the other Zia—Zia Rahman—Ershad stepped down as Chief of Army Staff and eventually resigned from the army in order to run for President. Shiekh Hasina changed her mind and decided not to contest the Presidential election, and Ershad won most of the vote, though the level of voter participation, while still debated, was probably very low.

1986 ended on a positive note, and the government claimed progress for the year. A parliament was elected, and only one major party boycotted, martial law was ended, and the full Parliament actually met toward the end of the year, though without the Awami League (which walked out early) and the BNP (which boycotted the election). A President was elected, though whether he was the genuine choice of the people is doubtful. Nonetheless, it would have been logical to assume that 1987 would be a more tranquil year. But it was the most turbulent one Ershad regime's had experienced.

---

18   Baxter, *Bangladesh*, p.112.
19   Ibid., p. 113, Table 9.1.

The Siege of Dhaka—Confrontation Grows

Despite all the political changes on the surface, nothing had really changed. The Army was still in charge, and Ershad had promised it would remain so.[20] The President still ruled in an arbitrary fashion through a compliant senior bureaucracy. The Cabinet was consulted infrequently, and there was little effort to treat with Parliament, even though it was a puppet, or even with the President's own party. The idea of consulting with the opposition got even shorter shrift. Admittedly, after the history of the previous four years, such discussions were likely to be fruitless in any case.[21]

Ershad initiated what became his greatest crisis (until his fall from power) when he arbitrarily introduced into his puppet parliament a bill to amend the Local Government Act, which provided for Army officers to participate in district development committees as non-voting members. The opposition was furious. This would give the Army, it believed, power over the resources at the disposal of the committees, it would make permanent the military's power in politics and, according to both Sheikh Hasina and Begum Zia, it would create a permanent garrison state.[22]

Demonstrations and strikes became an almost everyday occurrence. Though Ershad tried to find ways to temper the strife, and conceded several issues in hope of finding a *modus vivendi* with the opposition, civil order was slowly disintegrating. The boiling point was reached in late July 1987 when general strikes were declared protesting the government's attempt to revive its privatization policy, on which it had moved very cautiously since announcing it two years earlier.[23]

Demonstrations protesting various other grievances mounted in frequency and intensity over the next three months until, in November 1987, Dhaka was essentially shut down in a month-long general strike which was accompanied by serious violence.

This episode of civil disobedience became soon known as the "Siege of Dhaka."[24] Ershad could only respond by declaring a state of emergency, in

---

20   Ziring, *Bangladesh—From Mujib to Ershad*, p. 202.

21   Baxter, *Bangladesh*, p. 113.

22   Ziring, *Bangladesh—From Mujib to Ershad*, p. 203.

23   See above discussion on the new economic liberalization that Ershad began in 1982, which is covered in detail in Chapter 9, and which ended in failure in 1985. Trying to restart it in 1987 wasn't such a good idea.

24   As one illustration of the disruption and turmoil, the U.S. Embassy, which was still located in the heart of downtown Dhaka, was unable to open for business for about twenty straight days; the Ambassador operated out of an office in a more peaceful part of town

which he suspended fundamental rights and allowed the government to follow a far more muscular approach to halt strikes and demonstrations. Many people were jailed, and in early December Parliament was dissolved. The crisis subsided, though the violence continued into early 1988, but the political harm done to Ershad was terminal. That he hung on for another two and a half years is probably due more to divisions in the opposition than to his own resilience or strength.

Passions subsided for awhile, not because of any change of heart on the part of the opposition—or on that of Ershad—but because of fatigue and the need to meet other challenges. In order to retrieve a functioning government, a parliamentary election was held in early March. But the AL again joined the BNP in a boycott, and the result had no real meaning. Ershad and his Jatiya Party won a huge majority over a motley coalition of small (almost microscopic) opposition parties, a totally predictable outcome, and one that did not advance Ershad's prospects of gaining legitimacy. Naming a new Prime Minister did not help either in that effort.

Pushing along normalization, the state of emergency was called off in mid-April 1988. Still searching for support in his quest for legitimacy and to be a popularly elected President, Ershad appealed to religious parties by bringing Islam into the Constitution.[25] He had earlier said that he favoured basing the constitution on Sharia, and his puppet parliament passed a constitutional amendment in June that made Islam the state religion. While a step further towards institutionalizing Islam than Ziaur Rahman had taken the constitution, it fell far short of declaring Bangladesh an Islamic state, and far short of the Islamization that his Pakistani analog, Zia ul Huq was implementing. Nonetheless, it hardened further the attitude of that half of the opposition that was wedded to the idea of a secular state.

In the fall of 1988, devastating floods hit Bangladesh, perhaps the worst in a century. Twenty-five million people may have been made homeless, and more than half of the country was under water. The Ershad government handled the crisis very well, organizing an effective response, quite in contrast with their habitual policies.

But political legitimacy continued to elude the regime. In Ershad's case the ancient axiom that legitimacy can be gained by accomplishment had a very high threshold. His efforts continued to fall short because of his au-

---

in which the embassy's General Services section was located. Conversation of the author with Ambassador Willard De Pree.

25   Baxter, *Bangladesh*, p. 114.

thoritarian style and transparent ambition, as well as a growing perception that corruption was blighting Bangladesh. In July 1989, his puppet parliament passed another constitutional amendment that gave the President two further terms of five years in office. The post of Vice President was also made elective, and was to run concurrently with that of the President, and a new Vice President was appointed. This was Ershad's last constitutional alteration, and it was to assume an importance a year later in ways he could not have foreseen.

India: A Footnote Again to the Internal Drama

The Ershad era in Bangladesh was dominated by the political drama described above. Nothing really changed regarding the behemoth next door. The suspicion and skepticism of Indian designs and attitudes remained strong among most of the population—those who, for the most part, both Ershad and Begum Zia were trying to appeal to. The nostalgia for the days of the purely secular state of Mujib, and for the gratitude Bangladeshis felt in 1971 for Indian assistance in their war for separation, still motivated Sheikh Hasina and the Awami League. But even Sheikh Hasina found it politically expedient to steer a cautious course in talking about relations with India.

The most difficult issue between the two countries was one of long standing which had become increasingly neuralgic since the 1970s: refugees from the Chittagong Hill Tracts who had found their way to Northeastern India. Among these refugees were members of an armed Hill Tracts resistance group, which India had tolerated in its territory for a number of years.[26] In the mid-1980s, however, the Indians tired of the growing number of these refugees and the costs of hosting them and pressed Bangladesh to create the conditions for their return. Ershad sought a formula to do this, but it proved difficult. Measures to provide more autonomy for the Hill Tracts, to put an end to land-grabbing by Bengalis from the plains, and to boost the economy were not sufficient to bring most back.[27] A political solution would await another decade and the democratically elected Awami League government of 1996.

---

26   Kathryn Jacques, *Bangladesh, India, and Pakistan—International Relations and Regional Tensions in South Asia* (New York: St. Martin's Press, 2000), p. 135.

27   Baxter, *Bangladesh*, p. 109-10.

The Denouement—Ershad Meets His Match[28]

Ershad's opposition had rarely been able to agree among themselves long enough to bring him down. Perhaps it was the tide of democracy that was running high throughout the world, but the opposition parties were suddenly seized with a pragmatic understanding that they could only do so once solidly unified. They constructed an alliance based on a one-point agenda—to get rid of him through a campaign of escalating political pressure which would slowly bring the country to a standstill.

The opposition agreed that Ershad would be forced to resign, and a free and fair election for a parliament would follow. This was the first time that the two parties and their leaders had shown the remotest sign of civility toward each other, or cooperated on a common goal. Unfortunately it was not a harbinger of the future.

In October 1990, violent demonstrations broke out against the government, first on university campuses, especially at Dhaka University. These were organized by the perennially militant student wings of the two major parties. Smelling the political equivalent of blood, and sensing that events were tilting in their favor, the BNP and the Awami League increased the street campaign against the government. At one point, the BNP leader, Begum Zia, was mauled in a melee in front of the government administrative buildings, and was thought to have been injured.

Ershad was in a quandary: the demonstrations were spiralling out of control and he had to find a way to slow them down and ultimately to stop them. If he couldn't, an irresistible momentum would build to the point at which the government could not resist bowing to the Opposition's "non-negotiable" demand that he resign. He wrestled with the idea of declaring another state of emergency, which would give the government the constitutional powers it needed—curfew, arbitrary arrest powers, etc.—to apply "legal" force in quelling the demonstrations.

At one point he summoned the Ambassadors of major donor countries to sound out our likely reaction to the idea of declaring a state of emergency. A chilly silence greeted his entreaties. After what seemed like several minutes of mute disapproval (which could have been interpreted as mute acquiescence), I spoke out in unequivocal terms of the negative reaction of the

---

28   Much of what follows in this chapter is based on my personal observation and experience while US Ambassador to Bangladesh from August 1990 to October 1993. Footnotes 29 through 34 are simply elaborations on the text.

United States to the idea, saying my government would be much displeased by such a declaration. The Japanese Ambassador echoed my thoughts.

But Ershad was desperate at this point. He probably calculated that some donor governments might criticise such a declaration, but would go no further than ritual condemnation of his regime. He declared a state of emergency on November 27 and imposed a curfew. The country's economy shut down, which displeased those in the business community who had remained his supporters. But this did little to dampen the now inexorable pressure on him and his government to give way. Dhaka was ghost-like after the curfew at sunset, but during the day it continued to seethe with protests and demonstrations.

Ershad continued to seek room for maneuver. He sought neutral intermediaries to approach the opposition and try to broker talks so that he could work out a compromise solution. He approached me through his Foreign Minister, but I turned him down flat on the spot. Ershad may have tried his luck with other ambassadors, though none ever confided in me that he had. He found no takers among the diplomatic community or elsewhere.

His objective was to use talks as a means of cooling passions and probably to find a way to split the two major party leaders by engendering mistrust in each about the other's motives. Given the hostility that obtained then (and now) between the two individuals, this was an often successful strategy that he had deployed many times in the previous eight years.

The opposition had Ershad on the run, and knew it. When his last desperate gamble of trying to call out the army also failed, he was finished as President.[29] He couldn't count on the police to enforce the state of emergency and quell the violence and his resignation came within hours.

Ershad left office the same evening. When he made his intention to resign known to the opposition, talks did take place, but only to find ways to observe the constitutional niceties of presidential succession. His Vice President, Moudud Ahmed, first resigned from office, and the Chief Justice of the Supreme Court, Shahabudin Ahmed, was appointed to replace him. He was the compromise choice of the two major parties to be Interim Acting President. With him installed quickly as Vice President, Ershad re-

---

29   Perhaps not forever, as Ershad returned to politics later—after languishing in jail for awhile—took up the leadership of the party he had built, and is now an active participant in Bangladesh's poisonous politics. The rumor is that his price for collaboration with one of the two major parties is to be named President, although, unlike when he formerly held office, the position is largely ceremonial now under Bangladesh's parliamentary system of government.

signed the presidency, and Shahabudin became Acting President—all this within the letter of the constitution.

The Transition to Democracy

One of the reasons for the great optimism that swept the country was the new Acting President, Shahabudin, who was widely respected for his fairness and objectivity before his selection to run the country. He proved, in the event, to be the leader that Bangladesh needed to steer it toward democracy.[30] On his first day as President he announced a plan for the transition: a neutral administration, equitable and non-partisan law enforcement, a powerful election commission, a free and fair parliamentary election in February 1991 (in about three months), and a smooth and peaceful transfer of power to whichever party won the election. It all came to pass.[31]

Acts of reprisal began soon after, however. Former Vice President Moudud Ahmed's house was invaded at night by young toughs, and his wife and child forced to take refuge in a neighbor's house.[32] (Moudud had already disappeared.) Within a few days of his resignation, Ershad was charged with several crimes (some trivial), and he and his wife were led off to jail. Other officials of his government were arrested in the weeks after

---

30   Shahabudin was thought to have Awami League sympathies regarding policy, especially concerning its more secular platform, but all sides were confident that he would be steadfastly neutral and objective in his stewardship of the transition and the election: they were completely correct in that confidence.

31   I offer the following vignette as an illustration of the modesty and character of the man that the Bangladeshi parties had selected as their Interim President. In January 1991, the first Gulf War began with the bombing campaign against Saddam Hussein's forces in and outside Baghdad. On the first Friday after the bombing began, a large crowd was mobilised by an Iraqi-financed mosque to attack embassies of the governments of the coalition arrayed against Saddam. These Embassies were mainly located in the Gulshan and Baridhara suburbs of Dhaka, so diplomatic residences were within reach of the crowd also. The government, totally preoccupied with domestic concerns of the election, was caught by surprise. The crowd roamed the suburbs freely for a couple of hours and damaged the Saudi Arabian Embassy and the American Club (which I had closed as a precaution), and headed toward my residence. As soon as I learned of the crowd, I called the Presidency to request protection. The President's military aide-de-camp answered and gave the call to the President immediately. Shahabuddin took the call on the spot, understood the government's obligation thoroughly, and dispatched paramilitary forces which arrived within thirty minutes to stop the crowd in its tracks. (Interestingly, the crowd then dispersed and regrouped in front of the Iraqi Embassy where my French colleague, next door to that Embassy, observed Iraqi Embassy officers passing out money to the crowd.)

32   The house happened to be occupied by one of my staff, a USAID officer and his family. The next day I took a van, with the windows covered, to the USAID house, put Hasna Moudud inside, and took her to safety at her sister's house.

his government fell. Acts of vengeance in the countryside against officials of Ershad's Jatiya party multiplied.

Shahabudin's primary mission was to deliver a free and fair election. The government ran in neutral during the interim, though a technocratic cabinet he appointed kept government machinery turning over. He delivered on the free and fair election, and kept the nation confident that a new era was on the way. The two major parties prepared for a three month election campaign, with most observers believing that the Awami League had the superior grass roots organization and would win easily. This presumption strengthened after the AL put together an election alliance with like-minded small parties that agreed to cooperate in a joint election strategy.

The skillful and honest leadership of Shahabudin became a model for political transitions in the Third World. Moreover the concept of a neutral interim government to run the country and elections became embodied in the constitution during a later difficult transition. Observers of Bangladesh politics, and indeed many of the Bangladesh political class, assumed that this constitutional provision, which was designed to allow political power after an election to pass peacefully from one party to another without military intervention, violence, and/or international pressure would be the basis of a real and sustainable democracy in the country. Unfortunately Bangladesh's poisonous politics thwarted this hope, as we will see in later chapters.

The Election of 1991—A New Start? Or Deja-Vu All Over Again?

There were 300 parliamentary seats to be contested and filled. The AL had agreed not to put up candidates in 31 constituencies which its small party allies felt they could win against the BNP. The idea was that the small parties would not field candidates in the other 269 constituencies, leaving the AL to compete directly against the BNP and the other major parties. As in most Bangladesh political alliances, however, the temptations of winning a seat overcame the strategic goal of winning a majority for the alliance, and the small parties fielded candidates in other constituencies which took votes away from the AL.

The BNP avoided all such alliances before the election, whether by design or by accident, and contested all 300 seats. (Later it would forge an agreement with Jamat that gave it a majority in the new Parliament.) The party platform was considered by much of the electorate as more forward looking and fresh than its main rivals. It managed to portray itself as more pragmatic and less ideological, and wrapped itself in the Bangladeshi nationalism of

Ziaur Rahman as opposed to the Bengali nationalism of the AL, which was construed as pro-Indian. It also emphasized the party's Islamic leanings, though eschewing any idea of an Islamic state. The BNP leaders focused—or seemed to—less on the past martyrdom of their assassinated former leader than did the AL.

The BNP platform called for the continuation of economic policies favorable to private enterprise and privatization, as well as social development measures, including family planning, that Zia and Ershad had pursued (though mention of Ershad's role was avoided). In all, it was a platform that appealed to Bangladeshi voters, who with an irony reserved for countries in which political consistency is not always considered vital, remembered favorably the thirteen years of relative economic and social progress under Zia and Ershad, while repudiating the autocracy of military governments, especially of Ershad.

On the other hand, the Awami League seemed to campaign on a platform of nostalgia, one that almost deified the Party's founder, Sheikh Mujib, but more damagingly extolled his failed economic programmes that were, rhetorically at least, based on a socialist approach to development and economic policy. While there was a hard core of supporters for the League, its message, delivered much more stridently than that of the BNP, seemed to turn off many of the voters, especially those in the rural areas whose memories of the hard times under Mujib's reign, and of the 1974 famine, remained acute.

Thus the issues between the two major parties were rather sharply drawn, particularly those of economic and development policy. There was also a fundamental political divergence: the question of whether Bangladesh should have a presidential system or revert to a parliamentary one. During the campaign the BNP stood four square for the presidential system (after all, its founder, Ziaur Rahman, had believed in it), while the Awami League campaigned hard for reversion to a parliamentary one (even though its founder, Mujib, was the author of the switch from parliamentary to presidential). In the event, the decision was made on purely political grounds—who would likely win the presidential election.

The pundits were close to unanimous in predicting an Awami League victory, based on their assumption that its local party organizational base was were much stronger than the BNP's, but this proved badly off base. Although the popular vote was very close (31 percent for the BNP, 30.6 percent for the Awami League), the BNP won 140 seats because of the "first past the post" method of electing parliament—inherited from Westminster. The favored Awami League won 88 seats, the Jatiya Party 35, and the Jamat 18.

A Brief Period of Parliamentary Bliss

When Parliament convened, in late March, the first order of business was to elect thirty women members for the seats set aside in the constitution for them. The first political deal of the new democratic episode resulted in Jamat support for 28 BNP candidates in return for BNP support for two Jamat candidates. Thus the parliament began its life with the BNP holding 168 seats (an absolute majority in a house of 330 seats), the Awami League holding 88 seats, the Jatiya Party holding 35 seats, and the Jamat holding 20.

The second order of business for the new Parliament was to decide between the presidential system then in place or a return to a parliamentary form of government. With its 168 seats the BNP understood that, with that such a majority, it would control Parliament, and under a parliamentary system, the government. But a glance at the popular vote statistics made it less likely that it would have such control in the presidential system, after the two leaders squared off in a presidential election The BNP had finished with 31 percent while the Awami League won 30.6 percent, and if the votes for the small parties in its alliance were counted, 34 percent. Begum Zia, while undoubtedly still emotionally inclined toward a presidential system, but pressured intensely by her party leaders who saw ministerial and other high-level positions beckoning, let pragmatism rule and opted for a deal with the opposition on a parliamentary system.

It seems to have been the second—and to date the last—political compromise between the two parties, and the two leaders, in the modern political history of Bangladesh (the first being the one-point joint platform of the summer of the previous year when the two cooperated fully in the overthrow of Ershad). Each party put forth a draft constitutional amendment, and there were a number of differences between the two, one of the main one being the BNP's insistence on a provision that 10 percent of the cabinet need not be elected members of Parliament.[33]

With the approval of the leaders, Parliament formed a multi-party committee to find a compromise amendment that would gain the adherence

---

33   Begum Zia wanted this provision very much in order to allow her friend and trusted confidant, Saifur Rahman, who had served in the cabinet of her husband, to be in the government. It was a good decision, as we shall see, as Rahman became one of the outstanding Finance Ministers in the third world, in a very difficult economic environment.

of both major parties. According to the constitution, two thirds of Parliament (a majority that required the support of most members of both major parties) must approve constitutional amendments, and Bangladeshis continued their tradition of finding constitutional means of fine-tuning their political system.

Much to the surprise of most veteran Bangladesh watchers, the committee did reach a compromise that drew the support of both parties and leaders; the amendment passed the parliament with the required two thirds majority in early August, 1991, and won a large majority in a referendum the following month. Bangladesh was officially a parliamentary democracy again, sixteen years after the nation's founder, Sheikh Mujib, had changed it to a Presidential system. It took another constitutional amendment to get Shahabudin reappointed to his former job as Chief Justice. A BNP stalwart, Abdur Rahman Biswas, was chosen as the figurehead President by the Parliament. Begum Zia became the Prime Minister, and the Head of Government.

In the sixteen years since these compromises were brokered, there have no repeat performances. Bangladeshi politics reverted to the confrontational style of the Ershad and Mujib years, consultation with the opposition became the exception rather than the norm and real debate and compromise in Parliament were rarely tried. Instead the government used its majority to ramrod through legislation with no effort being made to find solutions that the other parties could live with.

Ershad as Henry IV

In many respects, Ershad resembles Zia ul Huq, his Pakistani counterpart, more closely than his predecessor in Bangladesh, Ziaur Rahman. But unlike either Zia, he spent almost his whole tenure fighting his enemies, trying to establish his legitimacy and shake off the verdict of most Bangladeshis that he was a usurper.

In effect Ershad ran an eight-year interim government, It accomplished very little, though it tried to move ahead on economic matters, because its energies and vision were sapped by the constant struggle to gain legitimacy and to survive. It simply marked time politically. But, as we shall see in Chapter 9, while the Ershad government trod water, the NGOs increased their delivery of social services, effective family planning spread to the far corners of the country, and education levels climbed, especially of girls. A social revolution was taking place while the politicians' attention was elsewhere.

Also like Zia ul Huq, Ershad's legacy was almost entirely negative. One of its most harmful aspects was the radicalization of a generation of students, and the even greater politicization of the already highly politicized universities.[34] His attempts to create a government counterforce to the students who usually led the opposition to his regime created a warlike atmosphere on the campuses which prevailed long after Ershad was out of power. And by bringing Islam more centrally into the constitution and forging links with the Islamists, he also helped to create the Islamist surge Bangladesh is witnessing today.

Ershad resembled Ziaur Rahman in one way: like him, he was convinced that while his power base lay in the Army, his political future depended on bettering the conditions of the multitude of rural peasants in Bangladesh.[35] Thus his disinclination to follow through on the economic reforms he promised, and seemed to believe in, was a historic failure (again more like Zia ul Huq). As was suggested at the beginning of this chapter, Ershad came to power at a propitious moment, but he squandered it in fruitless political confrontation over legitimacy. If he and his regime were to have ever gained a measure of legitimacy, it would have been through improving the quotidian conditions of the 70 percent of Bangladeshis who live off the land.

This chapter includes the beginning of the democratic era, not only to end on a happy note, but because it is a seamless part of the narrative of the Ershad years that led inexorably to the rise of electoral democracy. The cooperation of the opposition parties in overturning his government that began in summer 1990 extended to the constitutional arrangements under which Bangladesh would be governed in the electoral democracy that was inaugurated in autumn 1991. Mid-1990 to late-1991 was a time of great optimism for the people of Bangladesh and for their future, to which the author can personally attest. One almost thought that anything, and everything, was possible. As we shall see in the next chapter, this euphoria soon wore off.

---

34   Ziring, *Bangladesh—From Mujib to Ershad,* p. 167.
35   Ibid., p. 159.

6

ELECTORAL DEMOCRACY IS NOT ENOUGH

The post-Ershad electoral democracy that commenced in February 1991 became increasingly dysfunctional over the sixteen years of its troubled existence until it failed completely in early January 2007. During that period, the profile of political development in Bangladesh was, at best, flat—some would say retrograde. Bangladeshi political leaders and parties demonstrated vividly how, through bad governance and unconstructive and disloyal opposition, to undercut what should have been promising democratic development. Sixteen years of electoral democracy left the nation, politically, about where it was in 1991. In terms of political development, it is back to square one.

Bangladesh introduced in 1991 a novel and progressive concept—a nonparty, neutral caretaker government to oversee elections—that offered hope that the democracy that had emerged would deepen and endure. But this innovation had come about because of short-term political self-interest, not because the main political leaders believed in democracy. The Awami League (AL) and the Bangladesh Nationalist Party (BNP) could not even cooperate in the downfall of their most hated enemy, Ershad, until they had worked out how to ensure that neither would have an advantage in the election that would follow his ouster. This should have been a sign that more was needed than just a way to ensure free and fair elections.

In the two subsequent elections, 1996 and 2001, the mechanism worked well enough. The party out of power in the previous cycle triumphed over the party that had been in power, primarily because the latter had been so busy trying to ensure it would stay in power that it neglected to govern. The government was passed to the winning party peacefully and without violence or resistance beyond the usual carping by the loser alleging "rigged" elections—a claim always contradicted by the testimony of scores of international observers. But neither party ever accepted that the other had the legitimacy to govern if freely and fairly elected.

The caretaker government innovation was supposed to preserve electoral democracy while the institutions that are the foundation of true democracy were built and strengthened. But, as mentioned in the Introduction, hope outran reality. Institutions such as an independent judiciary, a working parliament, the rule of law, the art of give-and-take and compromise were further eroded by the toxic politics of Bangladesh (and by the pernicious leadership of both major parties). The parties ended up by degrading even the concept of the caretaker government in their passion to win elections at any cost.

After each of the three elections, both the government and the opposition reverted almost immediately to the politics of the past: 1) aggressive government behavior aimed at weakening the opposition; and 2) confrontation, demonstrations, and violence in the streets as the main elements of strategy and tactics by the opposition. The objective of the opposition was clearly to disrupt economy and society to turn the public against the government. An inevitable result (and possibly also an opposition aim) was pusillanimous policy-making by the government out of fear of alienating important bases of support.

Each election generated more heat than light as both major parties sought to undercut each other and gain the upper hand. The party in power had greater opportunity to pervert the electoral mechanisms, and in each election there was more encroachment on their neutrality—the election commission and the caretaker government. Over most of 2006 and into January 2007 such encroachments produced more stress than the system could cope with. The leaders of both major parties, intent on winning at all costs, steered a suicidal, all-or-nothing, course, resisting every entreaty and temptation to compromise. As in November 1975, Bangladesh was faced with the specter of chaos, anarchy, and serious civil strife.

In the end, only eleven days before the election was to be held, the Army once again intervened to prevent a slide into instability and violence. At its insistence, the pro-BNP President declared an emergency, postponed the election, and appointed a truly non-party, neutral caretaker government mandated to design a reform program that would lay the foundation for a stronger, and true, democracy. This includes fortifying the electoral mechanisms, in particular the Election Commission, and rooting out the pervasive corruption that was plaguing Bangladesh politics. The jury is still out on whether this attempt to build a modular democracy on a stronger foundation will work or not.

This chapter covers the period from the election of 1991 to the Army takeover in January 2007. It attempts to explain what went wrong and why the Army, which intended in 1990 to remain forever outside politics, believed it had to intervene again in the political life of Bangladesh. At the end of the narrative there will be brief description of the political events of late 2006 and early 2007 that led to the Army takeover. At the end of the chapter, I analyse how deep and pervasive are the problems that the new military/ civilian government must deal with to lay the basis for real democracy in Bangladesh when it turns power back to the civilians.

The Institutionalization of Violence and Street Action as Political Strategy [1]

The two major parties performed in identical ways when in opposition, setting the tone for Bangladesh's stalled political development during this third democratic episode. What the Awami League and its political allies did in 1991-1996 to unseat the sitting BNP government, the BNP did between 1996 and 2001 to unseat the sitting Awami League government. The Awami League followed exactly the same script after 2001 in trying to eject the BNP government, which won the election of that year.

The rules of the game in effective democracies allow the winning party, when freely and fairly elected by the country's citizens, the opportunity to propose and implement its programs in an atmosphere of free and full debate, in Parliament and among the public. This was completely missing from the Bangladesh politics, as practiced between 1991 and 2007. While power passed peacefully between parties in free and fair elections, all pretence to democratic governance was abandoned after the election. The opposition's objective was to force another election and return to power as quickly as possible. The natural state of Bangladesh politics during these turbulent years seemed to be: abjure other viewpoints; identify national interest with your party; and consider being out of power almost worse than death itself.

---

1   Much of the narrative of the following section comes from the author's own observations and analyses while serving as US Ambassador in Bangladesh or following the situation closely through official government and media reports from other posts, particularly Pakistan.

The non-democratic tools that both major parties deployed, while in opposition, to force a return to power always threatened, and often involved, violence. The periods between elections were almost always characterized by interminable and incessant disruption to the economy and to people's daily lives. Street power was the answer to all political frustration, it seemed. At the limit, these methods threatened the livelihood of ordinary Bangladeshis and their ability to feed their families. A second-level tactic was to boycott Parliament or to walk out of it over perceived (or alleged) political grievances.

The BNP Government of 1991-1996

For about six months, the Parliament elected in February 1991 was the epitome of democratic reason and effectiveness. For Bangladesh this political environment was not only unnatural, it was enervating. Before too long, it began to unwind and politics reverted to their usual zero-sum form. The "era of good feeling" lasted long enough, however, to resolve the fundamental question of which form of government, presidential or parliamentary, should obtain in Bangladesh. Parliament, while in this good mood, also elected the ceremonial President and passed legislation that permitted the President of the Interim Government (former Chief Justice) to return to the Supreme Court. For a while, political compromise seemed possible and extreme partisanship a thing of the past.

Political recidivism returned when the BNP implemented its substantive program in November 1991. Its first act was to abolish the local government system introduced by Ershad, based on the upazila councils.[2] (Ershad's system, which replaced the one installed by Zia that aimed to put local governments in charge of planning and implementation of local development projects, was believed by the BNP to have been designed primarily to allow Ershad to build up his Jatiya party.)

Perhaps if there had been a specific plan to improve local government, and a precise idea of what local units should replace the upazila councils, the criticism would not have been so immediate and virulent. But there were no specifics, and no plan. A detailed proposal to replace Ershad's local administrative system was only put forward in 2004 by the BNP government, after a hiatus of thirteen years. The doomed upazila councils were abolished because a year earlier his party had won majorities in the very same councils, in elections which the BNP and the Awami League had boycotted. This was more than the BNP could bear—the thought that Jatiya

---

2   See note 7 of Chapter 5.

would have a significant leg up in the next election because of its control at the upazila level.

The Awami League did not wait long to show its hand. In November, 1991, AL leader, Sheikh Hasina, wrote to the diplomatic corps criticizing harshly the BNP government's policies and suggesting that it should promote instead those of the AL. This seemed strange because the only policies that the government had laid out to that point were the continuation of privatization, an easing of the conditions under which private enterprise could operate, and an easing of of restrictions on foreign exchange transactions.[3]

The AL's street strategy began in early 1992. The proximate cause of the first set of demonstrations was the election of Golam Azam as leader of the Jamat-I-Islami party. Azam had left Bangladesh after the 1971 war of separation to live in Pakistan. He was charged with aiding the Pakistan army during that war, though this allegation was never proven.[4] The Awami League and its allies demanded that he be tried as a war criminal, and forfeit his Bangladeshi citizenship. Demonstrations to force a trial and/ or to influence the Supreme Court to uphold the claim that he was not a citizen began in June 1992. These went on, sporadically for about a year, but when the Supreme Court ruled that he was a citizen, the demonstrations stopped and did not recur.

But the opposition found many other reasons to continue demonstration and strikes. There were protests against anti-terrorist legislation that the government had promulgated to quell violence on university campuses. A vicious circle began: demonstrations to protest legislation designed to stop demonstrations. The universities were closed as much as they were

---

3   Despite the monumental government inertia in many areas, the Finance Minister, Saifur Rahman, continued to push Bangladesh toward a market economy and endeavored to create a climate which would attract more domestic and foreign investment. He fostered a close relationship between Bangladesh and the international financial institutions (the IMF, IBRD, ADB, UNDP) as well as the bilateral aid agencies that benefited the Bangladesh economy greatly. The author regards him as one of the most effective Finance Ministers he has observed in the third world. While Rahman had little support from his own party, let alone the opposition, he was *primus inter pares* in the cabinet, the most trusted advisor to the Prime Minister, despite his inability then to get elected in his native Sylhet. He was very effective in getting things done in the government, and the international community, including the author, counted on him to be the voice of progress and modernism not only on economic issues but across the board. He was our bulwark against the worst excesses and wayward, self-defeating policy directions (for example the occasional outbursts against foreign NGOs) the government was often inclined to take.

4   The Jamat i Islami (JI) party officially opposed the separation of the two wings of Pakistan, thus the war of separation, because of its overriding objective of a United Pakistan as an Islamic State. Whether Golam Azam aided the Pakistani army against Bangladeshi militants is open to question.

open.[5] The government was unable to stem the frequent partisan-inspired interruptions of social and economic life.

It acted, however, with dispatch and determination to quell the first outbreak of serious communal violence in almost thirty years. This came in the wake of the destruction of the Babri Masjid (mosque) at Ayodhya in north India by Hindu fundamentalist mobs in early December 1992. Demonstrations immediately broke out in Dhaka, and in the south east around Khulna. Violence against local Hindus and their temples quickly followed. The BNP government reacted quickly and forcefully to stop the trouble, and tensions subsided. A number of Hindus took the occasion to relocate over the border in Indian West Bengal, reducing their numbers in Bangladesh even further.[6]

Constant street action made the daily lives of most people increasingly precarious and the government's inability to quell the disturbances eroded its support. This first became manifest in January 1994 when the BNP was unable to carry the mayoral elections in Bangladesh's two major cities, Dhaka and Chittagong. Losing the two largest cities was a serious blow to the party.

In a parliamentary by-election in March 1994, the BNP appeared to reverse the negative trends by winning a seat that the AL had held until the incumbent died. The incongruity of the BNP victory (possibly rigged)

---

5   It was commonly said in Dhaka that it took seven years to get a three year university degree because of all the closures.

6   The percentage of Hindus in Bangladesh (East Bengal before Partition; East Pakistan between 1947 and 1971) has steadily declined from just below 30 percent in 1941 to under 10 percent in 2002 according to S.K. Datta, "The Recent Plight of Minorities in Bangladesh: A Post-Election Perspective," a paper presented by the former director, Central Bureau of Investigation of India, to an international seminar organized by the Center for Research in Indo-Bangladesh Relations, Calcutta, January 28, 2002. The percentages given in this paper are as follows:

year	percentage
1941	29.7
1947	23.0
1961	19.0
1974	14.0
1981	13.4
2002	9.0

Retrieved December 20, 2005 from http://www.acdis.uiuc.edu/Research/Ops/ spikier/ contents/ appendix _ 5.html. Other series on the Hindu population of Bangladesh pretty well track with these numbers but have fewer data points. The major difference comes only for the year 1971 which the government of Bangladesh lowball at 13.5% and Indian sources put at around 18 or 19 %. The government in Dhaka has some interest in a lower figure, but the discrepancy may also be explained by the fact that up to 10 or 12 million East Bengali Hindus may have taken refuge across the borders during the war of separation.

provided the Awami League the cause it needed to begin an all-out street campaign to bring the BNP government down. Demonstrations, often violent, general strikes, and walkouts and/or boycotts of the Parliament came with increasing regularity. Yet again the quality of daily life for the average person on the street deteriorated.

Several of the other opposition parties, including the Jatiya Party, joined the AL in the effort to unseat the government. In early May, the opposition began a permanent boycott of Parliament—permanent that is until the government agreed to its demands: that the BNP resign from power; and a caretaker government be appointed to see Bangladesh through another election. The idea of a "caretaker" or interim government to oversee elections had taken root intellectually and emotionally without having any base in the Bangladesh constitution or law.

A Relentless and Inexorable Street Strategy

However, government's primary objective in Bangladesh, as in many other countries, is to stay in office. The BNP tried almost everything to thwart the street strategy. It sought international mediation early on (the Commonwealth Secretary General came and stayed for weeks) and by the local diplomatic corps in an attempt to arrange a compromise that would bring the opposition back to Parliament and allow the government to live out its life.

Nothing worked. The two leaders, Begum Zia and Sheikh Hasina, refused to meet, and it is doubtful that any such meeting would have helped, given their mutual antipathy. The government resisted the demand for a caretaker administration, but then suggested its own version: five members from the government (including the PM) and four from the opposition to run the election. The opposition responded with a proposal for a caretaker government of five and five (but no Prime Minister) with the Chief Justice or similar neutral person leading it. This went nowhere.

The AL ratcheted up its efforts to unseat the government in late December 1994, when opposition Members of Parliament resigned *en masse*. The strategy was to cripple Parliament and bolster the increasing feeling in the electorate that the BNP government couldn't govern. One flaw of the resignation strategy was that it rendered impossible the demand that a caretaker government run the election because it reduced the number of MPs below that needed to pass the necessary constitutional amendment.

The impasse prevailed for another year. The government endeavored to use technicalities about the legality of opposition MPs' resignations to slow the momentum that had built up through its opponent's street strategy. Through 1995, the rising tempo and intensity of strikes and demonstrations against the government almost brought the economic life of the country to a standstill. The street strategy was working to perfection.

The Denouement

At some point in the middle of the year, the legality of the opposition's mass resignation from Parliament, and of the reason for rejecting the resignations, became moot because the constitution is clear that MPs who are absent for more than ninety days during which Parliament is in session shall lose their membership. Thus, by mid-year there was no choice under the constitution but to hold by-elections. These had to be held by September 18. However the opposition said it would refuse to participate—thus the dilemma for the government was how to hold serious elections without an opposition to contest them. It was not possible, but the government was able to put off the inevitable because serious flooding gave it reason to postpone the elections until December.

But the inevitable was only delayed by the rising waters. The BNP government threw in the towel, so to speak (a particularly apt metaphor in Bangladesh), in late November, 1995 when Prime Minister Zia requested that President Biswas dissolve the National Assembly. Thus, under the constitution, there was no longer a need for by-elections; instead there must be a general election within ninety days.

The election date was set by the Election Commission as January 18, 1996. Again the opposition boycotted, this time ostensibly on the grounds that there was too little time to file nomination papers. The real reason for the boycott was that it refused to contest an election under a BNP interim government, and continued to insist that a caretaker government oversee any election. The Election Commission tried to resolve the impasse by moving the election date to early February, even though this conflicted with the observance of Ramadan. Prime Minister Zia did her bit by offering again to resign thirty days in advance of the election.

All this was to no avail. The opposition had found an issue that united it and motivated its street soldiers to persist with and increase their demonstrations. It rejected all attempts to find a constitutional way out, insisting on an unconstitutional mechanism to ensure what it considered its right to run the government. What to do? The government had no real choice but to go ahead with the elections, which were again put off until February 15, 1996.

Given the opposition boycott, there were only BNP candidates standing in most places, so it won almost every seat and formed the government again.

The demonstrations and violence mounted. In this almost chaotic situation, the new Parliament met and quickly passed a constitutional amendment that was just what the opposition had been asking for: it provided that elections would be held under a neutral caretaker government that would assume office for ninety days to oversee the elections in an impartial manner. (One has to wonder if the opposition thought that it would win a free and fair election with such a majority that, once in power, it could rescind this amendment and return to the traditional practice of rigging elections to ensure its continuation in power, or whether it considered its hold on the electorate so solid that it would automatically win all future free and fair elections. In either case, it proved a costly mistake; it is perhaps yet another example of the law of unforeseen consequences disrupting political plans in South Asia.)

That done, the government resigned, and the new amendment took over. A caretaker interim government was appointed, led by the now constitutionally-mandated most recently retired Chief Justice of the Supreme Court. The "illegal parliament" of February, 1996—so called by the opposition which had boycotted the February election—had passed an "illegal" constitutional amendment that met its one-point, non-negotiable demand. So it put niceties aside and found the amendment legal after all, and went headlong into another general election in mid-June.

The BNP's Turn in the Wilderness

In the forlorn hope that a change in government would improve matters, Bangladeshi voters gave the Awami League a plurality of their votes, and of the seats in Parliament. The AL, with almost 34 percent of the popular vote, won 147 seats, not enough to control Parliament without help from other parties. It chose to join with Ershad's Jatiya Party, which it had been fighting in the streets five years earlier, proving again that power counts in Bangladesh politics, not ideology. The two parties had 178 parliamentary seats. With 27 women's seats, and an independent or two, the coalition finally added up to 210 of the 330 total seats in the Assembly, a comfortable majority. The BNP (which garnered nearly 31 percent of the popular vote) and its allies had 120 seats. As in 1991, the two main parties ran pretty even in the popular vote.

Hopes for a new era of better governance, more democratic procedures and responsible opposition were quickly dashed. The BNP leaders evidently saw no reason to deviate from the tactics and strategy the Awami League had used between 1992 and 1996. The new government was barely six months old when the BNP began its street actions. Though these were ineffectual in the beginning, they unnerved the government and kept it from concentrating on governing.

Throughout the first eighteen months of the AL government, the BNP-led opposition mixed "hartals" (general strikes) with walkouts and boycotts of parliament. None of these sparked any interest among the general public. The AL responded by attacking the BNP leadership and the party's most precious symbols to rub salt in the wounds of its recent defeat. It removed the bridge that led to the tomb of Ziaur Rahman, and it hinted broadly in public that it was thinking of changing the name of Zia International Airport. At one point, the government banned street demonstrations.

The AL government accomplished one important objective in 1997, concluding an agreement with the tribal opposition in the Chittagong Hill Tracts (CHT). This ended the twenty-five-year insurgency by the mainly-Buddhist tribes of that area of Southeastern Bangladesh. The government had restarted negotiations, which had been carried on sporadically by previous governments since Sheikh Mujib's time, on taking office a year earlier, and had conducted the talks in strict secrecy. Such secrecy was warranted because the agreement became a political football as soon as the BNP could make it one. By 1998, the BNP was attacking the accord for the secrecy in which the negotiations were conducted and the extensive autonomy granted the CHT governing body. The AL government was accused of eroding national unity, "threatening" the strategic location of the CHT, and blocking Bengalis from access to their natural resources. The CHT agreement became an ostensible cause of several hartals and street demonstrations.

At least the CHT was a real issue. After twenty-five years of insurrection that had led to many deaths, most observers believed that the agreement was a good step forward in bringing peace and development to a troubled part of the country. The government had taken a decisive step to solve a serious problem. The proper place to question the form of the agreement, of course, would have been in Parliament. The BNP chose to raise the issue primarily in the streets.

The AL also moved ahead in 1997 and 1998 on another important issue—making operational the long-dormant system of local government.

There had been no system of local rule since the BNP government, at the beginning of its tenure in 1991, abolished the Ershad system. Elections for the Union Parishads (Councils) were held in December 1997. Three seats on each Council were reserved for women, and the female voter turnout was 83 percent. Despite the fanfare, this new system suffers from the same problems and constraints as previous ones: the national government and bureaucracy are determined to control the local units and ration their resources accordingly.

The BNP's three main objectives for 1998 were the restoration of the floating foot bridge to Ziaur Rahman's tomb, regaining permission for political rallies in front of the press club in downtown Dhaka, and the withdrawal of criminal charges against some of its MPs. In a rare display of democratic politics and moderation, the two parties agreed to a compromise on these issues in March 1998, and the BNP returned to Parliament after a six-month boycott. This compromise lasted only a few months, however. Street action, hartals, boycotts, and walkouts continued through 1999 and 2000, as the law and order situation—often a function of political violence—worsened and became the main political issue. The BNP brought together other opposition parties, Ershad's Jatiya party (defected from the alliance with the Awami League) and the Jamat-i-Islami most prominently, in an anti-AL alliance.

By mid 2000, it became apparent that the AL government would conclude its regular five-year term, and that elections would be held on schedule in October 2001. The opposition alliance began to gear up for the elections by formulating a unified campaign strategy. The AL response was to fall back on one of its favorite attacks—branding the opposition as "anti-liberation."

A fierce election campaign was conducted under a caretaker government, which used the army for security. The BNP-led coalition, which ran on a strong law and order platform, won a huge majority of seats, though its share of the popular vote was only marginally higher than the AL which ran without coalition partners (41 percent to 40 percent). Yet again, neither of the main parties emerged from an election with a convincing popular mandate. The AL actually won four percentage points more votes than it had 5 years earlier, but the BNP coalition had wide support across many districts which garnered it 193 seats—an outright majority. The Awami League won only 62 seats, and the other parties 45. Despite the predictable whining by the loser, the election was declared as free and fair by a host of international observers.

BNP Back in Power; Déjà Vu All Over Again

Campaign promises are one thing, delivery is another. The BNP failed to get a grip on law and order, and it became much worse in the year after the election. In October 2002, the BNP government, admitting its failure, called out the army to crackdown on the growing bands of young men who had turned to crime, particularly extortion and robbery in the villages and small towns as a way of making a living. Some of these bands, but not all, had connections to the political parties and were used as tools of violence by the criminal element of the parties.

This army operation, called paradoxically, "Operation Clean Heart," raised profound questions about the political wisdom of once again, after some twelve years in the barracks and in UN peacekeeping operations, using the army for internal security. After a few months, however, the army declared victory and went back to the barracks. It had managed to slow the rise in lawlessness, but at some cost to its image after reports of politically motivated arrests and the torture of suspects.

In a pattern which has been repeated after almost every election, the new BNP government promised to repeal the Special Powers Act (SPA). This act is one of the legacies of Mujib, passed in 1974 when he was cracking down on the opposition, though it originally derives from the British Raj. It gave the government, usually through the district magistrate, the power to detain any person suspected of acts designed *inter alia* "to prejudice the sovereignty or defense of Bangladesh…to endanger public safety or the maintenance of public order…to create or excite feelings of enmity or hatred between different communities, classes, or sections of people…to cause fear or alarm to the public or any section of the public." Persons detained under this act could be held up to 120 days before the case was reviewed by an advisory board. The suspect had no right of legal representation. The board's report had to be issued within 170 days of the detention. If the board found that the detention is justified, the individual could be held indefinitely.

Such a law is a recipe for mischief. In Bangladesh, over 70,000 people have been detained under the SPA since its promulgation.[7] That amounts to about 2,300 people each year, on average, who have been detained, or almost 200 per month. About 99 percent of the detentions have been declared illegal by the Bangladesh High Court. Since Mujib created the SPA,

---

7   Amnesty International, "Bangladesh: Urgent Need for Legal and Other Reforms to Protect Human Rights," May, 16, 2003, accessed on December 21, 2005 at http://web. amnesty.org/library/Indexs.ENGASA130122003?open&of=ENG-BGD.

the BNP is more likely to promise to repeal it. The AL, though less emphatic and vague, has often hinted that it also would do away with the SPA. Whichever government is in power, however, finds the SPA too useful a tool to harass its enemies to carry out its promise to repeal it.

But the politics of confrontation continued as soon as the army marched back to the barracks. [8] The AL reverted to a hartal strategy—to shut down the entire country—which it had forsworn since 2000. At the same time, Parliament was often paralyzed by lengthy AL boycotts, walkouts, and almost as often by poor attendance of BNP members.

Crime, in particular violent robberies and extortions, continued to increase as governance deteriorated. The Bangladesh Bureau of Human Rights estimated well over 2,500 people were murdered in 2002 and perhaps more in 2003. [9] The catalogue of crimes the Bureau compiled included 160 murders related to rape, 112 to dowry, 102 to inter- and intra-political party violence, 126 to mass beating, 61 to bomb blasts, and 58 to police torture.

In the BNP's second term, governance worsened—continuing the trend that had obtained since 1991. The AL reverted to the time-tested strategy of street politics aimed at unseating a sitting government and/or ensuring that it can't govern. Hartals and more specific strikes occurred, almost on a monthly basis. Violence did not abate.

Parliamentary business was only possible when the AL was not in attendance. For example, the 14th amendment to the Constitution was passed in May of 2004 during a year-long AL boycott. [10] This reserves forty-five seats in Parliament for women, raises the retirement age of Supreme Court Justices from 65 to 67, and mandates that pictures of the President and Prime Minister be displayed in all government offices. [11] The AL objected to the

---

8   Amnesty International, "Mass Arrests in Bangladesh's Operation Clean Heart," *The Wire: Amnesty International's Monthly Magazine, Heart* (December, 2002) http://www.flonnet. com/f12112/stories/20040618001205200.htm.

9   Habib, Haroon, "A Year of Troubles," *Frontline,* 19, no. 21, (October 2002), http://www. flonnet.com/f1921/stories/20021025001404800.htm (accessed June 14, 2005). See also "2794 Killed in Nine Months," *The Daily Star,* September 30 2003, http://www.thedailystar.net/2003/09/30/d30930060352.htm (accessed June 14, 2005).

10   Author's note. The AL walked out of Parliament and began a boycott in June 2003 to protest what it called "hurtful remarks" that BNP leaders made about Sheikh Hasina and other AL leaders. These included assertions that the AL was creating "anarchy" and ruining the image of the country abroad.

11   See the next section of this chapter. The raising of the retirement age of Supreme Court justices was widely suspected to be one of the ways in which the BNP was attempting to sew up the next election through administrative and legal changes. This was thought to be the aim of Begum Zia's son, Tarique Rahman. He is now under arrest and investigation for alleged corruption by the military/civilian caretaker government which is conducting

amendment, particularly to raising the justices' retirement age (suspecting a BNP plot to put one of its adherents in charge of the next caretaker government), and to the requirement of a presidential photo in each government office (suspecting a BNP plot to get Sheikh Mujib's picture removed from government office walls).[12] But, being out of Parliament, it couldn't block the measure.

The AL returned to Parliament in mid-June 2004, perhaps because the 14th amendment had been passed when it was boycotting proceedings. Sheikh Hasina made it abundantly clear that parliamentary debate was not the chief method her party would employ in the political battles before the next election. She described her strategy publicly, "we will debate important issues in the House and gear up street agitation...."[13]

By late 2005, as disruptive as the AL tactics had been, responsibility for poor governance lay squarely with the BNP government. Among other problems, disunity (factionalism) and corruption had considerably dimmed its power to govern. A strong and dominant personality leavened with the ability to compromise in the spirit of party solidarity might have held the party together. Ziaur Rahman embodied both these characteristics, but they were missing from the party leadership of this dispensation.

The BNP government lost favor progressively as it was unable to deal with various structural problems, in particular a huge deficiency in energy production. The government had been unable to invest in electrical generating capacity, primarily because of corruption, and blackouts or load-shedding became common. This was particularly acute in rural areas, some of which received only 4-6 hours of electricity a day, while in Dhaka the blackouts lasted for 4-6 hours.

The factionalism of the present-day BNP is mostly explained by struggles for power, which in Bangladesh translate to struggles for resources. These occur mostly at the local level, and often involve brawls that result in dozens of deaths or injuries as local factions feud and fuss over power and the access to resources that it brings. There is also a generational split in the BNP between old-line stalwarts, most of whom remain loyal to the

---

a sweeping and inclusive campaign against the pervasive corruption of Bangladesh politics.

12 Author's note: as if anybody other than bureaucrats ever went into government offices anyway.

13 Sheikh Hasina, quoted in "AL Makes JS Comeback," *The Daily Star*, June 15, 2004. Accessed on June 22, 2004 at http://www.thedailystar.net/2004/06/15/d4061501011.htm.

memory and principles of the party's founder, Ziaur Rahman and the new generation of party loyalists led by Khaleda Zia's son Tariq Rahman. In addition, there remains a small faction exclusively loyal to Khaleda Zia herself. Problems of party unity appear pervasive throughout the BNP structure. One manifestation of this in the last BNP government was the size of the cabinet. It had sixty members for the first three years of the government— to accommodate all the party's myriad power centers. The Prime Minister has labored mightily to reduce that number, and succeeded in May 2004 in trimming it to fifty-one.

An example of the generational split in the BNP is the fate of long-time party stalwart (and one of its founders) A.Q.M. Badruddoza Chowdhury, who resigned as President in 2004, only a few months after he had been elected. Chowdhury evidently irked younger party regulars by trying, as President, to rise above partisan politics. He was accused by his BNP critics of showing insufficient respect to the memory of Ziaur Rahman. They threatened impeachment, even though constitutional experts believed that a President could not be impeached on such a charge. Chowdhury has formed a third party which later joined an anti-BNP alliance.[14] Aspects of this generational dispute were born of concern in the party about the move toward dynastic succession. Tariq Rahman was widely believed to be consolidating power to take over as Prime Minister after the next election— with the support of his mother. He appears to have been the driving force behind the all-out effort to ensure the reelection of the BNP through stacking the Election Commission and having a BNP partisan run the Caretaker Government. It was this uncompromising, no-holds-barred, strategy that led to the impasse and the escalation of violence which persuaded the Army to intervene on January 11, 2007.

Electoral Democracy Careers off the Rails—Enter the Army Again

Tension and friction escalated throughout 2006 as the two parties maneuvered to get the upper hand in the approaching election. The BNP government, which had been in power since 2001, would be running on its very poor record. Most observers believed that, barring a catastrophic mistake

---

14   Author's note: third parties have had little success in Bangladesh politics since the era of Ziaur Rahman. About fourteen years ago, one of the powers of the Awami League, Kamal Hossain, former Foreign and Law Minsiter under Mujib and drafter of the 1972 constitution, and a group of centrists broke off from Sheikh Hasina to form a third party, which went nowhere.

by the opposition, the BNP would surely lose the election if it came close to being free and fair. The latter seemed oblivious to its dismal record of governance and confident that it could engineer its reelection by administrative actions that would give it the upper hand at the polls. Early in the year it began a series of appointments and transfers of officials among local jurisdictions to ensure that supporters were in charge of districts that would be key to the election. Its appointments to the Election Commission were considered highly partisan. This provoked street action and threats of street action by the opposition, and the beginnings of a dynamic that ultimately led the Army again to takeover.

The Awami League had formed an opposition alliance; it sought partners in the campaign to unseat the government, unlike 1996 and 2001, when it ran by itself. These partners not only brought a unity to the opposition that is usually lacking, but several highly respected political leaders which leavened the AL's tendency to erratic political decision-making and a shrill image. Ultimately fourteen parties joined the AL in this alliance, which included former BNP stalwarts Badarudoza Chowdhury and Oli Ahmed, who had formed the Liberal Democratic Party (LDP) and Kamal Hossein, who had fled the Awami League in 1993 to form his own third party. Toward the end of the year, former President Ershad, with the bulk of his Jatiya party, also joined the alliance. Among other things, this collection of respected and experienced politicians seemed to keep AL leader, Sheikh Hasina, focused on the opposition's great advantage given the BNP's abysmal record.

The Election Commission had approved a voter's list that was seriously unreliable. Neutral experts, such as the US National Democratic Institute (NDI), estimated that it had 13 million more names on it than it should have had. After much strident rhetoric, a new list was prepared, but the courts found that it was deficient also and ordered the Election Commission to correct the old list. This was never carried out, either because the Election Commission did not want to, or was too incompetent to do so.

The tension built and the crisis became more acute when the time came for the Caretaker Government (CG), called for by the 1996 amendment to the constitution, to take over in late October. Over the preceding months, the two parties could not agree on the head of the CG (called the Chief Advisor), so the President, Iajuddin Ahmed, appointed himself. That he got away with it for a while was a surprise as he was clearly a partisan of the BNP, having been elected by a BNP-controlled parliament. About half of the advisors he appointed (the equivalent of a cabinet) were considered neutral, but those soon resigned and were replaced by more BNP partisans. Nevertheless, the opposition hung in despite the signs that the electoral deck was progressively more stacked against it. Sheikh Hasina and other opposition leaders probably believed that they could still win given the widespread disgust with the BNP's record, and particularly as long as Ershad could deliver his party's vote bank in North Bengal to the alliance. The BNP must have agreed because suddenly a long-dormant case against Ershad was revived and he was indicted almost instantaneously by a court. Almost as quickly, the Election Commission ruled that, as he was under indictment, he was ineligible to contest the election.

As it became clear that the opposition alliance probably could not win without the vote that Ershad would have delivered, the sentiment among its leaders changed to support of a general boycott of the election. The last one to be convinced appears to have been Sheikh Hasina, who announced a boycott on January 3 and an escalating schedule of "agitation" to stop the election. For about eight days, the situation deteriorated rapidly as neither side backed off. The BNP strategy was to force through a one-sided election that it would win easily (despite the unhappy precedent of 1996), and then to hunker down, rely on the Army to put down subsequent domestic agitation, and wait until the expected negative international reaction subsided. Its electoral alliance partner, Jamat-i-Islami, even offered to leave the alliance and run as the opposition.

The opposition strategy was not only to boycott the election, but through street violence to prevent it from happening, or at least to de-legitimize it in the eyes of the world. This political game of "chicken" had, however, an increasing number of human casualties as the violence mounted. The Army believed itself in the middle, about to be called on to put down violence through force, yet under warning from the UN that its peacekeeping duties might suffer if it used repression to support such an obviously illegitimate election. In addition, using force to quell the rising violence risked chain of command problems (Bengali troops being ordered to shoot Bengali demonstrators) that no army needs.

On January 11 it halted the slide toward anarchy and civil strife by intervening in the political life of the country for the fifth time in its history (three in the space of three months in 1975 and the fourth in 1982), and the first time in sixteen years. It was almost a stealth intervention. It began when the Army insisted that President Iajuddin declare a state of emergency, which suspends part of the constitution. Immediately after announcing the state of emergency, the President resigned from his day job as Chief Advisor in the Caretaker Government and appointed a truly non-party, neutral Chief Advisor, Fakhruddin Ahmed, who had been head of the Central Bank, after a long and distinguished career with the World Bank in Washington. The Army quickly ducked behind the Chief Advisor, to assume a role of "assisting the CG" in reforming the country. Nine other Advisors were quickly appointed who, with the Chief Advisor, assumed control of the day-to-day operations of the government. For the most part, these Advisors fit the constitutional requirement of being non-party and neutral.

As would have been expected after sixteen years of bad governance by both parties, and the looming threat of anarchy and violence, the public generally welcomed the intervention. Over the first few months of this new dispensation, the Army seemed to become progressively less shy about its role, though it maintained still that it was not running the government, only assisting the civilian CG to whom it had entrusted power. Nevertheless, the Army Chief of Staff, General Moeen U Ahmed, has been increasingly vocal in public about the aims of the Army/civilian CG. It appears to be the Army that is driving the anti-corruption campaign in which a number of big-time politicians, including Tariq Rahman, his mother Khaleda Zia, and Sheikh Hasina were detained for alleged corrupt practices.

The apparent aim of this hybrid military/civilian dispensation is to build a solid foundation on which an indigenous modular democracy can grow. The makeup of the foundation has remained in flux, but one rather large element is significantly reduced political corruption. To that effect, there have been thousands of arrests and detentions of big and small fish who are believed to be corrupt. The idea is to punish them as an example and to create an effective anti-corruption bureau with the legal authority, the scope, and the motivated individuals to enforce a strict anti-corruption code. The CG also vowed from the start to reinvigorate the judiciary and make it completely independent of the executive. Its legal independence was secured and reinforced early in the CG's tenure by implementing, eight years after it was handed down, the Supreme Court's order to make the administrative judiciary of the lower courts independent of the executive. The CG also wanted to improve the quality of the judiciary through, among other measures, ensuring that judges meet minimum educational and experience requirements.

The main elements of electoral reform are well known. The Election Commission must be reformed into a strictly non-party, neutral organism with the power to punish behavior that would pervert free and fair elections.

The voters list must be rectified to ensure it accurately reflects the voting public and both registration and migration can be adequately accommodated. And there must be a way to ensure that the Caretaker Government cannot be perverted to a partisan mechanism as it was in late 2006.

The agenda and timetable of the new military/civilian hybrid dispensation emerged slowly as it became accustomed to the idea of ruling the country. When the Army took over and quickly appointed the civilian CG, neither had worked out in any detail their plans or a reform program. It was, indeed, a work in progress.

Ideally they would construct institutions and procedures that address and correct the insidious and harmful structural and cultural problems of corruption and lawlessness that have come to dominate Bangladesh politics over the past two decades. In addition, the CG has to try to deal with and arrest the growth of Islamism, which has changed the tone of politics and society over the last fifteen years. These issues are surveyed in Chapter 10, which analyzes the options that the authorities in Bangladesh can deploy to address them.

The overarching question is how long will this unelected military/civilian government try to remain in power before it calls an election that would hand sovereignty to the people of the country? The answer depends on the length and depth of its reform agenda. At the time of writing, it seems to have grown from an original ambition to set the electoral mechanisms right before an election (perhaps this would take a year) to that of cleansing thoroughly the country's political culture by extirpating corruption and establishing the rules of the game.

The functionality between the agenda and the length of time to implement it works both ways. As the unelected government feels more comfortable and welcome, it will tend to augment its reform agenda. One thing that it might add to it is the idea of setting in place a paradigm for dealing with India, the behemoth that surrounds Bangladesh on three sides. That possibility will also be discussed in Chapter 10.

The concern, however, is that the feeling of "military exceptionalism" will take hold of the Army leaders—the belief that civilians cannot be allowed run the country by themselves. The Bangladesh Army would, if this attitude came to dominate, be clearly imitating the Pakistani Army again after rejecting such a mindset seventeen years ago. Instead of moving to a better democracy, in which civilian governments really govern as representatives of the people, as I suspect the Army meant to do when it took power away from the civilians on January 11, it would likely be replaying the Ershad era. In other words, it would not just be back to square one, it would be back to square one minus five.

7

ELECTORAL DEMOCRACY REVISITS PAKISTAN, 1988-99

The second "democratic" episode of post-separation Pakistan came after an eleven-year interregnum of military rule under General Zia ul Huq. The two democratic episodes are closely related in that many of the institutional and structural problems which attenuated the first democratic dispensation of Zulfikar Ali Bhutto—and contributed to its failure—were present, and magnified, in the second democratic dispensation. Benazir Bhutto, who inherited the leadership of the PPP from her father, and Nawaz Sharif, leader of a refurbished Pakistan Muslim League (PML), took turns in leading the four elected governments of the latter episode, and both were brought down, in part, by the institutional and structural problems that they inherited, and in part, by their own flaws.

None of these elected governments lasted more than three of their constitutionally mandated five-year terms, and none left office because it was turned out by the voters or by Parliament. The first three were dismissed by the two other power centers of the government working together—the President exercising his prerogatives under the constitution as amended during Zia ul Huq's military regime—and the army. The fourth was replaced by direct army intervention—a coup—after the constitutional provision permitting the President to dismiss a government had been rescinded.

Elected Governments Without Full Power to Govern

Brief mention should be made here of on how the legacy of the Zia ul Huq military interregnum affected the second democratic episode that followed it. Eleven years of military rule left to the succeeding elected governments three pernicious legacies: 1) it restored presidential power (to dismiss

135

governments and Prime Ministers) which had been removed by the Constitution of 1973; 2) it created, institutionalized, and (to some extent) codified a process of Islamization which inhibited social and political development, and produced an increasing tempo of sectarian strife that proved to be a major force in undermining the elected governments—and which continues to plague Pakistani society and the current government; and 3) it also strengthened the unwritten understanding that the army would have a role in governing the nation.

In addition Zia's eleven years in power also did little to reduce or solve the fundamental structural weaknesses of the state of Pakistan. It is virtually impossible to decide which of the various pernicious legacies inherited by the four democratically-elected dispensations of the years 1988-1999 was most important to their failure. All worked together to undermine the ability of democracy to sink strong roots and develop widespread adherence in society.

Structural Economic and Institutional Failure

One of the major problems that plagued the four governments of this period was the continually weakening economy and progressively lower economic growth, which averaged only 4.5 percent in this period—no more than 2 percent higher than the growth rate of population. This was exacerbated by serious and growing structural deficiencies in the economy and the deepening failure of economic institutions. Poor policy choices simply made the problems worse. (Democratic governments dread, in any case, making the hard choices necessary for dynamic economies.) And all four democratically elected governments oversaw levels of corruption that undermined investor confidence, as well as that of the general public, in their probity and intentions.

Structural and institutional deficiencies had been growing since the 1950s and were made much worse by the statist policies of the Bhutto regime. These deficiencies stemmed in large measure from lack of investment in and of attention (and interest) to the development of both institutions and human capital. A deteriorating economic structure and institutions were masked during the Zia ul Huq era by an external windfall—a huge increase in the inflow of foreign funds as a result of the war in Afghanistan against the Soviet invader and from Pakistani workers in the oil-producing Gulf countries—that buoyed the economy and relieved the Zia government from having to face up to the underlying economic deterioration over which he presided.

This windfall was running down when Zia ul Huq was killed in an as yet unexplained plane crash, and Benazir Bhutto was elected Prime Minister in 1988. Her PPP (Pakistan People's Party) government and its three successors had to deal with an economy that deflated after the war bubble burst. This brought out in stark relief the structural and institutional failure that they would have to address if they were to have a chance of restoring economic growth to the levels of the 1980s and earlier decades. One symbolic indicator of the economic deterioration is that, in the 1990s, the percentage of the Pakistani population under the poverty line rose by ten percentage points. From about 20 percent in 1990, the proportion of the population defined by international financial institutions as "poor," rose to about 30 percent by the end of the decade.[1]

The Democratically Elected Governments' Failures to Deal with Economic Crisis

For the democratic governments of Benazir Bhutto (1988-90 and 1993-96) and Nawaz Sharif (1990-93 and 1997-99) economic fragility required a constant struggle to improve an economy that was stagnant and gradually deteriorating. Pakistanis were slowly becoming poorer, which was a factor in the frequent changes of government. The two governments drew heavily on International Financial Institutions (IFIs) to wrest them from the economic doldrums. Their attempts to use IFI resources to push through austerity programs were marked by desperation rather than commitment, and the main consequence was to add to their already heavy internal and external debt burden—in itself a drag on the economy and especially on the development of the social/educational sector.

Benazir Bhutto came to power the first time in 1988, riding a wave of enthusiasm and high expectations in the West (and in Pakistan), and with a resolve to rectify the wrongs she felt had been done to her father. This determination seemed to extend to rectifying the wrong he did to the Pakistani economy. She abandoned the PPP's socialist goals that Zulfikar Ali Bhutto had instilled as principles of the party, and committed her administration to policies that would have undone his economic legacy—privatization,

---

1   Robert E. Looney, "Pakistan's Economy: Achievements, Progress, Constraints, and Prospects," *Pakistan: Founders Aspirations and Today's Realities*, ed. Hafeez Malik (Karachi: Oxford University Press, 2001), pp. 195-243

decentralization, and industrialization became the watchwords of her economic policy.

Implementation was, however, weak and incoherent. The privatization policy, for example, appeared more to provide patronage than to reform and privatize the economy in a serious manner. Bhutto's government had no other answers to Pakistan's growing economic malaise, and had achieved almost nothing in attempts to reform the economy when, for reasons covered below, her government was dismissed by the President in early August, 1990, less that two years after it had taken office.

The first administration of Nawaz Sharif took office in October 1990 with more ambitious plans to strengthen the economy, but also with more complicated and powerful economic challenges and problems. On the one hand, Sharif (who had a business background) adopted a populist approach to attack poverty and reflate the economy. He emphasized expanding small business. But his strategy required significant investment from private sources, which was not forthcoming. Reform and reflation of the economy remained Sharif's main concern throughout his three-year tenure. He tried both austerity and populist measures aimed at reflation. Nothing worked, primarily because the deep-seated structural problems needed fundamental and radical surgery, not the sticking plasters that Sharif (and Bhutto, in her turn) offered. Economic structures and institutions continued to weaken, and Sharif failed to address the root causes. While the faltering economy might have been an unspoken subtext, the proximate cause of his leaving office in April 1993 was an irreconcilable political dispute with President G.I. Khan in which the Army forced both to resign[2] (see below in the section on the judiciary for more detail on this).

Benazir Bhutto returned to power in October 1993—to take charge of an economy that had been set in the right direction by an interim government of non-partisan economic experts. Economically, her task was clearly to continue and sustain the incipient reform efforts begun by the interim government. That she, and her government, failed to do so can be ascribed primarily to politics. They faced many of the same economic problems as before—weak fiscal performance, sacrosanct military expenditures, growing internal and external debt, creeping unemployment (due in part to privatization), growing poverty, and continually tighter constraints imposed by IFIs as a condition for their support.

---

2   Talbot, *Pakistan: A Modern History,* pp. 327-8.

Corruption appeared to soar and became a key political issue while also eroding investor confidence. The reform effort of the interim government—which was able in its short tenure to ignore many political forces—was still in its infancy, and a weak infant it was without any support among the political parties. Moreover, the Bhutto government failed to strengthen the economy or to address its fundamental deficiencies. And again, while this may have been in the back of the minds of the new President, Leghari, Bhutto's erstwhile political ally, and the army, which probably recommended the action to Leghari, the second Benazir Bhutto government was dismissed in November 1996 because of political differences with the President—and the military. The growing corruption of Benazir's administration was certainly one of the principal factors.

After yet another interim government, the main achievements of which were in the political realm, Nawaz Sharif came back as Prime Minister in February 1997 with an overwhelming mandate from the voters. His government faced a financial crisis, which had been one of the main reasons his predecessor had been dismissed. Given his business background and electoral mandate, the presumption was that Nawaz would strengthen and extend economic reform and revivify the economy. However, his administration's approach was inconsistent, and its policy was implemented half-heartedly.

The problems of policy implementation were magnified by adverse external events: the almost-total cutoff of official capital flows and the accompanying swift drop in private inflows after the nuclear test of May 1998; an increasingly unserviceable external debt; a deepening trade deficit; and worsening domestic inflation—caused in part by the depreciation of the rupee. The upshot, precipitated by the nuclear tests, was probably the worst financial crisis of Pakistani history, which brought the government to the verge of international insolvency.[3]

The Zero-Sum-Game Nature of Pakistani Politics

Electoral democracy returned to Pakistan in 1988 amid a wave of domestic and international enthusiasm. Observers, swept away by the idea that democracy was the "end of history" and the almost-inevitable wave of the future, could be forgiven for assuming that so-called "democratic parties" in Pakistan would put priority on an overall goal of strengthening and deepening democracy. This would entail eschewing the all or nothing approach that seems always to have characterized Pakistani political culture. While

---

3   Looney, "Pakistan's Economy," *Pakistan,* p. 219.

competing vigorously against each other in the electoral arena, the parties needed to work together to subordinate the other two power centers—the army and the President—which had so often subverted democracy in the past. The urgent objective was to weaken the hold of those two actors on political power and embed in the polity a democratic mindset.

But this did not happen. Instead, until the second Sharif government came to power with a huge mandate and rescinded the eighth amendment, whichever political party was in power found it expedient to work with the army and the President against the opposition in an effort to consolidate and broaden its hold on office. This willingness to work with the army and President against the opposition only strengthened those competing poles of power, and led in each case to the dismissal of the governing party.

Benazir Bhutto and Nawaz Sharif followed the time-honoured Pakstani tradition of building their parties through patronage, which meant rewarding those who helped and joined—including from the opposition parties—while shutting out those who remained in opposition. It also meant harassing, and sometimes abusing, political opponents who refused to succumb to the blandishments of patronage. Benazir Bhutto took this approach to politics even further in her first tenure, from 1988 to 1990. In this case, the proximate cause was the power struggle between the Prime Minister (and her PPP), which had won a plurality of seats at the national level and led a coalition national government, and Nawaz Sharif (and his political alliance called the IJI), which had won the majority of seats in the Punjab assembly and, therefore, controlled Punjab.

Bhutto was determined that the PPP must control Punjab to control the nation. Whether this determination sprang from the knowledge that Sharif and the IJI would contest her power at the national level as long as he controlled Punjab, or whether she eschewed political cooperation and inclusion in any case is not clear. What is undeniable is that the struggle between the two was a prime cause of her failure and her dismissal from power in 1990. Seeking allies in the power struggle, she reached out to competing power centers, in particular the army, which allowed the military to strengthen its grip on foreign and security policy.[4] She did not challenge the military, for example, over its deployment of jihadi forces in Afghanistan or Kashmir.

The first Bhutto administration started with several severe handicaps. The army had entrenched itself in politics during Zia's regime and insisted

---

4   Talbot, *Pakistan: A Modern History*, p. 292.

on maintaining that behind the-scenes role in the transition to democracy as its price for allowing that transition to take place (and for Benazir and her PPP to take power nationally). She faced a President, Ghulam Ishaq Khan, with great powers (because Zia ul Huq had amended the constitution to give the Presidential office the prerogative to dismiss governments) who represented a hostile bureaucracy and who was probably hostile himself. And she faced an antagonistic Punjab government controlled by the IJI of Nawaz Sharif, a favorite of the army from the time of Zia ul Huq.

Bhutto's strategy could have been to try to neutralize the army and the President by some form of working arrangement with the other major political party, Nawaz and the IJI. The PPP did not by itself have the power in parliament to overcome either the eighth amendment, which gave the President the power to dismiss elected governments, or to pass important legislation (including rescinding the Islamization ordinances pushed through by Zia ul Huq which she had pledged to overturn). A cooperative arrangement with Nawaz and the IJI might have allowed her to pass some of her priority legislation and fend off the President and the military (though the IJI would probably not have been comfortable opposing the hudood laws). At the same time, the Prime Minister's need for a coalition with other parties to oppose the IJI in Punjab led her to continue patronage politics in the PPP and with coalition partners.[5] There seemed to be no effort on the part of either the PPP or the IJI to try to reach a working arrangement. On the contrary, the politics of confrontation remained the central thrust of both parties and both leaders.

The role of the ISI was possibly a factor in this struggle between Bhutto and Sharif and his IJI. It is commonly believed, at least by PPP partisans, that the IJI was created in 1988 by the ISI as a method to block Bhutto from power, or inhibit her power with a countervailing force, if she were elected. If this is so, it would explain why Sharif saw so little merit in cooperating with the central government and with Bhutto.

After winning the 1990 elections, Sharif faced the same two serious constraints on his ability to govern fully as leader of an elected government as had Benazir Bhutto: the army and the power of the President. In a sense, he was the army's creature—his political career in Punjab had been launched with the army's support during the Zia regime. It seems logical that he should have been able to work with the army, and with the President, when

5   Ibid., p. 294-5.

in power. But there was friction with both entitites during his first government and, with the army, it became much worse in his second term.

Confrontational politics continued to be at the center of both parties' political strategies, and the struggle often took on the appearance of a personal vendetta between the two leaders.[6] The culture of confrontation with the enemy and of allying with the enemies of your enemy progressively strengthened the hand of the military and weakened the elected governments of the second democratic episode. The confrontation with the Sharif-led opposition was again one of the three main features in the debilitation of the second Bhutto government—the others being the mounting law and order problems in Karachi and the perception of unbridled corruption. The non-elected competing power poles of the army and the President (a President of her own choice this time) remained binding constraints on the power of her government to control policies and to find political solutions to fundamental political problems—had Bhutto been interested in finding such solutions.

Sharif's huge majority in the National Assembly and Senate after the 1997 election gave him the power to eliminate one of the two non-elected power centers.[7] The Parliament rescinded the eighth amendment and thus reduced the President to the ceremonial role he had under Z.A. Bhutto. But the army's role as a non-elected power pole remained untouched, and when Sharif moved in 1999 to curtail that power, the army instead removed him.[8] With that, electoral democracy once again died in Pakistan and direct military rule re-emerged after eleven years of feckless, democratically elected, but undemocratic, government.

Islamization

Chapter 1 described briefly the role of Islam in Pakistan history and politics, and how it was used to persuade South Asian Muslims of the need for a separate Muslim homeland in South Asia. The sporadic creep of Islamiza-

---

6   The personal dislike may have started when the government of Z.A. Bhutto nationalized some of the Sharif family's properties during the nationalization wave of the mid-1970s.

7   It should be noted that in each of the four elections during this democratic episode, a smaller number of Pakistanis voted. In the election of 1997—in which Sharif received the "huge mandate" he claimed—about 35 percent of the eligible population voted. One could say that Sharif's "huge mandate" amounted to about 23 percent of eligible voters.

8   The army argues that Sharif's attempt to remove the Chief of Army Staff was unconstitutional, an argument it uses as legal cover for the military takeover, though it has used several others, including the so-called "doctrine of necessity," which basically means that coups are legitimate if they are necessary (but who judges whether they are necessary?).

tion since then, and the increasing pressure from the religious forces in society for an Islamic state, both in name and in substance, had a good deal of momentum by 1988. It was a process that could only be reversed with great political difficulty, an undertaking most elected governments would hesitate to initiate. It would be quite enough if the process had been slowed, even halted, by the four elected governments. Unfortunately halted it was not although the forces of Islamization were, more or less, held in abeyance during the first Benazir Bhutto government of 1988-90. She had promised during the 1988 campaign to roll back certain of the Islamic measures promulgated by the Zia ul Huq regime, particularly those relating to the rights and the role of women. She could not deliver on that because of her weak parliamentary position, and because her opposition, Nawaz Sharif and the IJI, used Islamization as a political weapon against her and her government. For example, the IJI supported and pushed a bill in the Senate in the last few months of Benazir Bhutto's tenure to introduce Sharia law as the basis of the Pakistani legal system.

The Islamization process made erratic progress under the two Sharif governments. To some extent, he pandered to the religious elements, but there may have been a rationale to that, though it is hard to discern. His coalition government included religious parties, which meant that he would have to make some gestures on Islamization. Moreover, some scholars believe that Sharif (or at least his political advisors) were moving in the second term—1997 to 1999—to form a center-right political movement as a counterbalance to the military in Pakistani politics. The aim would have been, ultimately, to subordinate the military to civilian political forces. This movement would necessarily have had to include Islamic parties if it were to have any political heft against the military.[9]

Sharif had to move cautiously and pragmatically since much of the Islamic law, which the religious parties wanted, appeared to contradict his economic liberalization measures.[10] The IJI government moved a Sharia bill through the Assembly and Senate in 1991 which pulled the legal system closer toward Islamic law, but did not replace the former with the latter. It left the previous system of law still intact and both were operative. In trying to placate his religious party allies yet preserve his economic liberalization measures and maintain the support of the business community,

---

9   Vali Nasr, "Military Rule, Islamism, and Democracy in Pakistan," *The Middle East Journal,* 58, no. 2 (Spring 2004), p. 200.

10   Talbot, *Pakistan: A Modern History,* p. 317.

Sharif pleased no one. The religious elements accused him of having no real commitment to Islamic principles, and the secular elements, including women's groups, minorities, and many business leaders accused him of being a fundamentalist. He felt so threatened by the latter that he publicly proclaimed that he was not a fundamentalist.

The huge majority Sharif and the PML won in the 1997 election could have reduced his dependence upon the Islamic parties and given him a relatively freer hand regarding Islamization. But despite this, as he moved to reduce the military's political power, he felt increasingly the need to cater to the Islamists. At the end of his tenure, in October 1999, he was threatening to amend the constitution to make Sharia the law of the land. This continues to be cited by the military as one reason why his government had to be removed.[11] A factor that exacerbated the trend toward Islamization during this second democratic episode was the increasing jihadi culture in the country. This resulted from the close Pakistani involvement in the so-called "jihad" against the Soviet Union in Afghanistan during most of the 1980s (and later in the jihadi involvement in the insurgency in Kashmir), which saw the introduction of more radical Islamist ideas into the society where they had some resonance among the poor, rural elements—along with the introduction of a large number of weapons. About the time the jihad against the Soviets was winding down, an insurgency in the Indian part of Kashmir was heating up, giving its protagonists another "jihad" to champion. The insidious creep of radicalization and Islamization in Pakistani society continued. Both Bhutto and Sharif went along with the army's policy of pursuing Pakistan's objectives in Kashmir through non-state actors—the jihadis—and, thus, lent strength to the radicalization of the polity—surely not what either leader wanted—and contributed to a potentially disastrous unforeseen consequence.

The role of the ISI cannot be overlooked in this context either. That agency's long-standing relationship with the jihadists is well known, and has even been admitted at times by former government officials. Whether the ISI makes the policy or only carries it out, its role in, and its responsibility for, the growth of jihadi culture in Pakistan is clear. It is the perfect example of the law of unforeseen consequences, which seems the dominant one in Pakistani politics.

---

11   The larger reason being that he tried to dismiss the Chief of Army Staff.

The Continuing and Age-Old Struggle Between the Center and the Periphery—Pakistan's Constant Undoing

Pakistani governments of all political stripes have been plagued, and undercut, by the unresolved problem of the power relationship between central and provincial governments. In essence, this is a failure to resolve political problems by political methods. This deficiency is also a symptom of a failure of accommodation among the provinces. In Pakistan, this problem is exacerbated by the imbalance between Punjab, with slightly over half of the nation's population, and the other three smaller, less populated, less resourced provinces. With its absolute majority of the population and domination of the army and bureaucracy, Punjab was often perceived by the others as defining its interests as those of the state.

In the twenty-four years of its existence, United Pakistan never solved this thorny issue,[12] a political failure that, as we know, led to a bloody civil war and a ruptured state in 1971. After this traumatic political breakdown, the result of not finding (let alone even looking seriously for) political solutions to political problems, it would seem natural that the political forces of the new, post-1971, Pakistan would have endeavored to strike a more accommodating posture, not only with political opposition at the national level, but more importantly with political forces in the provinces.

But none of the political forces—the political parties, the bureaucracy, the army—grasped the essential lesson of the separation of the former Eastern Wing. This deficiency of vision was one of the fatal flaws of the elected government of Zulfikar Ali Bhutto in the first democratic episode. The same deficiency underlay the inability of the four elected governments of the second democratic episode to resolve the ethnic problems of Sindh.

Benazir Bhutto's PPP government, 1988 to 1990, came to power just as the problem in Sindh between the Sindhis and the Mohajirs was becoming acute, and law and order was breaking down. The Mohajirs, represented by the political party, Muhajir Qaumi Mahaz (MQM), believed they were the victims of discrimination.[13] This had been brewing since the early 1970s when ZA Bhutto had implemented hiring quotas in the civil service for Sindhis. At about the time Benazir Bhutto took over the reins of government, the Mohajir/Sindhi rivalry turned violent.

---

12   Christophe Jaffrelot, "Nationalism Without a Nation: Pakistan Searching for Its Identity," *Pakistan: Nationalism Without a Nation* (London: Zed Books, Ltd., 2002), p. 7.

13   As it was then called. The MQM changed its name in later years to project a more "national," less ethnic image to Muttahida Quami Movement.

At the beginning of her tenure, Bhutto tried to resolve the problem and halt the violence by political means. The PPP concluded an alliance with the MQM to try to address the MQM's complaints about discrimination, working out agreements on education issues, job quotas, and domicile certificates. The MQM expressed satisfaction with the idea of ending the perceived discrimination, rather than insisting on recognition of another (separate) nationality.[14] The accord unraveled so quickly that historians question whether either of the parties meant it seriously.[15] The situation in Sindh became more unstable, with increasing resort to violence by both the MQM and the Sindhi organizations. The PPP government could not control matters, and the Sindh provincial government came to a standstill. To exacerbate tensions, the IJI began to use the Sindh crisis to undermine the Bhutto government. Despite longstanding animosities between the IJI and the MQM, they formed an alliance which aimed to defeat Bhutto in the national assembly in a no-confidence vote. While this failed, the MQM continued trying to undercut the PPP government. Violence and killings mounted in Sindh.

The crisis peaked in 1990 when, in a bloody incident in Hyderabad, Sindh's second largest city, over 40 mohajirs were killed, including many innocent women and children. A wave of mindless violence followed—much of it in Karachi—which served as the key element in the pretext the President, Ghulam Ishaq Khan, used (with the firm endorsement, if not at the behest, of the army) to dismiss Bhutto and her PPP government.

Sindh remained a festering sore under subsequent elected governments, none of which could broker a political resolution. The unceasing and seemingly unstoppable violence, most of which occurred in Karachi, Pakistan's largest and commercially most important city, was a constant threat to all four governments—often their biggest threat—during the second episode of democracy.[16] It has never really been resolved. Violence waxes and wanes, depending on the level of involvement of the national government, the state of its relations with the Sindhi and the Mohajir political forces, and whether the military with its more vice-regal approach to such issues is in charge.

It was another of the vicious circles that characterizes Pakistani politics. When the tide of crime and violence rose to intolerable levels, the army

---

14   Talbot, *Pakistan: A Modern History,* p. 304.

15   Ibid., p. 304.

16   Ibid., p. 342.

intervened.[17] In the short term this reduced crime and violence in Karachi, but served mainly to drive the militant faction of the MQM underground in the long-term—another unforeseen consequence that has come back to haunt subsequent governments. Since the military takeover in 1999, the struggle between the Mohajirs and the Sindhis seems to have cooled off. The main concern in Sindh in the past few years has been sectarian violence, especially in Karachi, involving Sunni and Shia militants against each other or targeting innocent civilians. Nonetheless, ethnic grievances continue to simmer under the surface.

The Unofficial Troika—Sharing Power with Two Unelected Power Centers

Two unelected power centers, the army and the upper reaches of the bureaucracy, have dominated governance in post-separation Pakistan. They have also occasionally cooperated against perceived competitors—including the few elected governments. They have, at other times, worked with elected governments, or other elements of the polity such as the feudal landlords of Punjab, against each other. But these two power centers have remained a constant of national politics, and a severe constraint to democracy. Their subordination to elected governments remains a necessary prerequisite of a successful rooting of democracy in Pakistan.

The bureaucracy was especially powerful in the early days of United Pakistan. Its influence was slowly reduced as the army became a more important political actor, but it always retained a hold on power because its interests overlapped significantly with the military and feudal landowners. Z.A. Bhutto "reformed" the bureaucracy and diluted its professional core, the Civil Service of Pakistan (CSP), believing it too powerful. After Bhutto's fall, however, the CSP regrouped and retrieved some of its power under Zia ul Huq and the elected governments of 1988-1999. This resurgence of bureaucratic power in the elected regimes was personified by the President, Ghulam Ishaq Khan, who had risen through the bureaucracy. He was President from 1988 to 1993, at a time when the office had the extraordinary powers accorded it by the previous military regime that wanted to check the power of elected governments. In a sense, such Presidential power exemplified democratic "checks and balances" gone haywire. It bore the marks of elements of the presidential system grafted onto a parliamentary one.

---

17   Ibid., p. 324.

In the army, the vice-regal mentality had been strong since the early days of United Pakistan and had never faded even in the days when Z.A. Bhutto had it in a subordinate role. It had been a political power center from early on (except for those first years of the Z.A. Bhutto government), and it found a natural alliance with the President, G.I. Khan. The President owed his power to the Zia regime, and represented institutions, primarily the bureaucracy, which also did not trust, and wanted to constrain, the power of elected governments. The President worked closely with the army to maintain those constraints, and with the army's connivance, or at its behest, dismissed the first two elected governments. This alliance of interests appeared to continue, in some fashion, when Khan was succeeded by Farouq Leghari, who had been a political ally of Bhutto but dismissed her and her government in November 1996.

Both Bhutto and Sharif sought to limit the ability of the two un-elected power centers to exercise those powers of dismissal, but until Sharif won the 1997 election by a landslide, and captured a huge majority in the National Assembly and the Senate, they could not do so. In 1997, Sharif used his huge majority to rescind the eighth amendment that conferred such power on the President. In 1999, the army asserted its determination to remain the arbiter of political power and national policy by removing the Sharif government in a coup d'état. When indirect manipulation and control through the constitutional powers of the President were not available, the army proved, as it had in 1977 when it took power from Z.A. Bhutto, that when it perceives that its political and corporate interests are threatened, it will move directly to defend them.

These four elected governments faced fundamental, almost monumental, challenges, which have been described above. To complicate their existence immensely, they did not have full powers to address those problems. The army insisted on a veto on many security and foreign policy issues (like India/Kashmir and Afghanistan), as well as the nuclear program. The President was reluctant to allow the elected governments much latitude on many domestic problems, especially the economy.

None of the four lasted longer than three years. In each case (with the exception of the army's direct intervention against the second Sharif government) some combination of the difficult issues listed above was the nominal cause:

- the stagnant and staggering economy and the inability to revive it and undertake structural and institutional reform;

- corruption;

- the terrible political problems in Sindh and the lesser ones in Balochistan and Punjab that affected law and order;

- the creeping Islamization and radicalization of society;

- and the hostile relationship with India which was exacerbated by the insurgency in Kashmir that began in 1989 and became the excuse for Pakistani clandestine intervention in what became a proxy war.

As backdrop to these serious issues, one perceives the structural weaknesses of the Pakistani political system:

- the zero-sum-game approach to politics;

- institutional failure;

- the inability to think in federal terms in a state in which there were quite diverse ethnic and regional interests;

- and the inability of the elected institutions of the polity to overcome the unelected power centers—the army and the bureaucracy.

We have seen in the previous and current chapters that the two military governments contributed both to the increasingly serious nature of the issues that plagued the elected governments and to the weaknesses which made it more difficult for the latter to come to grips effectively with the serious issues. In a sense, military intervention became a self-fulfilling prophecy as the very actions and behavior of the military governments of Pakistan helped create the problems that they used to justify their assumption of power—to restore "real" democracy.

The Judiciary Bounces Back—Into the Political Power Struggles—and Loses

The judiciary emerged from the Zia era with what might be described as a schizophrenic mindset. It was, on one hand, anxious to reestablish the more robust independence and review authority it had been given originally in the 1973 constitution; and it was, on the other hand, still traumatized from its experience of the previous sixteen years—during which the Bhutto government had whittled away at its independence and authority, and the Zia government had demolished these powers. This ambiguity also produced divisions in the superior judiciary between those judges who wanted to move faster and those who counseled prudence.[18]

---

18   Paula Newberg, *Judging the State—Courts and Constitutional Politics in Pakistan* (Cam-

Events of the second democratic episode forced the superior courts to work on two tracks. First, they had to deal with the past by hearing a number of cases from petitioners alleging illegal actions by the defunct military regime. And, second, they had to provide a transition into the new era of elective, semi-democratic politics by judging whether laws and constitutional provisions, particularly regarding the separation of powers, promulgated by the military regime were compatible with the new political process that had emerged after Zia's death.[19] Eager to restore its former reputation as well as its authority, the judiciary accepted many cases to review and decide. Some of these involved issues that probably should have been resolved by the political process through legislative action. Inevitably, the superior judiciary pragmatically tempered its verdicts in such cases. Such pragmatism seemed ingrained after such long practice.[20] Moreover, the political climate that had produced a hybrid constitution, the non-elected power centers that hovered intrusively behind the scenes, and the winner takes all nature of Pakistani politics were further reasons for caution.

Nonetheless, such judgments brought it sometimes into conflict with elected governments, which might ignore these rulings. Two cases involving the President's power under Zia's eighth amendment to dismiss the Prime Minister and the parliaments are an indication of the divisions in the superior judiciary and the thorny issues of transition that really required political solutions. The first challenged the amendment in the Karachi High Court, which upheld it on narrow, legal grounds and used the decision as a way to try to slow down the activists.[21] In 1993, however, Prime Minister Sharif appealed to the Supreme Court against his dismissal by President Ghulam Ishaq Khan. Sharif was restored to power by the Supreme Court which ruled that the President did not have the constitutional authority to dismiss him. This resulted in a constitutional crisis which was only resolved when the Army Chief brokered an agreement that both would resign and another election would take place. An interim government took the reins for three months, and the new election brought back Benazir Bhutto and the PPP to power.[22]

---

bridge: Cambridge, 1995), pp200-206.

19   Ibid., p. 201.

20   Ibid., p. 227

21   Ibid., p. 214

22   Ibid., pp. 217-220

This seeming victory for judicial activism was followed by another in early 1996. The second government of Benazir Bhutto, unhappy with the senior judiciary, had tried to bypass the normal agreed procedure that called for the Chief Justice of the courts to recommend judges. Bhutto had appointed three women judges to the Lahore High Court. The Supreme Court overturned this, and after accepting petitions challenging other judicial appointments, dismissed twenty High Court judges. In addition, the Court threw out the constitutional amendment promulgated by Zia ul Huq that allowed the President to transfer arbitrarily High Court Judges to the Federal Sharia Court.[23] This may have been the high point of judicial activism in post-1971 Pakistan. Nawaz Sharif and the PML were elected in early 1997, and came to power with a huge majority and a determination to overcome all opposition from other power centers. This included the judiciary, despite its constitutional role, if it got in the way. Almost immediately, conflict broke out between the Sharif government and an activist Chief Justice and superior judiciary. The 1996 cases that had checked executive power dramatically brought many in the senior judiciary to flex their constitutional muscles. The conflict mounted through the year over a series of executive acts, including a stringent anti-terrorist law designed to put down the rash of sectarian violence.

The growth of tension between the Executive and the Judiciary was mirrored by that between President and Prime Minister—which involved the courts, and which inevitably exacerbated their conflict with the executive. One of Sharif's first acts was to introduce the 13th amendment which rescinded the power of the President to dismiss the Prime Minister and the National Assembly. This put him and the President on an antagonistic course. In the complicated standoff that followed, Sharif's judicial opponents—the activist judiciary—took the early rounds, but Sharif fought back by finding a way to divide the judiciary along party lines. For a while, toward the end of the year, there were two Supreme Courts.[24] When the Chief Justice of the original Court indicated that the Court intended to proceed with a contempt trial of the Prime Minister, the Court was stormed by Senators and Members of Parliament of Sharif's party, and the justices forced to abandon the trial. This heightened the conflict with the President which had already sharpened over the appointment of Provincial Governors and others. The conflict escalated as Sharif consolidated his power

---

23   Talbot, *Pakistan, A Modern History*, pp. 347-8.

24   Ibid., pp. 362-3

until he was able, through the use of his strong-arm tactics and threats, to force the senior judiciary to remove the Chief Justice. He also forced the resignation of the President, by threatening impeachment.[25] The PML and Sharif seemed to have overcome all the power centers provided for in the constitution, but the non-elected, non-constitutional power center, the military, remained a barrier to his aspiration to full power.

The India Phobia—Obsession and Oscillation

In this eleven year period of elected government, the pernicious effect on Pakistani politics of the country's "conflictual beginnings" and its "demonization of India" was, perhaps, most manifest.[26] The "Indian syndrome" flows, like a subterranean current, through much of the period's political paranoia: it was the wellspring of the military's insistence that it must control policy, the excuse it used to do so, and to take a disproportionate share of state resources; it was the motivation for elected politicians to acquiesce to the military's proxy wars, questionable policies, and budgetary gluttony; and finally it led directly to the schizophrenic policies of the second Nawaz Sharif government which matched nuclear test to nuclear test in what can only have been a (self-flagellating) demonstration of Pakistani macho, then held out the olive branch to India with one hand and sent troops into a remote part of Indian Kashmir with the other.

The core problem of the "Indian syndrome" was, of course, Kashmir. It became much more neuralgic in the 1990s after it had been relatively quiescent during most of the late 1970s and 1980s. It revived as an active and festering problem because an indigenous insurgency broke out in Indian Kashmir in 1989. This was, in effect, a reaction to the election of 1988, which most Kashmiris believed to have been seriously rigged.

Not wishing to miss any opportunity to make life more difficult for India, the ISI (with, no doubt, high-level military support, and implicit if not explicit backing from the new civilian governments) wasted no time in recruiting young Pakistanis—many who had cut their jihadist teeth against the Soviets in Afghanistan—and sent them to help the insurgency. The

25 Javid Iqbal, "The Judiciary and Constitutional Crisis in Pakistan," *Pakistan—Founders' Aspirations and Today's Realities,* ed. Habib Malik (Oxford University Press, 2001), pp. 78-9

26 Jean Luc-Racine, "Living With India," *A History of Pakistan and Its Origins,* ed. Christophe Jaffrelot (London: Wimbledon Publishing Company, 2002), p. 116 is the source of these quotes and for some of the information in this section.

"proxy war" in Kashmir was, in many ways, an extension of Zia ul Huq's campaigns against the Soviets in Afghanistan.[27]

Thus the two elected governments of Benazir Bhutto and the first elected government of Nawaz Sharif, instead of making room to maneuver for a relaxation of tensions with India, found themselves in a deepening "cold war." The Indians accused Pakistan of exacerbating their problems in Kashmir (much of which, in reality, were self-inflicted) and Pakistan returned the compliment by asserting that the Indians were inflaming the problem (see above) in Sindh.[28] Fruitless talks, and clashes along the line of demarcation between Indian and Pakistani Kashmir, characterize the period between 1988 and 1997 with an occasional larger confrontation that threatened escalating into a crisis (in 1990 a crisis developed which led the US to send a special envoy to facilitate a de-escalation). Pakistan took the Kashmir issue back to the United Nations in 1994, to no avail.

Relations between the two countries became colder and tenser as the period wore on, though they were marked by brief periods of hopefulness, especially during 1996 when I. K. Gujral was the Indian Prime Minister. They had, perhaps sunk to a new low at the beginning of that year when, after Indian rockets killed nineteen people in a village in Pakistani Kashmir and the Indians tested a medium-range missile the next day. Concern was so palpable that Pakistani President Leghari felt it necessary to reassure the public that war was not in the offing.[29]

The election of Nawaz Sharif in 1997, for a second term, and of the Hindu nationalist party, the BJP, in India a year later didn't seem to change things much at first. The hostility continued unabated, and even grew worse. Shelling increased between the forces in the two Kashmirs, and late in 1997 the Indians deployed medium-range missiles along the border. The outside world watched these confrontations carefully because India was known, and Pakistan was believed, to have working nuclear weapons. They proved it in May 1998. The newly elected BJP government in India, driven to assert India's strength, tested three nuclear devices on May 11 and two more on May 13. For two weeks, debate in Pakistan was intense and Nawaz Sharif vacillated. Nationalists (including much of the military) and Islamic groups argued that Pakistani and Islamic pride and security demanded that Pakistan respond by testing its own nuclear devices. There

---

27   Ibid., p. 127
28   Talbot, *Pakistan: A Modern History*, p. 336
29   Ibid., pp. 336-7

was heavy pressure from the US and other Western countries, with explicit and tempting economic rewards, not to test. The Western entreaties also carried with them the threat of further economic sanctions if Pakistan did test. To the Western voices was added the fainter and weaker voice of the Pakistani liberal elements.

In the event, PM Sharif chose what he must have perceived as the politically safer way. Pakistan tested three devices on May 28 and three more on May 30. These tests provoked sanctions on both countries, and an intense diplomatic effort to get them to join the Test Ban Treaty and test no further. The sanctions hit much harder on smaller and economically weaker Pakistan (see above and Chapter 9).

Lahore and Kargil—Hope and Despair in the Same Timeframe

In retrospect, it appears that both Prime Minister Sharif and the new Indian Prime Minister Vajpayee desired, after these assertions of power, to change the tone of the relationship and instigate rapprochement, each for his own very different domestic reasons. The international pressure and the shock of the sanctions gave them the space to try. Vajpayee may have been thinking about his place in history, but also understood that India would probably never achieve the "great power" status it craves until it solved its endemic problem with its Muslim neighbor. Sharif probably wanted to reduce the tension and slow down the arms race (which Pakistan couldn't win), and also to reduce international pressure (and perhaps over time the sanctions) on Pakistan. And he may have calculated that this was the time, with General Musharraf in place as the new Army Chief, to improve relations with India. He assumed that Musharraf, a Mohajir, who on one occasion at least, had supported him in meetings of the Pakistani Corps Commanders, would be a political ally and less inclined to bring pressure from the Punjabi dominated Army against such a move.[30] The two leaders began to work towards breaking the impasse in the relationship, getting past the rhetoric and the mutual phobias. They agreed at a July 1998 SAARC meeting to reduce tensions between the two countries and in November agreed as a first step to resume bus services. Then, in a bold step, Indian PM Vajpayee travelled on the first bus to visit Lahore, in February 1999. This led to a

---

30   Hussain Haqqani, *Between Mosque and Military*, (Washington, DC: Carnegie Endowment for International Peace, 2005), p. 248

summit meeting which, for a few months, was considered a breakthrough and turning point in the historic hostility between the two countries.[31]

The Lahore Meeting agreement called for a resumption in the dialogue, the peaceful resolution of disputes, and provided principles for nuclear restraint. The outline of a process was laid down which was aimed at resolving the bilateral problems that had poisoned relations for so long, and particularly Kashmir. Equally important, in the long run, PM Vajpayee stated publicly that India "accepted" the existence of Pakistan, endeavoring to finally put to rest the major Pakistani fear that India still wished to reverse the 1947 partition, i.e. that it continued to deny the theory of a separate Muslim nation.

This era of good feeling lasted only about three months. In May, Pakistani troops were discovered to have occupied, since November of the previous year it turned out, the remote heights of a part of Indian Kashmir above Kargil.[32] These heights were normally occupied by Indian troops only during the summer due to the difficulty maintaining them in such harsh conditions during the winter. According to one former Pakistani military officer in the know, the aim was to give impetus "to the Kashmiri freedom movement," to entice India into sending more troops to its part of Kashmir which would weaken Indian ability to undertake a major offensive against Pakistan, and "create a military threat [to India] that could be viewed as capable of leading to a military solution so as to force India to the negotiating table from a position of weakness."[33]

---

31   Ibid., p. 249

32   The operation began just a month after General Musharraf took over as Chief of Army Staff—in other words about three months before the Lahore meeting and perhaps even before the agreement had been reached to start the bus service. While this might seem to absolve the military leadership of deliberately undermining the Lahore process, these military leaders knew that Prime Minister Sharif had initiated a process to reduce tensions, which even a small incursion seemed unlikely to foster. When the operation was discovered, the Pakistan Foreign Ministry claimed it was a "mujahideen" (jihadi) operation because, according to one of my very good sources, this is what had been briefed to them and the PM before the operation. But this was soon dismissed publicly by the military itself. Shaukat Qadir (see following endnote) writes that the Pakistani troops were about 1000 Northern Light Infantry fighters supported by 4000 providing logistical back up and "some local mujahideen assisting as labour (*sic*) to carry logistical requirements," (p. 25).

33   Shaukat Qadir, "An Analysis of the Kargil Conflict 1999," *RUSI Journal*, (April 2002), accessed on February 6, 2006 at http://www.ccc.nps.navy.mil/research/kargil/JA00199.pdf. In private conversations, other former military officers, who do not wish to be identified, dispute some of Qadir's analysis, claiming especially that the political aims of the Pakistan Generals who planned and undertook the Kargil operation were more limited than Qadir believes. Since, as even Qadir admits (page 26), the strategic operational plan and political objective for the operation were not developed until March 1999, four months after the incursion began, this must be taken seriously. In the beginning, according to

The occupation was, in some ways, a strategic threat, but the main problem was a political one.[34] While it may have been sparsely inhabited, and difficult to find on a map, the heights that Pakistan had occupied over Kargil overlooked an important transit point on the road to Ladakh and Siachen. While the Indians had opened a less vulnerable route somewhat earlier, this was nonetheless not the usual infiltration of a few jihadists into Kashmir. The Indian military could not let it stand (as some sources say that the Pakistani military leadership expected them to).[35] Moreover, the Vajpayee government had just lost a vote of confidence in the Indian Parliament and was serving as the interim government while preparing to contest another general election. A Hindu nationalist government facing reelection could hardly let this incursion go unnoticed or unanswered.[36] A fierce battle ensued for a number of weeks in which the Indian army took many casualties because the terrain was against them (the Pakistanis held the heights and the Indians had to attack up steep slopes).

The specter of escalation into a possible nuclear exchange haunted Western leaders, especially in Washington. The US and its allies put great pressure on Pakistan to withdraw, and equal pressure on India not to escalate. While some observers, including myself, thought that a nuclear exchange was unlikely, there was good reason to keep the pressure on PM Sharif.

Qadir, the primary objective was to "give a fillip to the Kashmiri freedom movement" (page 25).

34   In the author's view, Kargil was a monumental strategic miscalculation by Pakistani military leaders (and, to the extent they were complicit, the political leaders). It undermined, almost terminally, the promising Lahore process, and undercut Indian PM Vajpayee who had undertaken great political risk in pursuing it. He and other BJP leaders remained deeply suspicious of Musharraf after that, which hampered his efforts to improve relations after he took the political leadership a few months later. This suspicion must have extended to the political leadership while it remained in office as it seems clear that PM Sharif was briefed on the operation just after it started, though the extent of this briefing is not clear. (Qadir maintains that the operation was "casually broached with [the] Prime Minster...at some point in December [1998].") Why he let it go forward and/or did not pull it back later after the success of Lahore is a profound mystery. Kargil is a fascinating piece of South Asian history that awaits exploration by historians.

35   Racine, "Living With India," *A History of Pakistan and Its Origins*, p. 115. As Racine points out, the Kargil incursion, beyond the military and political challenges it represented, carried the implication that Indian troops are inferior and Pakistani troops superior, hardly an implication the Hindu-nationalist BJP could ignore.

36   The fall of the BJP could not have been foreseen when the operation began six or so months previously. Nonetheless, it proved to be another disastrous political miscalculation of the Pakistani military on a par with the 1965 war plan and the 1971 policy regarding East Pakistan. Though he has publicly indicated no remorse in his 2006 memoir, *In the Line of Fire*, (London: Simon & Shuster), President Musharraf's effort to improve Indian-Pakistani relations over the past 4-5 years has certainly suffered from the public and political suspicion of him in India because of the Kargil episode.

Pakistan had instigated this incursion—which had caused many casualties—that had destroyed the promising Lahore process and set back any hope of improved cooperation in South Asia for several years. The United States made it clear that it held Pakistan responsible for upsetting the peace in the region and for this backwards step away from a promising unfolding peace process between Pakistan and India.

It was a time of hyperactive diplomacy: I lost count of the Presidential letters urging withdrawal that I delivered directly, or via the Foreign Ministry, to Prime Minister Sharif. At the same time, I learned, Pakistani diplomacy was also active, and the two governments had opened a back channel to try to work out a reasonable solution that involved a Pakistani withdrawal and a renewal of the Lahore process. In late June, this seemed to be getting somewhere. The Pakistanis believed, or so they told me, that a deal was in the offing. President Clinton then decided to communicate with the Pakistani military. He sent General Anthony Zinni, Commander of CENTCOM, the military command that is responsible for military relations with the Middle East, East Africa, and Pakistan, to talk to General Musharraf and to Prime Minister Sharif. General Zinni had formed a positive working relationship with General Musharraf after the latter had been named as Chief of Army Staff the previous October. The two men met on the first day of Zinni's visit for most of the morning and through lunch. General Musharraf deferred to the Prime Minister on the final decision on whether to withdraw Pakistani troops. However, it seemed clear to the US side in the meeting that Musharraf's body language clearly indicated a desire to withdraw. He was anxious that Zinni see Sharif, and helped set up an appointment with the PM that the Embassy had been having trouble getting confirmed.

In the meeting with Sharif, Musharraf's body language conveyed the same message it had the previous day. Sharif was non-commital for most of the meeting. Then, suddenly, he changed tack and agreed that Pakistan would withdraw. At least, that is what all present on the US side thought he had agreed to. General Zinni went home with a positive message to report to President Clinton. In retrospect, I believe that the Pakistanis were confident, by the time Zinni arrived, that they had a deal with New Delhi. Its essence was that they would withdraw and the Indians agree to restart the Lahore process. Soon after General Zinni departed for Washington, they learned there was no deal. Pakistanis involved in the back channel diplomacy assert that the Indians reneged. The Indians claim that they never agreed, and there was a miscommunication which led to the Pakistani misunderstanding. The jury is still out on which of these versions is correct.

Diplomatic efforts continued, and culminated in the celebrated July 4 meeting between President Clinton and Prime Minister Sharif. This derived from a July 3 phone call between the two. In that meeting, during which the two leaders met with only an American notetaker, the Prime Minister agreed to withdraw Pakistani troops and President Clinton to "take a personal interest in the Kashmir dispute." It seems that the Prime Minister felt he needed some political cover domestically if he agreed to withdraw, and President Clinton's "personal interest" was the best he could get.

Kargil had many other negative results. In the long run, the most important may be its effect on domestic Pakistani politics. It was Kargil that underlay the dispute which led to the military coup in October 1999, removing Nawaz Sharif from power and restoring the military as the political master of Pakistan.[37] Ultimately this may be the longest lasting effect, as the military shows no signs of ever leaving power or of accepting full democratization. This will be covered in greater detail in the next chapter.

The Democratic 1990s in Muslim South Asia

After periods of military or quasi-military government since 1975 and 1977 respectively, Bangladesh and Pakistan joined the march toward democracy that highlighted the early 1990s. Pakistan was first in 1988: Bangladesh followed in 1991. Their friends and expatriates far and wide were thrilled and heartened, and they were, among other things, in the political vanguard of the Islamic world. Neither country completed the journey to full democracy, going instead from military government to something that resembled democracy, until one looked closer. Even the partial democracies they had become couldn't hold. Pakistan reverted to military government in October 1999, when the Army took over again and General Pervez Musharraf became head of government. And Bangladesh followed suit, in a very nuanced way, in January 2007. Yet, while they look again look similar on the surface, the similarity stops there—at the surface. The outlook in each is very different, *sui generis* cases that can't be generalized on the basis of their culture, religion, or geography.

Yet there has been one overarching similarity in the political development of both: elected governments have not been able to govern. In Paki-

---

37   There are other reasons for the October 1999 military coup, which will be discussed in Chapter 8.

stan, the root problem is a military that has been unwilling ever to give up power to civilian political parties, and has been allowed by the political class to get away with it. However, that string may be running out. The Musharraf government spent five years building a hybrid military government cloaked in civilian garb (modelled on Zia ul Huq's version of 1985-88), designed to keep to itself the power to make policy, only to see it come apart in 2007. Times change, and the model no longer works.

As this is written Pakistan is in existential crisis. On the one hand, it is struggling to find new formula for governance that will work for its political stakeholders—the military and civil society. At the same time, it faces a direct challenge to its sovereignty as a state from the jihadi extremists who have taken control of much of the Tribal Areas and parts of the Frontier.[38] The military has yet to step back from its determination to control policy, but civil society, led recently by the judiciary, has become more aggressive in pushing the Army back to the barracks. Late in 2007, the situation had unraveled to such an extent that President Musharraf declared an emergency, in effect a return to martial law that suspended parts of the constitution and civil rights, using this opportunity to get rid of some pesky judges. Ironically, it appeared that the government had undertaken a coup against itself.

Possibly Pakistan is working its way toward another version of hybrid military/civilian government, but any new dispensation must still face up to the state's growing vulnerability to jihadi extremists and their drive to convert it to an Islamist state. At the time of writing, the future of the country is much in doubt. The next chapter will cover this in more detail.

In Bangladesh, after fading from the political scene for seventeen years, the Army has again intervened in the political system. During its years out of power, it seemed not to have any interest in governing or in sharing power with a civilian side, and left civilian politicians in full power. However, on January 11, 2007, with chaos and severe instability threatening again (reminiscent of November 1975), governance rapidly deteriorating, and corruption a national embarrassment, the Bangladesh Army took over the state again.

It immediately handed over day-to-day government operation to a technocratic and truly neutral civilian interim government. The stated intention is to rebuild democracy, beginning with tightening up the rules of political behavior and strengthening the provision for a neutral, interim

---

38 Despite the rhetoric to the contrary about the danger from a hostile India, this is a real existential challenge to the Pakistan state, the first in 36 years, and it comes from the West, not the East.

government to ensure free and fair elections. It is an interesting experiment about which there is much skepticism, but the results are not in yet. It is a work in progress, in a true sense.

The major problem in those seventeen years was that opposition political parties wouldn't let the government govern. Whether the reform effort can construct democratic structures that allow the people to be sovereign, to choose the policies of elected governments, is still up in the air. To do that, the interim government and its military backer will have to find a code of conduct that drains most of the poison from the political culture. Otherwise the military/technocrat combination will return in a few years.

Three general elections took place between 1991 and 2007. Despite flaws that became more widespread in each succeeding election, these were essentially judged to have been free and fair. After each, power passed peacefully to the opposition despite a howl of protest from the incumbent party about cheating. That is half way to real, working democracy; the other half will be accomplished when those freely and fairly elected governments are able to govern effectively, with a loyal opposition raising issues, but allowing it to operate. This is what the interim setup is aiming to accomplish. It will be difficult. Political culture is such that gaining power is seen not as a way to implement a party's platform or ideology, but as a means of distributing resources to followers and keeping the opposition from power. In the long run, there is hope that Bangladesh's political culture will change for the better, as progress is made in education and other social development.

In Pakistan, the problem is more complicated and difficult. There is no sign that the praetorian nature of its military state is changing. The army appears to remain convinced that it is the only institution that puts Pakistan's national interest above regional, political, or personal ones, and that therefore it must maintain its grip on Pakistani governance. The way forward is to convince the Pakistan army to emulate the Bangladesh army while convincing the Pakistani civilian politicians not to emulate the Bangladeshi civilian politicians. But the depressing conclusion is that only some cataclysmic political event can evict the Army from the driving seat.

Deteriorating governance by the military and an inability to deal with the jihadi extremist challenge (which is the reason many Pakistanis welcomed the Musharraf government in the first place) has brought on the crisis mentioned above. The Musharraf chapter is the last in this book on the political development of the two countries. It would be tragic if the Musharraf period is the last chapter in the political development of Pakistan.

8

PAKISTAN'S SELF-FULFILLING PROPHECY: THE MILITARY BACK IN POWER

Though it is difficult to remember after eight increasingly tumultuous years, most Pakistanis, and many outside observers, welcomed the Musharraf coup of October 1999. As described in the previous chapter, Nawaz Sharif's second term had been a rough and fearful ride for much of the population. For the great majority, economic malaise was the most important factor. The Sharif government's erratic, and often badly thought out, economic policies (including his decision to test nuclear weapons, which unleashed crippling international sanctions) put the Pakistani economy into the almost-insolvent tank. For the secular political establishment, including a portion of the military, his determination to push through a constitutional amendment declaring Sharia the law of the land and his attack on the Supreme Court gave rise to visions of an absolutist Islamic state. For the Army as an institution, his drive to subordinate it politically was anathema.

It was, perhaps, this initial wave of enthusiasm and the benefit of the doubt it gave the fumbling start of the Musharraf dispensation that convinced the Army that the model of governance it had always held dear was still best suited to Pakistan. This model had, as its central core, that only the Army was fit to govern the country, though civilian fig leafs were a necessary accoutrement, *viz.* Ayub Khan and Zia ul Huq. Enthusiasm evaporated over the following three years, but this messianic view did not, despite the growing disrepair and dysfunction of the military government. In the end, President Musharraf lost all credibility and the Army much of its popularity.

The Musharraf interregnum was, in effect, just another phase in the ongoing cyclical process in which the military and civilian politicians shuttle in and out of office, while the Army rules no matter who sits in the President's chair. The Pakistani military has never, except between 1972 and 1977, allowed civilians to be in full control of the country, and each military dispensation has left the succeeding civilian governments with the same insoluble structural problems and no authority to solve them. In other words, in Pakistan, the very act of military intervention seems to have become a self-fulfilling prophecy.[1]

Musharraf took this ever tightening spiral to its logical conclusion—a political implosion that may very well end it. But at what cost is yet unclear. The possible outcomes are multiple and run from one extreme, a Salafist Islamist state, controlled by jihadis, that is a potential center for aggressive political Islam, to the other extreme, fragmentation into two or three parts, hostile to each other. Yet, as has been the case in Pakistan since its creation in 1947, there remain forces that can pull society back from the brink, among them an army that has yet to reveal whether its fissures are as deep and fundamental as other segments of society. If it can remain a coherent and modernizing force, and if it can change its mindset about how Pakistan should be governed, the Army could be instrumental in bringing an unbroken and unIslamicized Pakistan through this existential crisis to a new start.

"I Want to Thank You for Making This Day Necessary"[2]

Nawaz Sharif's clumsy attempts to subordinate the Army started the long slide into instability. His second term as Prime Minister and leader of the PML government brought rising tension between the elected civilian government and the Army. The antagoism was fueled by a series of problems, but the forced early retirement, in October 1988, of the previous Chief of Army Staff, General Keramat, was probably the most important. PM Sharif was angered by public remarks that General Keramat made in which he supported the idea of a National Security Council, widely viewed as a check on the civilian government's power to make policy. Sharif's arbitrary dismissal of its Chief stuck in the throat of the Army, and might have led to a coup at that time under a different Chief. To replace Keramat, PM Sharif appointed Lt. General Pervez Musharraf, over several more senior generals, probably

---

1   Though the Bangladesh Army has again intervened in the politics of that country as described in Chapter 6, I would argue that its previous periods of governance under Ziaur Rahman and Ershad did not lay the groundwork to make subsequent military interventions inevitable—as seems to be the case in Pakistan.

2   Yogi Berra on Yogi Berra Appreciation Day, in St Louis in 1947 at http://rinkwork.com/said/yogiberra.shmtl

because he thought that General Musharraf would be more docile as he went about chipping away at Army prerogatives.

The culmination of the growing dispute between the army leadership and the Sharif government came in the Fall of 1999 over which was responsible for the strategic disaster of Kargil (covered in more detail in the previous chapter). Both had blamed the other in the public media since mid-July when the army had withdrawn, under heavy international pressure (and probably because the military tide was turning against it), from the heights it had controlled on the Indian side of the line of control in Kashmir for a few months after a clandestine incursion during the winter. This political/strategic blunder also gave the opposition political alliance incentive and ammunition to attack the PML government.

Another Attempt at a Preemptive Solution to a Political Problem

The proximate cause of the October 1999 coup was an attempt by Prime Minister Sharif to resolve the dispute in his favor by removing Musharraf from command of the army and replacing him with a general known to be personally loyal to the PM. The attempt took place surreptitiously while Musharraf was abroad. Sharif evidently did not understand that General Musharraf would react much differently than his predecessor to being removed early, and that the Army remained determined not to let this happen again. The Army later claimed that the attempt to remove Musharraf was "illegal" and "unconstitutional" (as well as an attempt to humiliate it). The implication was that there would have been no coup if that illegal and "unconstitutional" act had not occurred.

While PM Sharif's intemperate move may have sparked the takeover, the Army had other concerns. These became clear once it had taken power. Musharaf's military regime made reform and retrenchment of the deteriorating economy and of a corrupt political system (to "reverse the rot") its primary goal.

The expressed need to clean up the mess in Islamabad seemed like an afterthought in the first few days after the coup. But clearly the Army brass had been stewing for some time about the state of the country, which it believed was in steep political and economic decline. The economic problems, which seemed only to get worse under each successive democratically elected government, were probably of most concern. Despite these long-standing worries, which may have led some of the officers to flirt with the temptations of direct rule, the Army appears to have moved against the civilian

163

government when it did in order to prevent Sharif's dismissal of Musharraf. It showed a clear lack of preparation for governing in the early days after the coup (though it had contingency studies going back many years). In the event it seemed to take weeks to put together a government.

In addition to concerns over national political and economic decline, the army may have had an even deeper (perhaps unconscious, and certainly un-articulated) reason for its dissatisfaction. It probably understood, on some level, that Nawaz Sharif was determined to reduce it to subordinate political status. He had succeeded in the early months of his second term in strip-ping the constitutional powers of the President over the Prime Minister. This reduced the indirect political power of the army, which had teamed with the President to dismiss the previous three elected government. The Prime Minister appeared to be using the popular discontent (also in the ranks of the army) over the Kargil fiasco to cut the army down to size. Evi-dently, he planned to consolidate his position by naming his own man as COAS. (He appears to have taken his text straight from the father of Benazir Bhutto, his mortal political enemy. Zulfikar Ali Bhutto had used the same formula, when in power in the early 1970s, to try to diminish the power of the Army.)

Whether the coup would have occurred later on anyway, Nawaz Sharif clearly triggered it in October by precipitately removing Musharraf from the post of COAS. He made things worse by not allowing the plane on which Musharraf was traveling to land. On October 12, 1999, the army took over the government without resistance, the plane landed with only a few min-utes of fuel remaining, and Sharif's nominee as the next COAS (General Ziauddin) had to remove the epaulettes he had only a few minutes earlier purchased in a bazaar. Sharif, his family, and his close collaborators spent the next fourteen months in jail before being sent into exile. General Ziaud-din remained under house arrest for several years before retiring.

Pervez Musharraf, 1999 to 2008—Zia Redux? or Ayub Khan All Over Again?

The second episode of military rule in the new (post-1971) Pakistan re-sembled, in form and political direction, the first.[3] Many observers see very

---

3   The discussion in this chapter covering the period 1998 to 2001 is based on the author's personal experience in Pakistan. Discussion of the period 2001-2002 is based on my proximity to Pakistani affairs while in the State Department Bureau of South Asian Af-fairs in Washington. The discussion of the period from late 2002 to the present is taken primarily from many conversations with Pakistani friends, from close reading of Pakistani

similar patterns of thinking and behavior in the Zia and Musharraf regimes. They resemble each other, especially in their actions to "reform" the political system. Nuanced differences, however, indicate that someone close to Musharraf had been thinking about how the Army could improve on Zia ul Huq and decided to avoid pitfalls that had characterized his rule. Musharraf's statements on the night of the takeover, according to the *New York Times*, justified the Army's action by claiming that Sharif had been attempting to politicize or destabilize the military.[4]

The new regime announced an "Emergency Proclamation" on October 14 which put the 1973 constitution (or what remained of it) in "abeyance," suspended the National Assembly, the Senate, the Provincial Assemblies, and all state office holders except the President. Under this proclamation, the military exercised all power, and its leader, General Musharraf, became the "Chief Executive" of Pakistan. Unlike Zia, early elections were not on the cards; they were promised at the end of a three-year period in which political institutions and the economy would be reformed. One striking similarity runs through the "political reforms" of both Musharraf and Zia: the misunderstanding of, and strong bias against, the un-predictability and messiness of democratic politics. The Musharraf regime seemed a carbon copy of Zia's in trying to construct a political system devoid of partisan politics—and of most mainstream politicians.

Though Nawaz Sharif had done pretty well in intimidating the judiciary and bringing it to heel, the new military government ensured that no attempt to assert real judicial independence would reappear. In early February 2000, the senior judiciary was required to take an oath of allegiance to the military regime which, according to some observers, "required the judges to violate the oaths they had all previously taken to uphold the 1973 constitution."[5] Six of the 13 Supreme Court judges refused to do so. (A

---

and international newspapers and other periodicals, which are identified where possible, and from two excellent recent publications: Steven Cohen, *The Idea of Pakistan* (Washington, DC: Brookings Institution, 2005), and Hussain Haqqani, *Pakistan—Between Mosque and Military* (Washington, DC: Carnegie Endowment For International Peace, 2005).

4   Celia W. Dugger, "Coup In Pakistan; The Overview; Pakistan Army Seizes Power Hours After Prime Minister Dismisses His Army Chief," *New York Times*, October 13, 1999. Accessed at http://topics.nytimes.com/top/reference/timestopics/people/m/pervez_musharraf/index.html?s=oldest&inline=nyt-per

5   International Crisis Group, *Building Judicial Independence in Pakistan* (ICG: November 9, 2004), p. 1. Accessed on January, 24, 2006 at http://www.crisisgroup.org/home/index.cfm?1=1&kid=3100

similar episode occurred during the emergency which Musharraf declared on November 3, 2007 and rescinded a month later.)

The government thought it could keep the judiciary under its close control by using the system of appointments, promotions, and removals. This has brought about great uncertainty among the senior judiciary. The Asian Development Bank reports, for example, that "junior judges of the High Court can leapfrog more senior judges and land in the Supreme Court in accordance with the wishes of the executive branch."[6] Jurisdictional problems and "creeping financial corruption" have also plagued the courts.[7]

The new oath was a prelude to the anticipated challenge to the October 14 proclamation that suspended National Assembly, the Senate, and the Provincial Assemblies. The case reached the Supreme Court in May 2000. The court, unsurprisingly, ruled that the coup was legitimate under the trusty "doctrine of necessity," a doctrine we visited in Chapter 4. In the decision, the Court also ruled that, despite its being in abeyance, the 1973 constitution was still the "supreme" law of the land, and while the Chief Executive had the power to bring "necessary" amendments by executive order, he could not amend "salient features" such as judicial independence, federalism, or the parliamentary system of government. The decision ratified the three-year deadline for a return to parliamentary rule.

The reformed political structure that Musharraf put in place looked, on the surface, almost identical to that created by Zia ul Huq—designed mainly to ensure the army's predominance in power. A "new" system at the local level was basically copied from Zia's formula for local rule through non-partisan councils selected by non-party elections.

At the national level, Musharraf's design of a new political structure differed only in degree from that of Zia. Instead of banning political parties, Musharraf sought to co-opt those politicians whose partisan loyalties were somewhat weaker than their political ambitions, and to freeze out those

6   Asian Development Bank, *Judicial Independence Overview—Pakistan* (Manila: ADB, 2003), pp. 69-70.

7   International Crisis Group, *Building Judicial Independence*, 1. The jurisdictional problems and the other inequities are illustrated in Human Rights Watch, *The Jurisdiction Dilemma* (HRW, 2005), accessed on January 24, 2006 at http://www.hrw.org/english/docs/2005/01/21/pakist10356.htm which describes the enormous miscarriage of justice in the now-celebrated case of the gang rape of Mukhtar Mai, a rape seemingly ordered by a village "panchayat" (council) for which convictions were overturned by the Lahore High Court only to have the Federal Shariat Court overturn the decision on jurisdictional grounds. The Supreme Court took over the case, probably on the advice of the executive which wanted to avoid further international embarrassment, and to avoid further jurisdictional squabbles between the courts in such a publicized case.

who remained loyal to the mainstream parties—the PPP and the PML. He set up a hybrid military/civilian, presidential/parliamentary system (a façade for military domination) in which he created a new party beholden to the military, a "king's party," (called the PML-Q) to run the civilian side of the government.[8]

Musharraf borrowed several tools from the Zia toolbox to accomplish his political goals. In June 2001, he issued CE Orders 1 and 2, in which he named himself to replace Mohammed Rafiq Tarar as President and formally dissolved the national and provincial assemblies. Until then, Tarar, who had been elected constitutionally by the national and provincial assemblies at the beginning of Nawaz Sharif's second term, in early 1997 had remained in place. Tarar was asked to resign when Musharraf apparently decided that being President, in conjunction with remaining Chief of Army Staff, would enable him to deal on a more equal basis with the Indian Prime Minister at the upcoming Agra summit. Dissolving the parliament, which had been suspended since October 1999, tidied up the package, as that would obviate any question of following the constitutional prescription for electing a new President. By keeping his uniform on while becoming President, he would maintain the army as his power base. Again, he emulated Zia ul Huq.

Despite the May 2000 Supreme Court Decision which appeared to limit his powers to amend the constitution, Musharraf promulgated in August 2002 a "Legal Framework Order" (LFO), which restored the power given the President by Zia ul Huq to dismiss the National Assembly, the Prime Minister, and the Provincial Assemblies without the consent of any elected body. There was little outcry about this despite the May 2000 Supreme Court admonishment that the "salient features" of the constitution should not be amended by the executive. Clearly Musharraf wished to ensure that the President had such power before the October 2002 elections produced a new National Assembly (one can never tell how an election will come out). The LFO was challenged later in the National Assembly but not by the judiciary.

The LFO also: 1) created a National Security Council, in which the military would be dominant, to vet important policy issues; and 2) recreated a political system that gives power over policy to the President and not the elected Assemblies. Musharraf extended for five years his term as President through a referendum that was of dubious legality, before the October 2002 election of National and Provincial Assemblies. And he remained as head of

---

8 The PML-Q has also been called the PML-QA, and is now called just the PML.

the army while also being President.[9] In other words, in politics, Musharraf is truly Zia ul Huq redux—the army followed, almost to the letter, its dated playbook.

The Other Musharraf—Fighting the Ghost of Zia

On close examination, in areas outside politics there were also striking differences between Musharraf and Zia. These stem from the very different visions and belief structures of the two military leaders and their principal advisors. One important difference is that Musharraf was specific and precise when the army took power in October 1999 about the timeframe for a return of civilian governance. He promised that direct military rule would be limited to three years. And unlike Zia, who reneged continually for eight years on the quick elections he promised when he took over in July 1977, Musharraf kept his word—sort of.

The political structure that he created after three years of direct military rule was neither a full-fledged democracy nor different in kind from the one that Zia created in 1985. In Musharraf's system, like Zia's, the President had the power to pick and dismiss the Prime Minister and the elected government. Musharraf remained President—while he kept his post as Chief of Army Staff, as Zia did. In other words, while he got the timing right (three years), there was only a limited return to civilian governance. A second difference is the seriousness, determination and resolve with which Musharraf tackled economic reform. In this respect, he resembles Ayub Khan rather than Zia ul Huq. This appeared to have been Musharraf's priority when he came to power, and the reforms he oversaw have been meaningful and important. (Chapter 9 covers his economic program.)

A clear and important difference between the two military regimes is that Musharraf appeared to have no interest in further Islamization of Pakistan, and indeed professed a desire to roll it back. Musharraf made several public statements against further Islamization and in support of greater tolerance and modernization. Nor did his military and civilian advisors show any sign of favoring Islamization. General Musharraf, himself, was viewed as having a moderate and modern outlook, unlike his military predecessor Zia, and over time he dropped from the ruling clique those military officers who

9   European Union Election Observation Mission to Pakistan, *Final Report of the EU Observation Mission to Pakistan* (Brussels: EU, 2002), pp. 10-14, accessed on January 20, 2006 at http://www.europa.eu.int/comm/europeaid/projects/eidhr/pdf/elections-reports-pakistan-02_en.pdf

were regarded as more like Zia in their personal piety and comfort with Islamization.

This did not deter the regime from emulating Zia and the previous civilian governments in using Islamist extremists for its own political purposes—behavior that certainly helps to strengthen the Islamists. This cynical use of extremists has turned out to be counterproductive, producing undesirable, unintended consequences, though these appear not to have been recognized by the army or the political elite. There was no progress in rolling back Islamization in Musharraf's years—despite much rhetoric—and some of the regime's political machinations (and miscalculations), inadvertently, gave the Islamists additional strength. Islamization made significant inroads in the Zia years (though it actually began in the elected government of Zulfikar Ali Bhutto), and it was further strengthened by the actions of the elected governments of Benazir Bhutto and Nawaz Sharif. Each used it as a way of driving a wedge between the Islamists and the military as well as getting an edge on the opposition. Under each of these governments, Islamization encroached more into society, as each believed it necessary to compromise with the Islamists to gain other long-term political objectives.

In trying to pursue his policy of "enlightened moderation," Musharraf ran head on into the heritage of Zia ul Huq. Each attempt by the Musharraf government to roll back Islamism came to nought because of the historical legacy inherited from all the previous governments. Though the majority of Pakistanis appears to reject Islamism as a political doctrine (and have turned out of office the Islamist parties that gained many seats in 2002), it is a conservative polity in which the mullahs have much influence on social issues.

Another apparent difference between the current and previous military regimes was that Musharraf did not, from the beginning of his regime in October 1999, to the declaration of emergency in November 2007, overtly attack the fundamental underpinnings of democracy—a free and unfettered press, open political expression, and freedom of movement. This changed fundamentally in November 2007 when he proclaimed an emergency (martial law by another name). This total change in direction is described at the end of this chapter.

The contrast between Musharraf's media policies in the first eight years to those of the Zia regime is, on the surface, stark. The Zia government exercised strict control of the media in this period and let up on media expression only in the second phase of his military rule, after the elections of 1985 had brought in the Zia version of hybrid government. Zia, in the

169

regime's early days, also sent a number of those considered political opponents to jail—behavior the Musharraf government did not emulate until the emergency was promulgated. The seemingly unfettered English language press—which only a tiny percentage of the population can read—was not the whole story, however. Things were never quite as rosy in the vernacular press, which heard from the government if it was perceived to stray too far into anti-regime rhetoric. Self-censorship is the usual way these papers stayed out of trouble. The main leverage the government used was withholding government advertising (since the government is the primary advertiser in newspapers); during Musharraf's early years, one large-circulation vernacular newspaper did not see any government advertising for over a year.

On the other hand, until the emergency, the government largely relaxed its tight control of available television channels. This was forced by the advent of satellite/cable television from the Gulf (and India), new channels that brought much fresh open political debate and discussion to the Pakistani public until they were restricted by the emergency. The downside was that their political content, as with much political discourse in Pakistan, was dominated by political Islamists. Thus the message for the average viewer was ideologically heavily weighted toward the conservative, often Salafist, view of the world. This is not to say that the elected governments of the 1990s were any more open to free expression of opinion. In fact, those of Nawaz Sharif were, if anything, less tolerant of contrary opinion. More journalists may have suffered under the Sharif government, which arbitrarily imprisoned, and sometimes abused prominent editors or writers of the English language press when angered by their criticism. Those governments also prohibited a long list of political opponents from traveling abroad.

The India-Centric Optic—Change in the Offing?

The Musharraf regime was different in one other important way, which has attracted much international attention. He and his military colleagues— unlike their predecessor military or civilian governments—seemed intent on resolving the long-standing political disputes and stabilizing the relationship with India. The Agra summit between Musharraf and Vajpayee broke the ice that had frozen relations for two years after Kargil. Though it did not produce any results, it went some way, at least, in "devillifying" Musharraf in India so that Indian leaders could work with him. However, relations became testy again and, indeed, very confrontational at the end of 2001 and in the first six months of 2002. A jihadist attack on the Indian Parliament in New Delhi in December 2001, again an example of the unforeseen consequences of fostering jihadi culture, led to a large mobilization of military forces along the Indo/Pak border and threatened to escalate into a shooting war, which evoked great international concern. The mobilization lasted about six months before things cooled off and, with much outside pressure, especially from the United States, both sides stood down.

At the beginning of 2004, both sides began to work diplomatically toward a process that could lead, if pursued seriously, to the eventual resolution of the many outstanding problems and to a normalization of relations. It seems as if Musharraf and his military colleagues concluded that the seemingly intractable hostility between the two countries was holding Pakistan back from modernization of its society and economy.[10]

Musharraf pursued a settlement often with flexibility and diplomatic finesse when Pakistan domestic politics permitted that. At other times, the shopworn rhetoric of the past crept back into use, but much modulated by the military strongmen. The Indian side has matched this some of the time and has seemed to drag its feet at other times, under both the BJP government under which the process began, and the Congress government which came to power in a surprise electoral victory in May 2004.

Whether this warming of the relationship and the gradual resolution of the problems between India and Pakistan will come to a fruitful conclusion, remains to be seen. There are very complicated issues that have proved, in the past, to be impossible to resolve. Primary among them is the Kashmir dispute, which is at the root of all the problems. It has in the past assumed an importance in the national identity of both Pakistan and India that made compromise solutions (the normal political method) unthinkable in both countries. Time will tell us if that perception is being overtaken by a more modern perception that, after sixty years, it is time for both countries to move beyond the parameters of the old dispute. However, the effect of the 2007 political crisis in Pakistan on relations with India is yet to be seen.

The possibility of a Pakistan-India rapprochement helped Musharraf domestically in the early years of his tenure. Perhaps most importantly, the confidence it engendered among domestic and foreign investors added to his generally sound macroeconomic policies to increase investment in the Pakistani economy. Much of the Pakistani establishment, which has long

---

10   Or, perhaps they have concluded that the military sees no further need to employ the "national security" *vis-à-vis* India justification to explain its political dominance.

considered the traditional frosty relationship with India to be out of date, backed Musharraf on his forward-leaning posture on India. This has been, perhaps, the only issue on which he had consistently solid support from the political establishment—though not from the Islamist parties or their jihadi offshoots.

The Road Map Back to Democracy Goes Via Some Familiar Looking Stops

Musharraf pledged, from the first days of the praetorian takeover, that the military government would restore "true" democracy, rather than the "sham" democracy, under which the nation had lived, he said, since 1988. He was pressed by the United States, and other industrial countries, to produce a "road map" of how the military intended to get back to democracy, but was not able to do so with any clarity. Pressures from Western allies prompted him to set up a unit headed by a retired general to find the formula for the military's "true" democracy. This unit produced a series of plans over the three years of direct military government which form the intellectual blueprint for the hybrid military/civilian political structure (which seems to be the military's version of true democracy) that came into effect with the October 2002 elections. It is not unlike the version of 1985-88.

It departed from Zia ul Huq's design in one major way: while the political framework Musharraf put in place was quite similar to that of Zia, he also designed a political party structure that allowed for a kind of partisan politics. This put into effect one of the military's long-held objectives—the exclusion of the two mainstream parties, the PPP and the PML (Nawaz), though they are supported by the majority of Pakistani voters. A "King's Party," the PML-Q was created, loyal to the military government, and after the election of October 2002, an alliance was forged with the combined Islamist parties (called the MMA).

In that election, the military worked against the two main parties, and the (perhaps) unintended consequence was the election of 53 Islamist candidates to the National Assembly (more than ever before). Islamist parties also won a majority of seats in the NWFP Assembly, and a plurality in the Balochistan Assembly. The unexpectedly high number of Islamist seats in the National Assembly made the Islamist parties a factor that the government had to deal with when setting up the parliamentary government.

The relatively large number of Islamists in the National Assembly and their control of two provincial assemblies, complicated the political life of the new military/civilian hybrid government structure and made Musharraf's stated goal of modernization of the country (what he calls "enlightened moderation") much more difficult. His early alliance with the Islamists Alliance in the Assembly ruptured after the first year. Later, in effect, he succeeded in splitting the alliance, as one half, the JI, was implacably hostile to him and the government and advocated street action to bring him down, while the other half, the JUI, prefers to coexist with him to preserve its political gains in NWFP and Balochistan.

The return to a more representative political structure began in early 2001, about eighteen months after the military takeover. Musharraf introduced a system of local government that was designed, it was claimed, to devolve power to the "grassroots level." The main features of the new local set up were local elected councils and an elected administrator, called a Nazim. Local elections were held in March 2001 to great fanfare. Six years later, however, the elected local governments have yet to get complete traction, after a number of startup problems.[11]

"Devolving power" to the local governments is a favorite mantra of Pakistani military governments. Musharraf's action harkened back to an almost identical action by Zia ul Huq, and even to somewhat similar political "reforms" introduced by Ayub Khan in the early 1960s. In fact, bringing political power to the grassroots is not the primary impetus of these devolution programs. They have been implemented in a "top down" fashion by the military governments in order to increase their power at the center. "Devolution" in the Pakistani context appears to mean transferring power from the provinces to the local level, but has generally not been supported by constitutional changes or by full financial devolution.[12]

9/11 Changes Much in Pakistan, But Not Everything

There is one other parallel with the Zia years. A war changed almost everything, and in so doing gave the regime a major increase in international acceptance and legitimacy, as well as more political space to continue to solidify the military's dominance of Pakistani politics. Overnight, Pakistan turned 180 degrees in some of its foreign policies, became a close ally of the United States, and reaped economic benefits from that new-found alli-

---

11   Not the least of which was the failure to provide resources and or a resource base (such as earmarked tax revenues) to the local governments.

12   Ali Cheema, Asim Ijaz Khwaja, Adnan Qadir, *Decentralization in Pakistan: Context, Content, and Causes* (Cambridge: Faculty Research Working Papers Series, Harvard University, John F. Kennedy School of Government, April 2005).

ance that boosted its economy. While the War on Terror was, in one sense, beneficial to the Musharraf regime and its political aims, it also had serious political costs—public opinion was from the outset, and remains, much opposed to the United States alliance. This forced the regime to go easy on some of its domestic reform agenda, but the serious consequence was the serious rise in public approval for the Taliban and Al Qaeda, which made it much more difficult to push back against encroachments of extremists in the tribal areas and other parts of the Frontier.

In the first two years of the Musharraf military regime, sectarian violence between Sunni and Shia hit squads seemed to be on hold. But by summer 2001, it was on the rise again. On August 14, two of the most extreme sectarian groups, Lashkar-I-Jhangvi and Sipah-e-Mohammed Pakistan were banned by the President. This action was probably good practice for what was to come. Despite the substantial public opposition, as well as the dissent of a few high ranking military officers, Musharraf did not hesitate after 9/11. He immediately joined the United States in the "War on Terror." He retired or sidelined the senior military officers who opposed his decision or who had been suspected of having Islamist sympathies. Musharraf was swimming upstream against a full tide of anti-American popular feeling, yet the revamped military hierarchy backed him without caveat.

The campaign against extremist groups continued and was intensified when it became clear that Sunni/Shia violence was deeply seated and would persist in the absence of harsher measures. Five such organizations were banned in January 2002, though this was mostly to mollify India after the jihadist attack in Delhi.[13] In November 2003, the President banned aother six jihadist organizations.[14]

Concurrently with the campaign against domestic extremist groups, the government's efforts to arrest foreign terrorists (Al Qaeda) began to show impressive results. However, anti-Musharraf setiment and rhetoric grew apace. These feelings were exacerbated by more military strikes against extremist positions in the tribal areas. This growing antipathy between extremists and Musharraf culminated in two serious assassination attempts against him—one of which came very close to ending his life.

---

13   The five were Jaish-I-Mohammed, Lashkar Taiba, Sipah-I-Sahaba Pakistan, Tehrik-I-Jaferia, and Tanzim Nifaz-I-Shariat-I-Mohammedi. A sixth, Sunni Tehrik, was put on a watch list. Mostly, however, the five banned organizations changed their names and were back in business. Their leaders and members, who were originally detained, found themselves back on the street in a month or two.

14   The Shia terrorist group Islami Therik-i-Pakistan and the Sunni groups Millat-i-Islamia Pakistan, Khudam-ul-Islam, Jamiat-ul-Fur, Jamiat-il-Ansar, and Hizbut-Tahir.

Building Hybrid Government in a War Setting

The all-too-familiar, carbon-copy transition from direct military rule to hybrid military/civilian government was complicated by the War on Terror—easier in some respects and more difficult in others. The external support and legitimacy the war gave was juxtaposed to the serious public disaffection with the government's unalloyed support for the United States against the Taliban and Al Qaeda. In January 2002, Musharraf announced that elections would be held that October—the third anniversary of the military takeover—as he had promised when he came to power. In April that year he concluded that he should not hold national elections until he had ensured that he would be able to remain as President over the long term, i.e. that he would not face an elected National Assembly that would, under the constitution, be able to remove him and elect someone else to the position.[15] He proposed to hold a referendum which would extend his term as President for five years—thus to 2007. The referendum was carried, the government claimed, by a large margin, though many believed it rigged.[16] It was viewed widely as unconstitutional, as it was clearly inconsistent with the constitutionally prescribed way of electing a President. Musharraf stated publicly later that the referendum had been a mistake.

The process of increasing the power of the President and creating, in effect, a hybrid Presidential/Parliamentary system began in June 2002. President Musharraf, newly strengthened by his victory in the April referendum, put forward for "debate" proposed constitutional amendments designed to increase the power of the office he held.[17] The most controversial would enable the President to dismiss the Prime Minister, and the government, without reference to the National Assembly. Such a provision had been added to the constitution by Zia ul Huq in 1984, and removed from it in early 1997 by the parliament in which Nawaz Sharif had a heavy majority. Perhaps his most important proposal was to set

---

15   The odds of this ever happening, given the predominance of the military and its proclivity to make elections come out the way it wants, seem infinitesimal.

16   Critics claimed the voting was marked by an overabundance of irregularities. The *Daily Times* reported on May 1 2002 that "blatant irregularities were seen at polling centers across Pakistan as both eligible and ineligible voters cast their votes, often more than once. Many voters openly queued up time and again to vote. In Lahore, a group of around a dozen people, each with both thumbs marked with indelible ink indicating they had already voted twice, turned up at one polling station to try to vote a third time...."

17   Where this debate was to be held, given that the only elected representative institutions at the time were the newly elected local councils, is an interesting question. They were, in any case, hotly debated in the press.

up a ten-member National Security Council, headed by the President, and including the Chiefs of the military services (also to be named by the President instead of the Prime Minister), that would have the power to overrule decisions of an elected government on "national security" grounds.

In July, Musharraf began to prepare for the October 2002 National Assembly elections by ensuring that he and those chosen by the military would not be encumbered by credible opposition. The President decreed that persons who had held the office of Prime Minister twice in the past would be prohibited from holding it in the future. This eliminated both Nawaz Sharif and Benazir Bhutto from contesting the elections, had they chosen to challenge all the other hurdles already in their path. The proposals, put forward in June, to increase the power of the President (euphemistically explained as increasing "checks and balances") were promulgated in August as the Legal Framework Order (LFO). These were rushed through whatever "debate" the government permitted in order to be in place before the October Parliamentary elections.

The election itself was not a great success from the military's point of view. It resulted, effectively, in a "hung" parliament—which was not able at first to organize itself to do business, or elect leaders. The PML-Q, the "King's Party," with 25.7 percent of the vote, did not win even a plurality in the National Assembly; it won 69 seats, the second highest total, two fewer than the PPP which received 25.8 percent of the votes and took 71 seats. The old PML of Nawaz Sharif garnered 9.4 percent of the votes and took 19 seats. The unwelcome surprise was the strong performance of the alliance of five Islamic parties (the Muttahida Majlis-e-Amal Pakistan—MMA for short) which, with 11.3 percent of the vote, won 53 seats.

Musharraf's first real taste of Pakistani politics began at this juncture. It took over a month for a governing coalition to be worked out which included some independents and smaller parties but depended on a rump group of wayward PPP members (called the PPPP) in coalition with the PML-Q. A carefully worked-out arrangement with the MMA ensured that the government could muster a majority in support of the Prime Minister yet preserved the independence of the alliance to assert its Islamist agenda. With this combustible combination, a civilian government was formed and the National Assembly could meet to elect (actually validate Musharraf's choice) a Prime Minister, Mir Zafarullah Jamali.

Hybrid Government Again

An impasse immediately gripped the new Parliament over the question of whether it would accept President Musharraf's August 2002 LFO, the package of measures increasing his powers. On this, the MMA joined with the opposition to demand that the LFO be submitted for legislative approval. He refused to do so, knowing that it could not muster the constitutionally required two thirds majority in both houses. The impasse continued for the rest of 2003, rendering the Parliament unable to conduct any business.

At the end of that year, Musharraf and the MMA struck a deal: the President agreed to retire from the Army and give up the position as Chief of Army Staff at the end of 2004 while remaining as President, to submit his holding of the President's office to a vote of confidence in the National Assembly, the Senate, and the Provincial Assemblies, to establish the National Security Council by an act of parliament. (as opposed to a decree by the President), and that any decision to dismiss the National Assembly would be referred to the Supreme Court within thirty days. The MMA, for its part, agreed that the rest of the LFO would be incorporated in the constitution as the 17th amendment without being contested in Parliament, to support Musharraf's program for modernization, and his government.

Musharraf began 2004 by winning, in January, the vote of confidence he had agreed to undergo in the above compromise. This, with the acquiescence of Parliament to the LFO that had occurred the previous month, fortified his hold on power. In April 2004, Parliament approved the creation of the National Security Council (NSC), which institutionalized the military's grip on government and its policy-making.

However the "military-mullah alliance" (the other "MMA") broke apart over the NSC vote, and Musharraf had to seek the votes of independents and breakaways from other parties. The MMA had had second thoughts, evidently. Then began the long colloquy in which Musharraf used the MMA's alleged perfidy, ultimately, to renege on his agreement to shed his uniform by the end of the year. Many of the same independents and breakaways helped the government to push through the Assembly the legislation that allowed him to retain his uniform, i.e. to remain as Chief of Army Staff and President simultaneously.

Trouble in the Minority Regions Again (Still)

The election of an MMA majority in the NWFP Assembly and an MMA plurality in Balochistan was, perhaps, a portent of coming trouble in the Frontier and the Tribal Areas (FATA) that border it and in Balochistan. There were also troubling signs of growing opposition in Sindh. The age-old problems between the center (Islamabad) and the minority provinces, that have roiled politics since 1947, heightened the fissiparous strains in Pakistan.

In the Tribal Areas, the writ of central government has always been weak and erratic. This legacy of semi-autonomy inherited from the British colonial regime that chose to exercise the writ of the Raj through payoffs and occasional punitive raids in those troublesome, freebooting areas, has come back to haunt the Musharraf regime. Successive Pakistani regimes since 1947 have chosen to follow the British example; they have been content to concede to tribal law rather than enforce the laws of Pakistan, and have not endeavored to promote development and education which would have weakened the hold of tribal leaders and law over time.

These areas, very fundamentalist in outlook and tribal in culture, became havens for the Taliban and Al Qaeda remnants that escaped from United States forces in Afghanistan. With the attention of the United States diverted to its war of choice in Iraq, Al Qaeda and the Taliban had the time and space in these areas (given the shelter they had been provided and which they enlarged through intimidation and territorial control) to catch their breath and regain the initiative. The Taliban have been infiltrating back into Afghanistan from their havens in Balochistan and FATA, and in effect waging a guerrilla war using terrorist tactics to overturn the government of Afghanistan, prevent the political and economic reconstruction of the country, and drive Western forces—the United States and NATO—out.

In addition, there has been a growing insurgency in Balochistan—a province that has a history of insurrections which have plagued the central government—that threatened the domestic stability and unity of the country.[18] The killing of Baloch nationalist leader, Nawab Akbar Bugti, in 2006 created a domestic political firestorm. Subsequent events have reduced the visibility of the insurgency in Balochistan, but it remains a highly sensitive issue for the federal government. As is almost always the case, the quarrel between the center and the provincials is over resources. The Baloch insur-

---

18   Amir Mir, "Balochistan: Dire Prophecies," *South Asia Intelligence Review*, 4, No. 30, Feb. 6, 2006, accessed on 2-6-06 at http://www.satp.orgtp/asir/index.htm.

gents seek a greater portion of their gas reserves and other natural resources. They have a point: most of the economic "rent" that these projects earn goes straight to the central government.[19]

Reaping the Harvest of Zia's Islamization

A serious commitment to Islamization began under Zia ul Huq. This provided the military government with some legitimacy and a support base, and became, in turn, entwined with the army and ISI's adventures in Afghanistan and Kashmir. There was a twenty-five year period when the entanglement of the Islamists with the military—the dominant political force of Pakistan—and thus with the government, embedded Islamism into Pakistani society, and transformed it into a country that is much less tolerant, much less pluralistic, but more militant and violent.

After September 11, 2001, Musharraf's government needed to reverse those trends if Pakistan were to escape becoming a pariah state, viewed by the United States and its allies as an enemy that harbored terrorists and fostered terrorism. Returning to the vision and concept of Jinnah was squarely in Pakistan's best interests—for its economic as well as its political future. Moreover, harking back to Jinnah appeared to accord with Musharraf's personal preferences, given his professed inclination toward a moderate, modern version of an Islamic state. In his efforts to reverse the hard-line characteristics of the more Islamized Pakistan, Musharraf advocated policies of "enlightened moderation," namely a society ordered more along the lines that Jinnah envisioned. He often invoked Jinnah in his public exhortations about the need for a moderate, tolerant society in which extremism and sectarian violence must be curbed.

Two problems have significantly inhibited progress on "enlightened moderation" and posed enormous challenges for Musharraf and his government in moving society away from the rigidities of religious orthodoxy that Islamists have slowly imposed on it and on the mindset of much of its population. The first is the length of time that Islamization has had to sink its intellectual and scriptural roots into society. It will take sustained heavy lifting and much political courage to pull them up. Neither the elected governments of 1988 to 1999, nor the military government of Musharraf, have

---

19   The economic definition of "rent" is the profit from that comes from a differential advantage in production; in this case the differential is the location (in Balochistan) of the energy resources.

been able (or much inclined most of the time) to push back the Islamization process that became institutionalized under Zia ul Huq.

The second problem is that Faustian political bargains with Islamist elements have continued, despite Musharraf's rhetoric about the need for "enlightened moderation." These bargains have a long tradition in Pakistani politics, having been practiced by civilian governments going back to Liaquat Ali Khan in 1949 and to military governments of the Ayub Khan vintage. Governments since the late 1970s have exacerbated this by using extremist, jihadi groups—offshoots of Islamist parties—as tools of Pakistani foreign policy. This has had domestic repercussions in the inevitable spillover of jihadi culture into Pakistan's domestic life. The pattern is that the broader national interests of a Pakistani state that resembles the one envisioned by Jinnah have been constantly traded off for narrow, short-term political gains.

The Musharraf government was no exception to this rule. It used jihadi groups as its predecessors had in Kashmir until it became counterproductive to do so, as the peace process with India advanced over the last few years and the war on terror made it inadvisable. The problem is that the military cannot always control its erstwhile jihadi partners. There is always the potential danger that a jihadi group, acting completely on its own, will carry out an act of terrorism that will undermine the budding peace process.

The President and his government pushed for "enlightened moderation" primarily with rhetoric. Declarations of intent were its main weapon, though it also banned many hard-line, extremist groups, and tried to curtail the relationship between them and the military intelligence agencies. But sustained political action to grind down the hard edges of Islamization is not as easy as government rhetoric might suggest. The Islamists, preying on a pious and uneducated public (in a country in which two-thirds of the population is rural) have thwarted, through the mullahs to whom much of the rural populace pays great respect, each proposal designed to advance "enlightened moderation" which they find threatening, In every case, the government has discerned—rightly or wrongly—a groundswell of opposition that it did not care to face.

Musharraf, perhaps intemperately, called for changes in the blasphemy law in 2000, and then backed down in the face of Islamist criticism. There have been other about-faces after bold, assertive rhetoric about spreading "enlightened moderation." The government gave way, for example, in the face of an Islamist demand that the bearer's religion be inscribed in Pakistani passports, and was loath to take action to enforce the law in other cases. The only case in which Musharraf has shown resolve and follow up is the amendment to the Hudood laws.[20] This reduced blatant discrimination against women, but it stands alone as a success in pushing back Islamism.

Connected with his rhetoric about "enlightened moderation" was Musharraf's seeming obsession with the international image of Pakistan. His public statements indicated that he wished that image to be one of an enlightened and moderate state. This perception was continually tarnished by events that are often related to the tribal *mores* of many parts of Pakistan (which "scriptural" retrogressive Islam has found reason to support). In cases that have attracted Western attention and criticism, the President tended to blame the victim for tarnishing Pakistan's image abroad rather than the *mores* which led to the incident.[21] These cases have usually involved violence or discrimination against women which, as will be seen in Chapter 9, are serious and widespread in Pakistan.[22]

Musharraf was not helped in moving "enlightened moderation" by his choice of political friends. His main political allies for the year or so after the elections of 2002 were the Islamist alliance (the MMA), and the PML-Q that he had created. The MMA was, by definition, opposed to the concept of "enlightened moderation," viewing it as secularism in disguise. Though a rift soon opened between more hard-line elements of the MMA

---

20 Even on this there was great drama. The proposal to amend the Huddood laws, which were described in Chapter 5, was announced with great fanfare, though it was limited in scope only to repair some of the worst parts of these laws. However, even those limited proposals were resisted by many of the PML-Q's government supporters. The government's vacillation evoked much outrage in the English language press. See *Daily Times* editorial, "Retreat in the Face of Extremism?" Thursday, August 10, 2006. Access http://www.dailytimes.com.pk/default.asp?date=2%2F10%2F2006. For detailed expositions on the Hudood Ordinance see "Pakistan—Women in Pakistan Disadvantaged and Denied Their Rights" (Amnesty International, 1995), accessed on http://web.amnesty.org/library/print/ENGASA330231995 and Rana Riaz Saeed, *The Controversial Hudood Ordinance 1979* (Pakistan: Development Advocates & Lobbyists, December 2004).

21 The two most celebrated recent cases involve Mukhtar Mai, who was gang-raped at the order of a village council in Punjab for an alleged infraction of her brother (in fact, he was innocent of the charge) and a female doctor who was gang-raped in Balochistan, allegedly by Army officers, and also persecuted as if she were the offender. Both these women courageously resisted the effort to sweep these terrible acts under the rug and fought back through the courts or the media. In each case, the President publicly criticized the victim as someone who wanted to tarnish the national image.

22 In these cases, and in many other similar ones, there is an intertwining of Islamic scriptural doctrine (as interpreted by conservative or fundamentalist clerics) and tribal mores, which is little understood in the Western world. This is not to excuse, in any way, the acts themselves, which are reprehensible by any standard. They should be punished under any system of justice that recognizes international law and human rights. But such acts tend to tar Islam with a brush that is, perhaps, a bit too broad.

and Musharraf, he remained bound to the more conservative political elements because of his dependence on the new PML (the former PML-Q melded with a number of smaller PML factions), which comprised the more conservative elements of the old PML. It has been at the bottom of some of his retreats from policies that offended the Islamists, namely attempts to undo the blasphemy law, and he had to override strong PML opposition to push through the amendment to the Hudood laws.

2007—Things Fall Apart

What President Musharraf and his military/civilian team did not seem to realize is that, in replicating Zia ul Huq's hybrid governing structure, they had built a system that was inherently unstable in 21st-century South Asia. It was one that implied continual stress between a military determined to maintain its political power and the privileges that power had brought, and a civil society that no longer responds to the "national savior" stereotype of the country's armed forces and is increasingly unwilling to cede sovereignty to them. The forced stability of the Musharraf regime could not last, particularly when the President made known his ambitions to continue both as President and Army Chief, which foreshadowed permanent military domination of Pakistan's politics. Musharraf's case would have been much stronger with the public and the outside world if he had earned the legitimacy that a record of political success generally brings. Except, however, on economic growth (covered in Chapter 9), his record as described above was mediocre at best. And while the macro-economy looked much improved, poverty remained stubbornly high, and the bulk of the benefits seemed to go to the well-off; the perception of most Pakistanis was that the rich had become richer.

His political reforms were clearly, to the Pakistani political class, borrowed from the past and designed to maintain the military in power. Devolution was a sham, which aimed only to reduce the political power of the provinces and increase it at the center. "Enlightened moderation" was a hollow mockery as the extremists continued to gain ground against the writ of the state. Hybrid government itself was a fig leaf for military government. There had been no discernable progress in people's fundamental needs such as public education, health care, women's rights, or civil rights. During the last two years of his first term in office, President Musharraf became a good democrat in one sense. He spent much of 2006 and 2007, the last two years of his five-year first term, running for reelection. As the election approached, his political troubles mounted, and he became more isolated. His ability, and perhaps desire, to pursue coherent and forward-looking policies, either domestic or international, diminished. His search for political allies widened to include former political enemies. And his political enemies began to coalesce against him. Uncertainty surrounded his political future and that of the country.

His strategy seemed to consist solely of finding reasons and ways to continue as both Army Chief and President. His attempts to arrange that politically by shifting his alliances and legally by interfering with the Supreme Court brought down his carefully constructed hybrid political structure even sooner than it would have deconstructed on account of its inherent instability. Once his system began to unravel, it did so at ever increasing speed until, in early November, he felt that he could only save himself and the military's dominance by running what was, in effect, a military coup against his own government. On November 3, 2007, the Musharraf era of benign military intervention effectively ended when, speaking as Army Chief, he declared an emergency and suspended the parts of the constitution that delineate civil and political rights.

A number of adverse developments came together to cause the system suddenly to implode. The precipitate cause came when Musharraf, intemperately, tried to force the Chief Justice of the Supreme Court to retire by referring him to a judicial review panel for unprofessional conduct. Musharraf evidently felt it necessary to get rid of this Chief Justice as he feared the judge would lead the court to upholding the plaintiffs in several cases which challenged his wish to remain in uniform while being President. Under the Chief Justice, Iftekar Chowdhury, the court had ruled against the government on a range of cases involving the disappearance of persons suspected of terrorism. Justice Chowdhury refused to retire, and was instead suspended and, for a while, placed under house arrest. The resulting protest, initiated by the country's lawyers, provoked an escalating series of strikes and demonstrations that began to draw the political parties into the fray. Musharraf was forced by the ensuring political uproar to respect a court decision that restored Chief Justice Chowdhury to the bench just as these cases were about to be heard by the court. That was probably the precipitate cause of the emergency proclamation which placed those parts of the constitution under which the suits could be tried into temporary limbo. A number of unfriendly justices were dismissed when they refused to take a loyalty oath (a repeat of a similar oath in 2000).

In the same time period, the charade that he called "enlightened moderation" was revealed to domestic foe and foreign friend alike as an empty box. He failed in his attempt to control the Taliban in Tribal Areas and eliminate Al Qaeda by deploying the Pakistani Army in the region. The latter did not want relish the fight and retreated after several months under the cover of "agreements" with the tribal leaders to stop Taliban incursions into Afghanistan. These agreements were generally regarded as worthless, and proved within only a few weeks to be so.[23] This inability, or unwillingness, on the part of the Army and the government to push back against the extremists, and to prevent large-scale Taliban incursions into Afghanistan to attack United States and NATO has soured the good relationship Musharraf had with the West after 9/11. The probability that he would ensure that the elections came out his way also put his Western allies in a bind: they needed Pakistan's cooperation against the terrorists, yet couldn't turn a blind eye to the likelihood of a rigged election. [24]

Western governments and observers often appeared more concerned also with jihadi extremist encroachment on the state's writ than the political establishment in Pakistan. The jihadis continued to expand their sphere of influence, not only in tribal areas, but in the surrounding so-called settled areas. The government had actually lost control of much territory west of the Indus River by the end of 2007. Winning it back would prove costly, as was demonstrated by the Army's decision to retake the Swat valley, a mountainous and very scenic area. The military campaign to recover Swat cost the Army many lives, and a few helicopter gunships.

The Army and the government faced and face extraordinarily complicated issues in deciding how and whether to respond to jihadi encroach-

---

23 In frustration, the United States or NATO forces are thought to have struck unilaterally at al Qaeda leaders in the tribal areas, though the facts surrounding these strikes are vague and ambiguous. It has not been clear whether there was any prior consultation. Pakistan has, on one occasion, said there wasn't, and on another claimed the deed for itself. Nor is it clear if any of the al Qaeda leaders were killed as a result of the strikes. The only thing that is clear is that the domestic fallout against Musharraf is intense each time it happens

24 That the Taliban and al Qaeda have sheltered in the tribal areas and along the border in remote areas of the Frontier and Balochistan and been aided by sympathetic elements of the local populations seems undeniable. This creates tension between the Musharraf government and the United States on one hand and additional tension between the government and its Islamist critics on the other. The United States presses for Pakistani government action in these areas against Al Qaeda and the Taliban, but when the government acts it has a difficult time because of local support for the terrorists and complications this causes in domestic politics. When it goes too slowly or carefully, it encounters problems with the United States, its major ally.

ments. The primary challenge is to the Army itself; clearly this is a severe test of its loyalties, and its reputation for discipline. Despite the fact that most of the jihadis are of the Salafist school of Islamic thought which rejects the Sufism that runs through the Islam of most Punjabis, who make up the great bulk of the Army, its Punjabi majority appears reluctant to take on the extremists. Moreover, over 20 per cent of the force is Pashtun and convincing such troops that the mainly Pashtun Taliban are the enemy is also an uphill task.

Keeping Army discipline intact is not made any easier by the political atmosphere that certainly affects some of the officer corps. The so-called War on Terror includes the internal struggle in Pakistan against these jihadi elements, which is commonly viewed by the great majority of the Pakistani public as America's war. This is part and parcel of the general rejection of American policy in the Islamic world and the widespread approval of Osama bin Laden and acceptance of his declarations that the United States is out to destroy Islam. The public view on this is certainly also the Army's view. These attitudes would complicate any government's anti-extremist policy. The Musharraf government seemed paralyzed by the complexities and often took no action until it was too late. There was no better example of the Musharraf government's ambiguity and paralysis on the question of spreading jihadi extremism than the Lal Masjid, or "Red Mosque" controversy. Musharraf and his team showed an unfathomable weakness and vacillation in the face of a long and humiliating provocation by two extremist clerics who set up mosques and madrassas on land belonging to the state in the middle of Islamabad, the capital. The message from those mosques was at the outer limits of radical Islamist hortatory rhetoric. Waves of madrassa students, especially from an Islamist girls school, were sent into other areas of the city to intimidate citizens whom they believed werer not living according to the precepts of Sharia law. Through a long and troubling confrontation, the government chose to negotiate rather than impose its writ. Finally, it acted with force, but it had waited so long that the clerics had been able to reinforce their students with well-armed jihadi fighters. The human cost taking down this mosque complex after a long period of indecision and waffling was far higher than it should have been.

Overlaying these developments, which were rapidly eroding whatever political foundations the Musharraf dispensation had after eight years of steadily deteriorating governance, was his search for a political alliance that would keep him in power. He appeared ready to jettison his "King's Party,"

185

the PML-Q, if the right partner came along. Most of the attention centered on Benazir Bhutto and her PPP. The rumor of a possible alliance between the two were circulating much before Musharraf's political troubles began. I first heard of the virtues of such a deal while visiting Lahore in the spring of 2006, and in those days it was inspired by an optimism that considered these two political leaders as "like-minded" moderates and that a coalition of moderate forces would be a strong political force that could put Pakistan on a sustained, progressive path of political, economic, and social development. The deal envisioned by the moderates was nothing less that a radical realignment of the Pakistan political spectrum. It was believed that it would bring together the large and small political parties which are moderate and, more or less, secular[25] (the PPP, MQM, and ANP) and the political actors— Musharraf and the moderate officers of the Army—with the authority and means to push back Islamism.

This alliance of the like-minded would supposedly give Musharraf the political support, if he has the will, finally to deliver on his rhetoric to bring about a more moderate society and reduce not only extremism but intolerance and the encroachment of Islamism on Pakistan. This promise would have considerable support among voters. With the PPP adding its rural vote bank in Sindh (and its declining vote bank in Southern Punjab) to the MQM's vote bank in the urban areas of Sindh, this combination would probably have had a comfortable plurality in the National Assembly. In retrospect, it left out one important thing: the unwillingness of either leader to play second fiddle to the other.

Talks went on between the two camps for about a year and seemed, to outsiders at least, only to get serious when Musharraf began to run into political trouble. For a time in the spring and summer of 2007, when Musharraf was trying to balance the political fallout of his action against the Chief Justice with the need to find some way to push back against the jihadis, it looked as if a deal would be struck. One factor that inhibited Musharraf, it now appears, was the Army's dislike and distrust of her and of her long-deceased father.[26] A deal would have included the government dropping the court cases for corruption against her and her

---

25   To the extent that any of the political parties can afford to be known to the public as secular. This word has a somewhat different meaning in Pakistan politics—suggesting that they do not favor making Pakistan a more "Islamist" state than it already is.

26   Musharraf was quoted later in the Pakistani press as admitting that Ms. Bhutto was extremely unpopular with the Army. *Daily Times* article of January 14, 2008. See www.dailytimes.com.pk/default.asp?page=2008\01\14\story_14-1-2008_pg1_1

husband (charges she always labeled as "political") and allowing Bhutto to engage in political activity. Musharraf would have likely received her party's support in the Presidential election. Ms. Bhutto's insistence that he agree to take off his uniform at some future time was thought to be the sticking point during this period. The deal was never consummated. As Musharraf's political position steadily eroded after the confrontation with the judiciary and the lawyers and his continued loss of government writ to the jihadists, Bhutto appeared to elevate her price. Musharraf probably found the cost of a coalition with her too high (possibly an agreement that she would be Prime Minister). How much the Army's dislike of Bhutto was behind Musharraf's unwillingness to pay that price is not clear.

She returned dramatically to Pakistan in October under threat of death from the jihadists after the Musharraf government agreed not to prosecute her and allowed her to lead her party in the upcoming election. She narrowly escaped death on her first day back when a suicide bomber killed about 140 people around her car, but missed her. There remained talk of a deal with Musharraf after the election, but the possibility of that seemed to evaporate after he declared the emergency on November 3.

The rest of the story of the Musharraf years is well known, and the denouement is yet to come. Under severe pressure from abroad as well as domestically, Musharraf rescinded the emergency and restored the constitution in mid-December. He has not restored the judges he forced out. He was sworn in as President and has retired from the Army to be a civilian President. For the first time in eight years, the Pakistan Army has a new Chief. Though the new appointment is said to be Musharraf clone, we will see what happens if the Army concludes that supporting him is not in its long-term interests. What happened in November 1990 to President Ershad in Pakistan's former other half, Bangladesh, might be instructive.

Benazir Bhutto was assassinated on December 27, 2007 at a political rally in Rawalpindi. Her death is still being investigated as this is written, but the attack had many of the hallmarks of the Al Qaeda/Taliban/jihadist groups that have killed so many people in the last few years in Pakistan. She had many flaws, and was not the perfect vehicle for the moderate hopes and aspirations of the Pakistani people, but she was the only consistent voice of moderation and resistance to the steady jihadi encroachment on the Pakistani state. She had a mass following that had only grown in her absence, or perhaps in the courage of her return. Flaws and all, she spoke to some interior part of a great many Pakistanis who want only to live a better, peaceful life in the 21st century and who saw her as the embodiment of those hopes. Without her, the voice of moderation in Pakistan may be still.

9

ECONOMIC AND SOCIAL DEVELOPMENT AND THE NGOS

Economic Underachievement in Bangladesh

The Bangladesh record in economic development has been, after a disastrous first five years, one of continual improvement and rising economic growth. The country, its private entrepreneurial sector, and its people have escaped from the "basket-case" category (perhaps they never deserved to be in it) with the help of international and bilateral donors, NGOs, and under the direction of some pretty good economic leaders. The World Bank summarized its progress in 2003 as "remarkable."[1] On the other hand, Bangladesh remains a consistent economic underachiever, mainly because of its seriously deficient governance.[2] This has been a constant drag through all the Bangladeshi governments after Ziaur Rahman. Governments have been unable, or unwilling, to build and strengthen economic institutions, and thirty-three years after independence, almost half the population is still counted as below the poverty line. In fact, it is striking that social development has progressed more rapidly than the growth of income and the reduction of poverty. According to the World Bank, "Bangladesh's faster gains in human development than in income growth result from the public policies that have complemented the remarkable energy of the grassroots level...channeled by the country's nongovernmental organizations and community-based organizations, many of which are world leaders in their innovative ideas and operational methods."[3]

---

1   World Bank, *Bangladesh Development...*, p. i.

2   World Bank, *Bangladesh Growth and Export Competitiveness*, pp. 3-4.

3   Ibid, *Bangladesh Development...*, p. i.

The economy is much more vulnerable than it should be, after thirty-three years, to the vagaries of the world market and to the degradation of the environment that high population density has produced. For example, in a country in which agriculture is the backbone of the economy (70 per cent of the population still makes its living on the land), soil fertility is being degraded by the intense utilization of land, poor farming techniques, and deforestation. Yields are beginning to decline, and it is unclear if the great successes of the past decade, the achievement of self-sufficiency in rice and all food grains, can be sustained.

Mujib's Populism—Politics, Not Ideology

The Mujib government seems to have set out to prove that Bangladesh was, indeed, a "basket case." The Awami League government came to power in 1972 with its left wing strengthened by the war, and Bangladeshis expected a radical departure from the policies of the past. Unfortunately Sheikh Mujib lacked the vision and coherent ideology to set Bangladesh on a stable and realistic economic course. Governing was not Mujib's strong point — he has been characterized as a leader "whose mobilization capability greatly exceeded his administrative skills."[4] His objective was to please his main supporters, the rising Bengali middle classes—the so-called "vernacular elite"—whose interests were mainly in the rural economy, and were anything but socialist. His strategy to satisfy the AL's vocal left wing but not offend his main supporters was to nationalize most of the industrial assets of Bangladesh but not touch the rural economy.

In the first two years of independence, fiscal and foreign exchange constraints seemed to be forgotten, or wished away. But this could only be temporary. Economic laws reasserted their dominance after a couple of years of grace provided by foreign donors and a favorable international climate. As international assistance wound down to more sustainable levels by 1973, the economy started to come apart. Economists agree that overly expansionary fiscal and monetary policies are at the root of the severe macroeconomic problems that brought the Bangladesh economy to its knees in 1974 and 1975. Fiscal policy was a disaster. An unknown but huge deficit in 1972 was followed by an even larger one, recorded at 16 per cent of GDP, in 1973. The money supply expanded by over 70 per cent in 1972 and 16 per cent in 1973 as the banking system provided large amounts of

---

4   Stanley A. Kochanek, *Patron-Client Politics and Business in Bangladesh* (New Delhi: Sage Publications, 1993), p. 83.

deficit financing and international donors very large inflows of foreign assistance.[5] The accumulated pressures drove inflation up to 59 per cent in 1974 despite better fiscal and monetary performance. "By the third quarter of 1974, Bangladesh was on the verge of defaulting on her outstanding commitments for payments for imports, for which there were no funds."[6]

With some fanfare, Mujib had created a Planning Commission with four leading academics. It began its work in what can only be described as a "hothouse" atmosphere, with unparalleled freedom of action and produced in a few months the first Five-Year Plan, "determined to effect fundamental structural changes."[7] The Commissioner argued for total socialism—for the "socialist reconstruction of Bangladesh."[8] Mujib and his cabinet opted for a radical program of nationalism as his industrial policy, but "rejected similar proposals for land reform and changes in land-tenure relationships."[9] In a single day, in late March, 1972, the government's holdings of industrial and commercial assets jumped from 34 per cent to 92 per cent of total assets.[10] Much to the surprise, evidently, of the Planning Commission, the response of the private sector to the announced objective of "socialist transformation" was to take its money elsewhere—either abroad or to other economic sectors, such as trade or construction, where such restrictions did not exist. The implementation of these policies was spotty and unenthusiastic, at best. By mid-1974, the economy had collapsed and famine was approaching. Bangladesh became the laboratory for the study of famine as primarily an economic phenomenon, caused by mistaken economic management. The amount of food produced and available in Bangladesh in that year was greater than the year before or the year after, yet there was a severe famine that year.

In a hyper-inflationary situation, consumers wanted to make sure they had a supply of food before the price went even higher. Farmers held grain off the market waiting for the price to rise. In essence, it was the lack of confidence in the government to control inflation that set loose what could

5   In fact, Bangladesh became "aid-dependent" at that point, using aid inflows to finance budget deficits, a habit that it has never completely kicked.

6   N. Islam, *Development Planning in Bangladesh: A Case Study in Political Economy* (London: Hurst and Co., 1977), p. 146.

7   Ibid., p. 77.

8   Ibid., quoting from Rehman Sobhan and Mufazzer Ahmed, *Public Enterprise in an Intermediate Regime: A Study in the Political Economy of Bangladesh* (Dhaka: Bangladesh Institute of Development Studies, 1980).

9   Ibid., p. 80.

10   Ibid., p. 81.

be described as rational responses on the part of consumers and producers. Those without resources to buy higher priced food were the victims. As usual, there is a wide range of estimates as to the number of victims of the 1974 famine, but not about who they were: clearly they were the poor. Help from international emergency assistance began to arrive in August, but it came too late for more than 100,000 people who died of starvation. July 1974 represents the point of inflection; the socialist/populist experiment was over.[11]

The Long Slog Out of a Deep Hole

Succeeding governments have slowly worked back from the economic hole that Sheik Mujib and the AL dug for the country after independence. It has been a slow progress away from statist policies and orientation, and the path has been erratic, albeit in the direction of market orientation and an emphasis on the private sector.

Zia's Economics: Pragmatism and Politics

When he came to power in November 1975 as Chief of Army Staff and Deputy CMLA, the Ziaul Rahman's martial law government faced a major economic crisis. Macroeconomic tools—money creation and budget deficit financing—were still wildly expansionary. Zia moved slowly and cautiously toward the position of the donors, industrialists, and bureaucrats. He especially needed the international donors, whose aid and support was vital to stabilizing the economy. Also a shift away from policies identified with Mujib provided a rationale for the army retaining power.

He gradually adopted an economic policy that was broadly reminiscent of policy under Ayub Khan in United Pakistan from 1958 to 1968. He knew and felt comfortable with this policy, which had been successful in raising growth rates. It encouraged private sector growth, emphasized export-oriented industry, and rapid export growth.

Zia added to the Ayub model an emphasis on agricultural production. His government boosted subsidies to the agricultural sector, and he spent much time traveling to promote self-help programs to increase the production of rice and other food crops. Rural production increased as a result. His "market-friendly" economic policies brought about accelerating growth,

---

11   Hossain, "The Economy: Towards Stabilization," *The Zia Episode in Bangladesh Politics,* p. 69.

which has characterized the economy since the late 1970s. Slowly and erratically, successive governments liberalized agriculture and trade and deregulated industry. Despite the halting and stop-and-go implementation, the result has been faster, and steadier, growth over the 25 year period that followed.[12] This has been "a key element in poverty reduction."[13] Zia turned Mujib's industrial policy on its head, gradually pointing the country toward a private sector orientation. This policy, which was expanded as he grew politically stronger, resulted in the sale of over 350 enterprises in the seven succeeding years; at one point in the mid-1980s, academics pointed to Bangladesh as a model of divestiture.[14]

Ershad's Economics—More of the Same, and More

General Ershad needed justification for his military takeover, and constantly cited a stagnant economy as the main cause. He claimed that there was a need for a new (non-democratic) government to be in charge and make the "harsh" decisions deemed necessary to pull the economy from the doldrums. This was reminiscent of Mujib's excuse for changing to a one-party presidential system. The government continued to lean on this "economic" justification throughout Ershad's eight-year tenure, and spent much time and political capital on the economy—to little avail.[15] Ershad's fiscal and monetary policies were carbon copies of Zia's. It was industrial policy that the Ershad government used to justify the coup. It took him only three months, until June 1982, to announce a "New Industrial Policy" (NIP). Mostly it just built on what Zia had already started, but was made to look more aggressive.[16]

This policy turn did not appear to reflect any particular ideological predilection on Ershad's part, but instead his political need for support from the business and military establishment. It also reflected the continuing pressure from the international community, especially the multilateral and bilateral

12   World Bank, *Bangladesh Development Policy Review* (Washington: IBRD, December 14, 2003), p. ii.

13   Ibid., pp. 3 & 7. The Bank says that "not only is Bangladesh's growth volatility the lowest in a sample of 151 countries, it also declined over the past three decades."

14   Elliott Berg, World Bank economist and expert on privatization, in conversations with author.

15   Achtar Hossain and Anis Chowdhury, "Monetary Policy," *Policy Issues in Bangladesh*, 79 (New Delhi: South Asian Publishers Pvt. Ltd., 1984), p. 43.

16   Kochanek, *Patron-Client Politics*, pp. 95-102. This and the following paragraphs on Ershad's industrial policy are taken mainly from this valuable source.

lending agencies, to move economic policy toward more efficiency and reliance on the private sector as the main engine of growth.

By 1986, its highly competitive export industries had become the engine of the Bangladesh economy. The large number of parastatal, high-cost import-substitution industrial units, completely uncompetitive in the world economy, were an increasing drag on growth. Ershad promulgated Revised Industrial Policy (RIP) that emphasized privatization, not the political hot potatoes of disinvestments and denationalization. It was probably the right policy at the wrong time. It had little chance of implementation in the confrontational politics of 1986-90.[17]

Economic Policy and Performance by the Elected Governments

In the past sixteen years, the economic performance of the elected governments has generally been good. Policy direction has been consistent and growth mostly around 5-6 per cent, averaging 5.7 percent since 2001, according to the World Bank. Growth per capita doubled after 1990. Average per capita growth was 1.5 per cent between 1973 and 1989; it averaged 3 per cent in the period 1990 to 2001, and about 5.5 per cent after 2001.[18] Per capita GDP rose by about 25 per cent in fiscal years 1992 to 1999. Real GDP grew by almost 40 per cent in the same period, about 4.8 per cent per year.[19] In part, this better record on growth reflects sound macroeconomic management under the direction of strong finance ministers. In particular, the Finance Minister in the BNP government of 1991 to 1996, Saifur Rahman, who had the complete confidence and backing of the Prime Minister, set the course for good economic progress. Exports grew explosively between 1990/91 and 2004/05 by almost 300 per cent. As a per centage of GDP, exports increased by over 100 per cent in the 1990-2002 period, from 6.12 per cent to 14.28 per cent. Over $2.3 billion in exports went to the United States, Bangladesh's largest export market, in 2002-2003.[20] These were led by the ready-made garment industry, which grew at over 10 per cent each year of the period. This sector now employs around 2 million Bangladeshis

17   Kochanek, *Patron-Client Politics*, p. 101.

18   World Bank, *Bangladesh Growth and Export Competitiveness* (Washington: IBRD, May 4, 2005), p. 7.

19   World Bank, *Bangladesh PSRP Forum Economic Update* (Washington: IBRD, November 2005), p. 41.

20   Ibid., p. 30, export growth. World Bank, *Development...*, p. 9, for percentage of GDP. Sadiq Ahmed and Zaidi Sattar, *Trade Liberalization and Poverty Reduction—The Case of Bangladesh* (Washington: IBRD, May 1 2004), p. 21.

directly, and possibly another million in "through backward and forward linkage activities," primarily women from the rural, landless poor.[21] The Asian economic crisis of the mid-1990s brought growth lower because of the competitive devaluations of Southeast Asian exporting countries and the fall in the prices of jute, shrimp, and leather. Growth recovered smartly to a steady 6 per cent, as the dynamic export sector (garments, shrimp, frog's legs, etc.) continued to pull the economy along.

Serious structural and political issues cloud the economic future, however. The closure of loss-making state-owned enterprises has stalled as elected governments of both parties have not wanted to take on the labor unions or the bureaucracy. The tax/GDP ratio is the lowest in the Asian region despite formal tax rates that are about equal to other countries. A cloud of uncertainty hangs over the exports. Serious infrastructural issues and fear of an unstable political situation have diminished orders of this bell weather sector.

Growth Without Development in Pakistan

Pakistan inherited the more developed, industrialized, and dynamic parts of the economy of United Pakistan when the East separated from the West in 1971. It failed, however, to build on that inheritance or the momentum of the 1960s when, under Ayub Khan, United Pakistan experienced strong economic growth. The "Islamic socialism" that Zulfikar Ali Bhutto introduced in 1972 aimed at addressing the inequality that had built up in the previous decade. But it was both too radical a solution and seriously perverted in execution.

The legacy of Bhutto's economic program has proved difficult to overcome. His policies seriously damaged the economic structure and created a constant need to undertake difficult reform and retrenchment which came in fits and starts and may have made things worse. During much of the thirty-seven years since separation, Pakistan benefited from windfalls which made it easy for governments to avoid difficult decisions. The Pakistani diaspora in the Gulf states, Europe, and the US has contributed much in the way of remittances to their families in Pakistan. This has grown over time, though there has been an ebb and flow depending on the government's policies. And on two different occasions large amounts of assistance from friendly governments coincided with a high tide of remittances from expatriate Pakistanis, further disincentivising governments from undertaking necessary reform.

---

21   World Bank, *Bangladesh Growth and Export...*, p. 3.

Bhutto Starts It Off with a Bang

Bhutto launched a new development strategy, designed to be more equitable. At its core was highly centralized government control of the economy. Imports and exports were tightly controlled, as were the prices of agricultural commodities. The key policy was the nationalization of major Pakistani economic assets—banks, insurance companies, and larger industrial enterprises in ten basic industries. By 1974, the state was producing about 20 per cent of Pakistan's non-agricultural output.[22]

Industrial production fell in 1972, rose in 1973 and 74, before falling again in 1975 and 1976.[23] Budget deficits swelled as nationalized industries performed poorly and needed public monies to cover costs. The government took to borrowing heavily from abroad, as well as domestically, to cover the deficits.[24] Deficit financing became the key to meeting the gap, and this fueled inflation, which hurt Bhutto's primary constituency most—the poor and the lower middle classes. This poor economic performance worked against Bhutto's redistributive politics. Growth averaged 4.3 per cent per year during Bhutto's term in office, down from an annual growth of 5.4 per cent in the Ayub years. Private investment in large-scale manufacturing fell by nearly 50 per cent over the period and annual manufacturing growth dropped to under three per cent, down from 10 per cent in the 1960s. Behind these dismal performance figures was a sea change in investment patterns—the share of public and private investment actually reversed themselves from the 1960s. Public investment rose to 70 per cent of total investment, while private investment contributed only 30 per cent.[25]

Agricultural production per capita actually declined during the Bhutto period. The much heralded land reform fizzled away to nothing. Bhutto's land reform plan had enormous loopholes, primarily in limiting holdings by individual, but not by family. Thus, the great landowning families retained most of their holdings by spreading them out among many family

22   Marvin Weinbaum, "Pakistan: Misplaced priorities, missed opportunities," *India & Pakistan—The First Fifty Years* (Cambridge and Washington, Woodrow Wilson Center Press and Cambridge University Press, 1999), pp. 91-2.

23   International Monetary Fund (IMF), *International Financial Statistics(IFS)*, 1979 edn, pp. 327-31.

24   Weinbaum, "Pakistan: Misplaced priorities," *India & Pakistan*, p. 92.

25   Robert E. Looney, "Pakistan's Economy: Achievements, Progress, Constraints, and Prospects," *Pakistan—Founders' Aspirations and Today's Realities*, Hafeez Malik (ed.) (Karachi, Oxford University Press, 2001), pp. 203-5.

members. Those families that did lose land were political enemies of Bhutto, and their land often wound up in the hands of his political allies.

Missed Opportunities in the 1980s

The military government of Zia ul Huq, unlike that of Musharraf later on, did not take the difficult actions that would have set the economy on a healthier course, despite the windfall of external resources available to it. Zia made no effort to undo Bhutto's extensive nationalizations, nor confront the bureaucracy made more powerful by all the new, if unproductive, state enterprises it had to manage, nor take on the workers in these state industries.[26] The resource windfall came from two extraordinary circumstances. First, international aid levels soared as Western countries, and others such as Saudi Arabia, transferred large sums to or through the Zia government in the multilateral struggle against the Soviets in Afghanistan. For example, assistance from the United States to Pakistan after 1982 totaled about $5 billion, making it the third highest recipient of US aid during that period. Second, and more importantly, between 1975 and 1985, Pakistanis abroad, mainly in the Middle East, remitted over $25 billion to their families back home.[27]

Instead of directing this bonanza towards investments in infrastructure and education, a consumption boom was fueled. This certainly made the Pakistani economy grow faster, and appear healthier on the surface. Economic growth shifted into high gear again; from 1978 to 1983 the economy grew by an average of 6.3 per cent, well above the average of the Bhutto years. In the 1983-88 period, it grew even faster—by 6.6 per cent. Large-scale manufacturing grew at 16.6 per cent over the latter period. Unemployment was eased dramatically by the flow of workers to the Middle East.[28]

The Roller Coaster of Electoral Democracy

The elected governments of Benazir Bhutto and Nawaz Sharif were unable to solve the serious economic problems or correct the structural deficiencies they inherited. Each tried a different approach—which was part of the problem. The fundamental structural weaknesses of the economy that emerged into plain view in the 1990s are classic developing-country problems. They

---

26   Weinbaum, "Pakistan: Misplaced Priorities…," *India & Pakistan*, p. 93.
27   Looney, "Pakistan's Economy…," *Pakistan—Founders,"* p. 210.
28   Ibid.

can be summed up as a serious gap between national consumption and national production. In other words, Pakistan continually consumed more than it earned and financed this by borrowing. But, as the problems became progressively more serious, they also became progressively more difficult to correct without wrenching reform—the kind that democratically-elected governments find nearly impossible to undertake. The result was a series of stop-gap measures, sometimes backed by the international financial institutions, but undertaken with no real commitment by governments that just wanted to get through yet another bad patch. Pakistan became known in the IFI community as a "one tranche country."

The military continued to take a disproportionate share of revenue for its "security responsibilities," while the social sector, including education, as usual, was starved of resources. The already seriously deficient stock of human capital became worse (an underdeveloped, undereducated population) which, apart from the social and political implications, has led to a uncompetitive labor force *vis-à-vis* its neighbors and the Asian region.[29]

Benazir Bhutto, in contrast to her father, emphasized the private sector as the driver of economic activity in Pakistan when she came to office in 1988. She wanted to shift the focus of government policy to providing economic and social services. For this, she needed substantial economic growth, led by the private sector, and additional resource flows. She proposed policies of trade liberalization and reform of the fiscal and financial systems, as well as a long list of state enterprises to be privatized. None of it came to pass.[30] Nawaz Sharif came to power backed by a new political elite: industrialists of a recent vintage, traders, smaller entrepreneurs, and others of the urban middle class. To please this new political elite, both of his administrations aimed at energizing the private sector as the engine of growth in the economy. In his first term, this would be done through privatization, deregulation, and reform of the economic structure. His program of privatization, however, as with his predecessor, became a method of rewarding political friends and a source of corruption. Sharif sought to liberalize the economy, and privatize the large para-statal sector, but he combined this with populist measures that often contradicted his stated objective of liberalization. In

29 Sadiq Ahmed, "Explaining Pakistan's High Growth Performance over the Past Two Decades: Can It Be Sustained," *World Bank Policy Research Working Paper* (Washington: World Bank, 1994), pp. iii and 40, http://wwwwds.worldbank.org/servlet/WDConstantServer/WDSP/IB/1994/08/01/000009265_397071616141607/Rendered/PDF/multi0page/pdf (accessed 6-15-2005).

30 Ibid., 219.

addition, the government failed to address effectively the large and growing budget deficit.[31] An important reform of the financial sector began under Sharif. His government brought in experienced Pakistani banking experts who had been working in international banks abroad to take control of the mostly insolvent state-owned commercial banks and to "clean them up" to prepare them for privatization.

Musharraf—Ayub Khan All Over Again[32]

When Pervez Musharraf took power, the economy was certainly a subtext in the Army's mind yet his economic reform program is the strongest accomplishment of his time in office and the one that outsiders find most impressive. But even the economic accomplishments of his tenure have their critics. They point out that Musharraf's economic policies parallel closely those of Ayub Khan in their emphasis on growth and negative impact on income distribution and poverty alleviation.[33] It is possible that the growing and glaring income disparity is, in part, responsible for the escalating political crisis he faced throughout 2007 which triggered the implementation of martial law on November 4. Nonetheless, Musharraf's economic reforms boosted economic growth rates impressively. His government stuck firmly to the reform program, not only through the phase of direct military rule, but through that of hybrid electoral politics. This was particularly striking as this government inherited the long-standing and firmly entrenched structural deficiencies that the previous governments had been almost totally unable to solve.

The government's macroeconomic stabilization measures cut to the heart of the structural problems that had plagued Pakistan for almost two decades. The reform of the banking system and the privatization of the banks, which the Sharif government had started, was accelerated and has proven highly successful.[34] The Musharraf regime was less successful on the fiscal

---

31   Ibid., p. 214 and Wienbaum, "Pakistan: Misplaced Priorities…," *India & Pakistan*, p. 94.

32   The bulk of this section is based on the author's experience in Pakistan from 1998 to 2001, and on Pakistani issues since then.

33   A smaller number of analysts worry about the lax monetary policy that has characterized the last few years. See footnote 35 below.

34   World Bank Document, *Implementation Completion Report (IDA-35170) on a Credit in the Amount of SDR 239.5 Million (US$300 Million Equivalent) to the Government of Pakistan for a Banking Sector Restructuring and Privatization Project* (Washington: World Bank, 2005), 4, http://www-wds.worldbank.org/servelet/WDSContentServer/WDSP/IB/2005/06/17/000160016_20050617110622/Rendered/PDF?32589.pdf (accessed 6-15-05).

side. Strict fiscal discipline has been imposed and tax revenues have risen. However, revenue performance still does not compare well with other developing countries of its income level. Perhaps the greatest success of the Musharraf reforms has been on external accounts. Pakistan was in danger of defaulting on its external debt service at least three times in the 1990s under the elected democratic governments.[35] However, foreign exchange reserve levels have dissipated badly as global food and energy inflation, as well as the political uncertainty of the past six months take their toll.

Economic growth, which was 4.2 per cent in the last months of the Sharif government—slightly lower than the average for the years of electoral democracy—rose to 5.1 per cent in the first four years of the Musharraf government, to over 8.4 per cent by FY 2005 and has been in the 6-8 per cent range in subsequent years.[36] How the current political turmoil will, over the long-term, affect this solid achievement is unclear. But the numbers usually left at the bottom of macroeconomic charts tell a more worrisome story. They speak of a disproportionate share of the gains from this high economic growth going mainly to the "haves." "Poverty incidence," as it is sometimes labeled, remains stubbornly high, at over 30 per cent of the population; and data seems to indicate that it is growing.[37]

Analysts of the International Monetary Fund (IMF) give Pakistan, in the Musharraf years, about a "B+" for economic reform, but warn that much remains to be done. They point out, for example, that "[m]uch has been done in recent years to improve the business climate in Pakistan…," in comparison to other South Asian countries, "[but] it lags…significantly behind [countries in East Asia]." These analysts give credit for the policy changes and reforms that have led to a boost in domestic investment and to the export boom that have helped raise the economic growth rate in the past few years. On the other hand, they warn that the basis of this rapid growth is thin and fragile, and probably not sustainable, if among other important

---

35 Mushtaq Kahn, "9/11, Pakistan's Economy, & the IMF," Public Presentation at The Woodrow Wilson Center for International Scholars, January 10, 2006 (unpublished). Figures come from the annual publication of the State Bank of Pakistan.

36 Ibid. for the 2005 estimate. For the other number in the paragraph, Cheema, *Macroeconomic Stability*, p. 16. Cheema's figures are supported by Henri Lorie and Zafar Iqbal, "Pakistan's Macroeconomic Adjustments and Resumption of Growth," *IMF Working Paper* (Washington: IMF, 2005) who project growth in the out years to be near 7 percent. See also Jay Solomon, Zahid Hussain, and Saeed Azhar, "As Growth Returns to Pakistan, Hopes Rise on Terror Front," *Wall Street Journal*, November 9, 2004 (New York), p. 1.

37 Cheema, *Macroeconomic Stability*, p. 16.

factors, agriculture, which represents almost 25 per cent of the economy, does not increase productivity.[38]

In Social Development, the Tortoise Becomes the Hare

Social development indicators for Bangladesh and Pakistan are often unreliable and inconsistent. Nonetheless, there is a real difference between the two countries. In Bangladesh, most social development indicators have been moving, generally, in the right direction for the better part of two decades. Most of the important elements of social progress and modernization are on the upswing. In Pakistan, the story is different. For most of the past three decades, Pakistan achieved little in social development, and occasionally it regressed, especially under the military rule of Zia ul Huq.

The Metaphor Is Population Growth

Demographers and other social scientists continue to debate why Bangladesh has leapt ahead in family planning. The "supply side" view is that government policies permit donors and NGOs to provide contraceptive material freely and without hindrance.[39] Those favoring the "demand side" argue that societal perceptions are that the costs of child rearing have increased dramatically and induced people of child bearing age to wish to limit family size and therefore demand contraceptives.[40] "Cultural" explanations cut across the demand and supply theses and present persuasive evidence that a combination of historical, cultural and political circumstances engender an openness to change and innovation in Bengali society that often runs "counter to ... socioeconomic circumstances." [41]

A key determinant of success has been the constant policy, of all the governments since Zia Rahman, aiming to bring about a significant decrease in the growth of population (an unusual political continuity for Bangladesh). This was combined with an understanding of the need, and a willingness,

---

38   Henrie Lorie and Zafar Iqbal, *Pakistan's Macroeconomic Adjustment and Resumption of Growth 1999-2004*, IMF Working Paper (Washington: International Monetary Fund, July 2005), pp. 11 & 24.

39   This explanation is favored primarily by donors, who have funded family planning programs, the recipient governments and NGOs, who have carried out the programs.

40   See, for example, M. R. Montgomery and J. B. Caster line, "Social Networks and the Diffusion of Fertility Control," *Policy Research Division Working Paper no. 119* (New York: Population Council, 1998).

41   Alaka Basu, Alaka Malwade, and Sajeda Amin, "Conditioning Factors for Fertility Decline in Bengal: History, Language Identity, and Openness to Innovation," *Population and Development Review,* vol. 26, no. 4 (Dec. 2000), pp. 761-94, quote on 764.

to allow international and bilateral donors as well as international and domestic NGOs to take over and formulate a large part of the family planning program. The average annual compound rate of population growth
from 1971 to 2003 is just over 2 per cent. The year-to-year growth rate has
decreased continuously since the early 1970s, and dipped below 2 per cent
for the first time in 1990. It is now 1.7 per cent.[42] This remarkable decline
means that the growth rate of population is now below the South Asia
level, and would, if sustained, reduce pressure on resources.

A host of reproductive health statistics illustrates this impressive decrease
in the population growth rate, both absolute and relative, that Bangladesh
has registered in just over two decades. A sharp reduction of the fertility
rate is the critical factor. Since 1975, according to World Bank figures,
Bangladesh's fertility has declined by 55 per cent and its population growth
rate by 31 per cent. At the first level of analysis, the increased use of family
planning methods, especially contraceptives, are the proximate cause of this
decline in fertility. The supply of family planning materials and measures,
especially contraceptives, increased, as did information from and exhorta-
tion by the government and the NGOs. Initially, perhaps, the disruption
in the traditional patterns of rural life during and after the war of separation
brought about a new societal perception, that the costs of child-rearing
had increased. Extended families living together became less of a pattern as
land became scarcer. Young couples that in the past would have remained
in an extended family compound migrated to the cities. Moreover, poorer
women, widows and those without husbands who would have been available for helping with child-raising, left the villages to seek employment,
especially after the famine years of the mid-1970s.[43] In this situation, the
costs of parenthood are no longer shared among a larger family group but
fall more squarely on the parents.

The dynamic of bearing fewer children has its own momentum. As the
practice of limiting children in a family comes to be more common, more
couples find it socially acceptable and take up the practice. Soon it becomes
the norm. To some extent, this can be tracked through the "contraceptive
prevalence rate," the use of contraceptives by women between 15 and 49
years of age. In Bangladesh this rate had risen to 54 per cent by the final
decade of the 20th century, above the average South Asian rate, and twice

---

42   World Bank, *World Bank Development Indicators* (Washington: IBRD, 2004), pp. 38-9.

43   Martha Alter Chen, *A Quiet Revolution—Women in Transition in Rural Bangladesh* (Dha-
        ka, BRAC Prokashana, 1986), pp. 60-2.

that of Pakistan.[44] The "cultural" thesis, adds another element to the explanation. Recent studies have found parallels between political/social innovation in West Bengal and social innovation, primarily involving population control, in Bangladesh. They posit that Bengali culture, history, and language identity has meant, in both West Bengal and Bangladesh, that social change and innovation are more acceptable, and often welcome, than in other South Asian cultures.[45]

The bottom line is that, in Bengali culture, there is "a willingness to change...." This began with the elites and spread to the general population, in part because of more intense interaction between elites and the general population based on national feeling and common language than is common in other South Asian cultures in which, "socioeconomic differences are not attenuated by a similarly strong sense of cultural identity."[46]

Education and Health

Bangladesh made great strides in educating its population during the 1990s. Government efforts intensified significantly, and private initiatives remained critical to the progress that has been made. Government expenditures on education totaled about 15 per cent of total expenditure, and rose significantly in the past two decades of the twentieth century. For Bangladesh, however, the grim reality in education is that the glass is also half empty. At the turn of the millennium, half of its male population and two-thirds of its female population over 15 years old are still illiterate.[47] According to the World Bank, primary school enrollment reached a decade high in the mid-90s, and has fallen since. A vast distance remains to be covered to deliver a level of education and literacy required by its development needs. In the health sector, as in most of the social development sectors, "Bangladesh's achievements are also impressive," given its "adverse initial conditions, high population density, vulnerability to disaster, and low stock of natural resources."[48] These achievements represent "extraordinary progress," ac-

44   World Bank, *World Bank Development Indicators 2004*, pp. 96-7.

45   Basu, Malaweke, and Amin, "Conditioning Factors for Fertility Decline, *Population and Development Review,* p. 764.

46   World Bank, *World Development Indicators 2004*, p. 72.

47   Ibid., p. 84.

48   Anil B. Deolaikar, *Attaining the Millennium Development Goals in Bangladesh* (Washington, World Bank, 2005), p. 3.

cording to the World Bank, but this is inhibited severely by the "problem of governance."[49]

The bad news often concerns children. The infant mortality rate has decreased sharply, but is still very high. The number of children under one year of age who die per 1000 births fell from 129 in 1980 to 54 in 2000 (48 in 2002). For children under five, the mortality rate also remains high (109 in 2000).[50] In 2000, only 13 per cent of births in Bangladesh were attended by trained health staff, though this is up from 8 per cent in 1997. This is one reason that the mortality rate of mothers is one of the highest outside sub-Saharan Africa at 392 maternal deaths per 100,000 live births in 2000.

The reduction in the mortality rate is due to its high immunization rate for measles—77 per cent in 2002 as contrasted with 57 per cent Pakistan. Also the per centage of pregnant women that seek pre-natal consultations with trained health workers doubled in the 1990s. Nonetheless, at least one mother in three gives birth without ever having seen a trained health worker. Half of the babies born in Bangladesh in 1995 were considered "low-birthweight" infants. Thirteen per cent of Bangladesh children under five were severely underweight in 2002

The high incidence of water borne diseases undoubtedly affects mortality rates and longevity expectations. The high incidence of cholera in Bangladesh is well known, as is the superior treatment of the disease developed there. There is also a high incidence of hepatitis A and C. Clearly, the "improved" sanitation and water sources are not improved enough. Moreover, millions Bangladeshis in almost all of the country's 68,000 villages are threatened with a slow death from arsenic poisoning from tubewell water presumed safe only a decade ago. Finally there is the modern scourge of the third world, HIV/AIDS, which appears to be spreading in India. The governments of both Bangladesh and Pakistan appear to know next to nothing about this rapidly spreading disease, and seemingly don't want to. UNAIDS, the UN agency that monitors and combats HIV/AIDS, estimates the prevalence rate in the population between ages 15 to 49 as below 0.1 per cent in Bangladesh. The same agency has conducted surveys

49   Ibid., pp. i, iii.
50   The World Bank, *World Development Indicators* (Washington: IBRD, 2004), p. 42. Unless otherwise indicated, all data in this section are taken from the same source. Figures in this publication show that 77 per cent of women in the labor force are in the agricultural sector, but such numbers have only been collected recently in Bangladesh; there are no numbers from prior years for comparison.

in Bangladesh which indicate that 29 per cent of men and 22 per cent of women in the 15 to 24 year age range understand that a healthy-looking person can transmit HIV/AIDS.

Women's Development

Bangladesh is well ahead of Pakistan in women's development as the above figures make clear. One important component of women's progress is their access to the labor market, especially to income-earning jobs in industry and the services, and to some control over family income. Development experts, and NGOs in the field, argue forcefully that when women provide and/or control family income the family expenditure pattern is more socially productive. Women who have some control over family income see that children are sent to school, better clothed, better fed, provided better health care, and generally raised with a promise of social uplift.[51]

Women have traditionally been a large part of the labor force in Bangladesh—much more so than in Pakistan. In the country's earliest days in 1972, there was little reliable data, but women probably made up over 40 per cent of the Bangladeshi labor force. By 1980, this had grown to over 47 per cent, and over 70 per cent of women participated the labor force. This is in sharp contrast to Pakistan.[52]

While working is not a new experience for the women of Bangladesh, until the 1980s, almost all of this employment was in agriculture, much of it by the women in landless families working as labor in fields owned by someone else and paid, more often than not, in kind. Today the structure of women's employment has changed. Large numbers of women, mostly those from the rural, landless poor, now work in export industries where they earn a salary that they take home to supplement, and quite often solely provide, the family income. The very successful export industry for ready-made garments which, as mentioned above, employs about 2 million employees directly and another million indirectly, about 90 per cent of which are women. A significant part of the half million workers in the frozen shrimp export industry, almost all from the rural, landless poor, are women. Women's income has also been bolstered by the extensive micro-credit programs of Grameen Bank, BRAC, and many others. These micro-credit institutions serve mainly poor

---

51   Mark M. Pitt, Shahidur R. Khandker, and Jennifer Cartwright, *Does Micro-Credit Empower Women?—Evidence from Bangladesh* (Washington: World Bank, 2003), pp. 29-30.

52   World Bank, *World Development Indicators 2004*, p. 42.

women and provide them a major source of income, boosting their say in family decisions on schooling, health, etc.

In covering the issues of women's development, we cannot avoid discussion of violence against women—a significant problem in both Bangladesh and Pakistan. In Bangladesh, there is no doubt that violence against women is widespread. The anecdotal evidence is extensive (i.e. newspaper and other media reports), but the hard information is not; it appears the government does not collect such data.[53] It seems that in our comparison, violence against women in Bangladesh, while lamentably high and perhaps growing, is not as bad as in Pakistan. This is a relative statement that does not intend to let Bangladesh off the hook for its own poor record in protecting women from violence.

There are only a few studies of violence against women, and some of them date back a decade or so. A very comprehensive report, from 1993, indicates that the most common form of violence against women is domestic—suffered in the household. Women are quite commonly, across socio-economic class lines, battered by their husbands. A seasonal pattern has been noted by researchers: beatings rise in frequency during the "kartik" (the hungry season from August to October).[54] Women's deaths relating to dowry squabbles are also common, usually engineered to look like kitchen accidents or suicide. Acid throwing attacks were said, in this report, to be on the rise. The increase in such attacks may result from women being more visible now, having transgressed the boundaries of "purdah," given their employment and the NGO programs that promote their development.[55]

The statistics for rape are totally unreliable. They come from police reports of a crime that is often not reported to them. Rape is notoriously underreported because of the social stigma attached to it and the concomitant lack of sympathy for women in the criminal justice system. Sadly, very out-of-date statistics show that 35 per cent of the cases reported involved minor

53   Rachel M. Marcus, *Violence Against Women in Bangladesh, Pakistan, Egypt, Sudan, Senegal, and Yemen* (Sussex: Institute for Development Studies, University of Sussex, BRIDGE Report no. 10, 1993), p. 4. See also Sally Baden, Cathy Green, Anne Marie Goetz and Meghna Guhathkurta, *Background Report on Gender Issues in Bangladesh* (Sussex: Institute for Development Studies, BRIDGE Report No. 26, 1994), pp. 79-84 for violence against women in Bangladesh and for general background.

54   Rachel Marcus, *Violence Against Women...*, p. 5.

55   Habida Zaman, *Violence Against Women in Bangladesh: Issues and Responses*, Women's Studies International Forum (January/February 1999), vol. 22, Issue 1, 40.

girls.[56] A law that requires a medical examination of a woman immediately after a rape is a severe disincentive in Bangladeshi culture to reporting it. Unlike Pakistan, there are no laws on the books in Bangladesh that foster violence toward women. Nonetheless, the culture places women at a distinct disadvantage, and helps to legitimize such violence. Moreover the legal system does little to protect women. They are intimidated from complaining to police, or showing up in court if they do complain to the police, and the courts routinely dismiss cases in which the complainant does not appear.

There are also laws designed to protect women, but enforcement is weak. The most important among these are an act that outlaws the abduction of women and acid throwing attacks on them, one which mandates capital punishment for killing a woman victim of a rape and one that mandates capital punishment or life imprisonment for murder or attempted murder over dowry. These all date from the early 1980s.

Has Social Failure Weakened the Pakistani State?

Social progress has been more limited in Pakistan. The World Bank staff puts it this way: "Pakistan lags behind countries with comparable per capita income on most of the social indicators.... [t]his is true both of the effort expended (eg. expenditure on public health) and outcomes (e.g. infant mortality).... [It has] failed to achieve social progress commensurate with its economic growth."[57] Pakistani social indicators have lagged behind those in Bangladesh for reasons not clearly understood. Certainly the influence of religion in the culture is an important element (including the role of Islam and of the mullahs who set social horizons for much of the population), but why has this been less influential on Bangladesh culture? Many observers point to the persistence of feudalism in Pakistan.

One important difference between the two countries is the heterogeneity of Pakistani society, in contrast to the homogeneity of Bangladesh. A heterogeneous society, such as Pakistan, finds it harder to form a national consensus around social objectives. In such a culture, the attitude of government cannot be omitted as an explanatory factor. Pakistani rulers, whether civilian or military, have consistently been ambiguous and often uninterested in social development. For example, family planning has not been a social objective that had complete support in society. In practical terms, this

---

56   Rachel Marcus, *Violence Against Women...*, p. 5.

57   World Bank, *Pakistan Development Policy Review—A New Dawn?* (Washington: IBRD, April 3, 2002).

has meant that NGOs have been less effective in promoting demand for contraception, and that the cacophony of the many vested interests that oppose family planning, including many religious leaders, as well as the leaders of feudal society, have inhibited the government from providing unwavering support for such programs.

This is the most striking contrast between Pakistan and Bangladesh, and it runs the gamut of social programs from family planning to women's development. In all, it is a picture of an almost incomprehensible absence of vision on the part of Pakistan's leaders and political class on how to strengthen the country and society—and on how to develop a nation from a collection of competing nationalities.

Population Growth—Beginning to Decline?

Well after most other countries in South Asia had begun to bring down population growth rates, Pakistan was recording growth rates approaching three per cent. Fortunately these have declined in recent years, but remain well above average in South Asia. The average annual compound growth rate of Pakistan's population between 1972 and 2003 is about 2.45 percent, and the country has lagged far behind in reducing fertility.

There is in every society an ideal family size which places a limit on the fertility transition of society. The hurdle that Pakistan must cross to reduce the fertility rate further and the population growth rate even lower is to somehow effect a change in Pakistani society's ideal family size. Most Pakistanis themselves say they want enough children to ensure two sons. Decades of increased urbanization, and more importantly, a sharp and lasting reduction in infant mortality, may be necessary to bring this ideal family size down.

Education and Health

In Pakistan, the effort to increase access to education for both males and females may be just beginning. The per centage of government resources devoted to public education increased only marginally in the Musharraf years despite much rhetoric to the contrary.[58] (In Bangladesh, expenditures on education almost doubled through the 1990s.)

World Bank figures show that budgetary resources allocated by the Pakistani government to education decreased as a percentage of GDP over

---

58   World Bank, *Pakistan Public Expenditure Management—Strategic Issues and Reform Agenda* (Washington: IBRD, January 28, 2004), p. 1.

the decade of the 1990s.[59] The NGO, Human Rights Watch, reports that, "[Health and] education (especially for women) have been consistently receiving diminishing allocations in the budget (among the lowest in the third world) and much of what is to be distributed disappears through institutionalized corruption."[60] School enrollment remains far below the norm for the region and lags behind Bangladesh. The more startling contrast is in the figures for female enrollment in primary school. In the 2001-2 school year, the per centage of females enrolled in primary school in Pakistan was 48 per cent.[61] In contrast, in Bangladesh in that year, there were 90 per cent of the eligible females enrolled in primary schools.[62] The gender gap is found primarily in Pakistani rural schools; in urban schools roughly the same per centage of females and males are enrolled.[63]

One recent study, which involved field surveys in twenty-five villages in Punjab and NWFP, revealed interesting data on educational practices in two provinces of Pakistan. Among the many constraints on access to education, it appears that "supply side" problems loom very large for a majority of children. According to the survey, 63 per cent of the male children at the entry level face some sort of supply constraints (i.e. a lack of facilities such as buildings, teachers, or teaching materials). Female children face even higher constraints: 82 per cent do not have access to girls' schools in their village.[64]

This same study found that entry into primary school was the most important factor in whether a child remains in school long enough to become functionally literate. While, overall, male children average 6.6 years of schooling and female children 1.6 years, that increased for those who ac-

59   Ibid., p. 1.

60   Human Rights Watch, *Crime or Custom? Violence Against Women in Pakistan (August 1999)* quoting 17th unnumbered page of The Women's Environmental and Development Organization, *Mapping Progress: Assessing the Implications of the Beijing Reform* (New York: WWEDO, 1997), accessed on 6-15-05 at http://www.hrw.org/1999/pakistan/Pak-html-06.htm#P434_82204.

61   World Bank and International Development Agency, *Joint Assessment of the Poverty Reduction Strategy Paper—Pakistan* (Washington: IBRD, February 12, 2004), pp. 67-88.

62   World Bank, *World Development Indicators*, 84.

63   World Bank, Pakistan-*Country Gender Assessment; Bridging the Gender Gap: Opportunities and Challenges*, (Washington: IBRD, October 2005), p. 44.

64   Y. Swaboda and M. Loshkin, "Household Schooling Decisions in Rural Pakistan," *Policy Research Working Paper 2541* (Washington: IBRD, February 2001), p. 15. In the villages, the authors explain, Pakistani culture requires single sex schools. Parents are unwilling to send their daughters to school if they must cross a major road or river as they may risk breaking purdah. Also, there are insufficient qualified female teachers to teach female students in the villages. In other words, supply side constraints explain some of the gender differences in Pakistani education.

tually entered school to 8.8 and 6.0 years respectively. Another way to put it is that, while the probability of children entering school is low—64 per cent for males, and a very low 24 per cent for females—the primary school graduation rates for those who enter are very respectable—82 per cent for males and 69 per cent for females.[65]

The gender gap closes after secondary school for females in Punjab, i.e. their school progression rates almost equal males. In NWFP, however, this is not true. As expected, educational patterns are explainable, in large part, by family income and/or asset ownership, as well as health. The other factor that seems to have some bearing is sibling order. Younger sisters, for example, receive more primary education depending on the number of older sisters they have who may marry early or go into domestic work (usually non-paying). A parallel for males is that the larger the number of older brothers the more the chances for the younger brothers to finish primary school and enter secondary school. Often a family decides that a younger brother ought to have more education and he benefits from the financial support of his elder brothers, drawing on their earnings.[66]

The implication is that there is an unsatisfied demand for education at the primary and secondary levels in Pakistan—unsatisfied because the public education system is so under-resourced, and therefore underdeveloped. The infrastructure needed to offer all Pakistanis who desire it a basic education is not there. The profound deficiencies of the public education system in Pakistan have led many observers to conclude that the slack was being taken up, in part, by the many Islamic schools, madrassas, that appear to have sprung up in the last thirty years. This conclusion has been challenged in recent years, and conclusive evidence is yet to be published.

A recent study, commissioned by the World Bank, suggests that the large numbers of Pakistani youth that were assumed to be matriculating in madrassas may have been exaggerated. This research was undertaken by a team of academic econometricians and derives its estimates from household survey samples. It is hotly disputed because of its methodology, and its estimate that only about one per cent of the school population in Pakistan attends madrassas. Many other social scientists believe this figure is misleadingly low.[67] Whatever the number of students, the rapid growth of

---

65   Ibid., p. 15.

66   Ibid., p. 17.

67   Tahir Andrabi, Jishnu Das, Asim Ijaz Khwaja, Tristan Zajonic, *Religious School Enrollment in Pakistan*, WBS3521 (Washington: IBRD, February 1, 2005).

madrassas does give cause for concern. A recent article indicated that there are over 11,000 madrassas in Pakistan, an increase of close to 5,500 in the past five years. Since these figures are bound to be disputed, I repeat them only to demonstrate the extent of the escalating growth of madrassas in recent years. The number of madrassa students, according to this article, is about 685,000, which would amount to just over 2 per cent of the student population of Pakistan. This would be about twice the per centage estimated by the World Bank study, but still at the low end of other estimates.[68]

More interesting, and perhaps more worrisome, is the breakdown given in this article among madrassa students by the schools of Islamic thought that inspire and fund the seminaries. Almost 450,000 of these students attend madrassas which follow the Deobandi school, a reformist, scriptualist brand of Islamism. Less than 200,000 attend Barelvi madrassas, which follow a softer, more Sufi-influenced brand of Islam. Thus two-thirds of madrassa students are being inculcated with the less tolerant and more rigid ideology of rejectionist, jihadi Islamism. Other observers point out that madrassas of any variety tend to "insulate...pupils from society and to cocoon them into a rejectionist discourse."[69]

The numbers of madrassas and their students notwithstanding, they bear careful scrutiny and their curricula ought to be reformed. Some have served as handy recruitment centers, and in a few cases, training centers, for young men to be indoctrinated in the militant version of Islam. While some madrassas teach militancy, others feature a broad curriculum, which though emphasizing study of the Koran, also teach courses in science, mathematics, and technical skills such as computer science. Most of these have been in existence for many years, and draw students on the basis of their broader curriculum and their reputation for quality education. The vast majority, however, are more recent in origin, more narrow in scope, mainly turning out clerics with few skills to prepare them for the modern world. The Musharraf government vowed to reform the madrassas, especially to modernize and broaden their curricula, but moved very timidly to carry out that pledge before it began to unravel in March 2007.

In general, health sector statistics in Pakistan look very similar to, if not slightly better than, those in Bangladesh. Neither country has anything to

---

68   Khaled Ahmed, "Second Opinion," *Daily Times*, February 9, 2006. Ahmed is quoting an article by Abdul Majeed Salik, in *Jang* on January 6, 2006 written in Urdu. Accessed on February 9, 2006 at http://www.dailytimes.com.pk

69   Ibid., p. 2.

brag about regarding the general health of its population.[70] As in Bangladesh, children suffer the most. The higher child mortality rates, which appear contradictory, probably reflect lower immunization rates in Pakistan. In 2002, only 57 percent of Pakistani children had been immunized against measles, 20 percentage points lower than in Bangladesh. It is also due, in part, to fear-mongering facilitated by the mullahs about a "western conspiracy" to make Pakistani women infertile.

Women's Development

While data on progress in women's development has many gaps, overall Pakistan shows up poorly in contrast to Bangladesh, as little headway was made in overall women's education during the 1990s. The percentage of females enrolled in primary school increased marginally in that decade to 46 per cent, a level that is still less than half of those eligible to attend. Almost as striking as the gender gap is the urban/rural gap. In urban areas, girls and boys have almost identical enrollment rates in primary school; in rural areas, the girls rate is nearly 20 per centage points less than the boys.[71]

Unlike Bangladesh, women in Pakistan have traditionally made up a much smaller part of the labor force—though their participation has increased somewhat in the thirty-four years since separation. Only about 25 per cent of Pakistani females over ten years old are in the labor force. The structure of women's employment also differs in Pakistan: there are few in industry, thus few who take home salaries with the influence that gives over family spending patterns. Though the numbers employed in industry appear equivalent, it is mostly cottage industry in which women in Pakistan are employed, i.e. carpet-making, and weaving, usually made at home, with the help of the rest of the family (including the children). Nor is access to micro-credit nearly as extensive in Pakistan as in Bangladesh (details below).[72]

Finally, violence against women is equally—and probably more—widespread in Pakistan than in Bangladesh. The data is sparse, unreliable, and out of date, but probably understates most of the problems because it is not reported accurately. We rely for data mostly on NGOs specializing in human rights, including Human Rights Watch, the Human Rights Commission of Pakistan, and the random media reports. These sources estimate

---

70   World Bank, *World Development Indicators*, p. 108. Unless otherwise indicated, data in this section are taken from this source.

71   World Bank, *Pakistan—Country Gender Assessment*, pp. 44-8.

72   Ibid., pp. 86-98.

that 70 to 90 per cent of Pakistani women experience domestic violence, much of which is disguised as "accidents." As in Bangladesh much violence against women in Pakistan is related to dowry disputes. Very different, however, is the prevalence of honor killings—those related to the perception that some action on the part of a woman has sullied the honor of the family. This is often because of a romantic attachment—or the belief there was one—to a male not approved by the family. Honor killings are rarely prosecuted. Often the preferred method of avenging family honor is rape—especially when the woman victim is of another family, or another class or clan. The cultural and social mores which give rise to such violence are similar to those in Bangladesh. They begin with the traditional family structure that grants supremacy to men and subordinates women. This engenders endemic domestic violence, which is "a structural rather than a casual problem." The structure of the family is the problem, because it is "a structure that is mirrored and confirmed in the structure of society, which condones the oppression of women and tolerates male violence as one of the instruments in the perpetuation [of] the power balance."[73]

There is, perhaps, one difference. The Hudood Ordinances, though they were modified in a confusing political struggle, continue to give legal sanction to women's' subordinate status.[74] Zia ul Huq introduced the Hudood Ordinances in the early 1980s to provide a legal underpinning for the cultural and social structures that assume the subordinate status of women. They were a logical part of his Islamization program, which also introduced Sharia courts. The egregious parts of these ordinances have disappeared after last year's political battle. No longer is a woman required to produce four male Muslim witnesses to prove rape and be absolved of adultery; no longer does reporting a rape open the victim up to being charged with adultery. But though improved from the human rights perspective, they remain on the books as symbols of how women still do not have equal rights and are vulnerable to the whims of a male-dominated society.

The Difference Is Direction

Neither Bangladesh nor Pakistan have any reason for self-congratulation when it comes to social development. Both come very low on the UN's ranking of counties' human development indicators (Bangladesh is ranked 138, and Pakistan 142). The difference between them is small, and it is one

---

73   Ibid., p. 30.

74   The Hudood Ordinances were discussed in detail in chapters 4 and 8.

of direction rather than absolutes. In 1975, their human development index numbers were almost identical. From 1980 through 1990, Pakistan's index number increased more rapidly than Bangladesh's; it appeared to be progressing faster socially. From 1990 through 1995, though a gap remained between the two, it did not increase. From 1995 through 2000, the situation reversed itself completely; Bangladesh's human development index overtook that of Pakistan. It has moved further ahead in the past five years.

Pakistan is a patchwork of regional and ethnic cultures in which social development, especially for women, has often run counter to ingrained cultural practices and strongly–held social attitudes, among which is the low level of education and literacy of women. This is complicated by the feudal structure of society which, though changed and modified by economic modernization, remains strong in rural areas, and sees little self-interest in social development of its labor force.

As elsewhere, including Bangladesh, Islamists in Pakistan generally oppose aspects of social development that conflict with their "civilizational" agenda. The basis of this agenda is a rejection of "animalistic" western culture, which must be kept out, whether it is imported by westerners or by Pakistanis who have been tainted by exposure to the West. Social development is often associated with western culture because it deals mainly with women's development. Often, in Islamist literature, the ideal of the urban Muslim woman of leisure (though perhaps immured) is contrasted with working class western women or some distorted version of the western "liberated" woman.[75]

Islamist opposition to most forms of modern social development, as we understand them, is aided in Pakistan by the lack of both a coherent and unified civil society and a strong consensus among the political class for modernizing society. It is not primarily pressure from Islamist political parties—although this has been important politically at various times—but the passive resistance from much of the leadership of the feudal society that has fatally undercut the promotion of social development even by moderate governments that espouse the principle. The "Faustian deals" that Pakistani political leaders have made, both military and civilian, have been an added factor, historically, that have strengthened the Islamists politically and often led to the sacrifice of social development goals for other political goals.

---

75   Barbara Metcalf, "Islamic Arguments in Contemporary Pakistan," *Islamic Contestations* (New Delhi: Oxford University Press, 2004), p. 247. The Islamists also condemn "modernism" as the source of many of the ills in Islamic societies, and this becomes also a basis for resisting social development.

There are some other important differences which help explain the divergence between Bangladesh and Pakistan, though not completely. The more homogenous nature of Bengali society and culture appear more open and welcoming of change, and this has allowed social innovation to spur social progress. (There are obviously lags between innovation and progress, and this would explain why Bangladesh seemed to be falling behind in the 1980s.) Also, Bangladesh's very vibrant civil society has spawned and nurtured a wide variety of active and creative NGOs that have essentially taken over from the government in the delivery of most social services. Even the attitude of the administration, though it may be changing, has heretofore fostered the growth and activities of these NGOs. This also took time to grow and mature, but is the basis now of rapid social progress.

NGOs exist in Pakistan and have operated there since United Pakistan became an independent state after partition in 1947. Yet they have never become central to social development as they are in Bangladesh. This chapter goes on to examine NGO activities in both countries, and why their role, and their impact, is so different.

NGOs in Bangladesh—Reaching Deeply Into the Heart of Society and Culture

NGOs are involved in every kind of social uplift in Bangladesh, and the country is perhaps best known, at least among development *cognescenti,* as a laboratory for almost every kind of NGO that aims at improving the lot of the poor. This is not so in Pakistan. There NGOs play a decidedly minor role, and this possibly has had a very deleterious impact on the country's hobbled social development.

The most notable and celebrated NGO product in Bangladesh is microcredit, the provision of small, uncollateralized loans to the rural poor, mostly women. A large majority of Bangladeshi NGOs have microcredit programs in their repertoire, though many also feature other kinds of income-generating projects, as well as social service programs such as education, especially of girls, women's development, family planning, and health. The microcredit concept has been copied worldwide, even in the United States, and is part of the NGO repertoire in Pakistan also, but much less successful.

The best-known microcredit organization in the world is Grameen Bank of Bangladesh, which invented the concept, and started solely as a microcredit institution. It has branched out to many other areas of social uplift in the 28 years of its existence. Technically, Grameen is not an NGO, in that it is registered with the government as a bank, and has government representatives on its board. The concept that its founder, Mohammed Yunnus, began with is so simple and self-evident that we look back and wonder why we didn't think of it. Yunnus reasoned that what the poor lack, to improve their lot in life, is money—or specifically, access to credit. They lack access to credit because they have no collateral with which to secure a normal commercial loan. Grameen began, and remains mainly, a lender of very small loans to the rural poor, mostly women, without collateral.

Most academic studies have concluded that microcredit programs have made a serious and sustained positive contribution to Bangladesh development.[76] Rahul Amin, a social scientist who has studied and written extensively on NGOs, observes, "women who receive collateral-free credits for income generating activities from the NGOs, or who become NGO members, are more likely to undertake new income-generating activities, raise their income, and productivity, empower themselves, adopt family planning, reduce infant and child mortality, prevent childhood diseases, and attain self-reliance in meeting their socio-economic and other welfare needs than their comparable non-beneficiaries."[77]

Rural women who are the beneficiaries of microcredit programs, according to Amin, "not only increase their …income and empowerment, but also …overcome the socio-economic barriers to fertility regulation and primary health care utilization…[and that] many of these effects are likely to reinforce each other, creating a self-sustaining momentum of socio-economic development…."[78] The question is not *whether* they contribute positively to development, but *how*. Studies that analyze their impact agree that microcredit is positively correlated with improved standards of living…and with a wide range of favorable [social] developments," such as an enhanced

---

76 At least the author has found no serious dissenter to this conclusion. This would not be the case if the discussion were about the political implications and impact, since some academics and government officials have reservations on that score. It is noteworthy also that the NGOs, through their microcredit programs and income-generating projects especially, contribute to growth of national income of Bangladesh. Kendall W. Stiles (see footnote 79) cites a 1998 study by Mohiuddin Alamgir, *Contribution of Grameen Bank to Gross Domestic Product of Bangladesh: Preliminary Estimates* (Dhaka: Program for Research on Poverty Alleviation, 1997) as estimating that the "multiplicative" effects of Grameen alone added one per cent to Bangladeshi GDP in 1997.

77 Ruhul Amin, *Development Strategies and Socio-Demographic Impact of NGOs: Evidence From Rural Bangladesh* (Dhaka: University Press, Ltd., 1997), p. 115.

78 Ibid., p. 116.

sense of worth among women beneficiaries, female voter participation, reduced abuse in the household, and an increased sense of freedom.[79]

But analysts have not been able to choose definitively a primary causation from among those theoretically possible: 1) increased income itself; 2) peer pressure of the group dynamics among the beneficiaries; 3) or the enhanced status of contributing regularly to family income. There are also the questions of whether the income benefits the woman or the household, and whether the borrower ever really gets debt-free, or is always dependent on microcredit to maintain income levels. Moreover some analysts question whether microcredits actually reach and benefit their supposed target—the poorest of the poor. There is also evidence that people at that income level do not ask for such loans because they are ill-equipped to use them productively. Many NGOs argue that by lending to women slightly higher on the income scale who have the ability to use the loans productively, the poorest of the poor will benefit from the higher income of the village (a new version of the "trickle down" theory). Other NGOs such as BRAC are changing the package for the poorest of the poor by providing income-producing items free and training on how to turn them into income.[80]

There are presently 14,000 NGOs in Bangladesh registered with the Ministry of Social Welfare. Whether this total includes those registered with other ministries, or the 840 registered with the NGO Bureau, is not clear. There are probably a few thousand more that are not registered with any government agency because they are too small or are financed totally from local donations or trusts, and which perhaps call themselves something other than NGO. About eight NGOs claim memberships of over 100,000, and there are also eight which show cumulative microcredit disbursements ranging from $7.6 million to $527.8 million—not counting Grameen which towers over the microcredit NGOs with cumulative disbursements of over $2 billion.

The positive social and economic impact of the extensive and growing NGO programs is uncontested. From microcredit alone, the rural poor now receive more than $200 million each year. Stiles points out that, "by the late 1990s, the amount of NGO money reaching the rural poor surpassed state-funded programs...." His conclusion is very telling in our

---

79   Kendall W. Stiles, *Civil Society by Design: Donors, NGOs, and the Intermestic Development Circle in Bangladesh* (New York: Praeger, 2002), p. 48.

80   Celia Dugger, "Debate Stirs Over Tiny Loans for World's Poorest," *New York Times*, April 20, 2004, pp. 1 and 8.

comparison: "[P]rograms of NGOs have enabled them to reach deep into the heart of Bangladeshi society and culture."[81]

The Politics and Economics of an NGO Showcase

For long periods of time in the late 1970s and the 1980s, the state found it very useful to have NGOs supplementing the delivery of social services to the poor (because of its inability to provide such services widely or efficiently). But it seems almost natural that, at some point, the growing power and influence of the NGOs would be perceived as threatening. This has been exacerbated by the rapidly increasing support that NGOs received from foreign donors over the past 10-15 years. Where the state has wanted to secure or strengthen its legitimacy through patronage, NGOs dispensing social services that attenuate such patronage are perceived as threatening by governments. Most NGOs appear to make strenuous efforts to avoid partisan politics (a difficult task in Bangladesh, a society in which everything seems partisan). After all, the state has potent leverage in the threat to use its power to enact new laws regarding the implementation of projects. However, the state's strength *vis-à-vis* the NGOs is limited. Both sides know this, which strengthens the incentive to reach a *modus vivendi*. Episodic periods of tension in the 1980s and through most of the 1990s interfered very little with NGO operations, notwithstanding the fact that governments seek continually to limit their political influence.

With over seven million rural poor Bangladeshis receiving almost $200 million in microcredit loans as well as an increasing volume of other social service deliveries each year, the tension between the state and NGOs (and thus the donor agencies) is likely to become more constant and continue to grow. Neither side can count on winning consistently. The 1991 BNP government of Khaleda Zia tried to bring the NGOs to heel, but the policy failed because, in such extreme circumstances, NGOs always receive the strong support of foreign donors—which the government needs as much as the NGOs.

The dilemma is that the state cannot allow itself to be sidelined by NGOs because they are unable to replace the state in many of its responsibilities: guarantor of whatever rights there are; provider of national infrastructure. As Kendall Stiles observes, "a state reduced to 'franchising' or privatizing

---

81   Stiles, *Civil Society by Design*, p. 48.

service delivery as a result of a reduction in state capacity will likely [lose] control over national policy."[82]

Not all social scientists are convinced that NGO activities in Bangladesh are an unalloyed benefit to the country. These dissenters worry that the prominent role of NGOs is, in the long run, pernicious to the country's political development, in particular to the maturation needed for real democracy to evolve and strengthen. Have the NGOs, in a sense, usurped the role of a wider civil society? Have they developed an unnecessarily antagonistic relationship with the private commercial and industrial sector? Have they so marginalized the state (aided by the state's notorious incompetence and corruption) that it is weakened beyond repair? A state which worked efficiently and transparently would be the patron and enabler of NGOs, and not their rival. That is not the case in Bangladesh. NGOs have become important there because they meet a need and a demand for social services and income generation projects that only they have been able to provide. The NGOs are not forcing their programs on the people; in fact, they are hard pressed to meet the demand. As Stiles observes, "...it is obvious that the millions who receive microcredit do so voluntarily, and often enthusiastically (the ultimate vindication of the program from a democratic standpoint)."[83]

A high volume of NGO activity may actually divert resources from community organizations that are devoted to improving the lot of the poor.[84] This diversion can even affect national professional organizations. Stiles cites organizations such as lawyers, academics, journalists, and other professionals which have been weakened by the growth of NGO influence and support.[85] Some social scientists who seek more utopian solutions to the socio/economic distress of the poor argue that NGO activity attenuates the desire of the people for change. They may reduce the pressure on government to improve its effectiveness and/or to change or even overhaul the political structure. This may be exacerbated by donors' aversion to revolutionary solutions.

NGO programs, especially the microcredit initiatives, are faulted for undercutting political mobilization of the lower strata of society. Such ar-

---

82   Ibid., p. 128.

83   Ibid., p. 124.

84   Ahmed Kamal, "NGOs and Civil Society," paper presented at the March 1, 1999 meeting of the European Commission/NGO Dialogue Project in Dhaka.

85   Stiles, *Civil Society by Design*, p. 122. Much of the discussion in the three subsequent paragraphs comes from Stile's analysis on pp. 122 and 123.

guments seem to ignore the political and social context in Bangladesh and confuse Bangladeshis' desire for a better life with a revolutionary zeal for a new society. A more valid empirical concern is that NGO activities can create divisions among the poor, as their delivery of social services and microcredits inevitably favors some groups over others. This is a concern that an efficient and effective government could alleviate.

Economists dealing with development have occasionally expressed concerns about the way microcredit is used as an income-generating device for the rural poor. One question is whether the increment to the income of microcredit borrowers from the income-generating projects these credits finance is sustainable. To rephrase the issue, do microcredits lead to one-shot increments in income, such that the credits must be continually repeated to sustain the new level of income? Is the ultimate result a dependency on microcredits and a perpetuation of debt? A second, macroeconomic unknown is whether microcredits, the social benefits of which are very clear, undercut the holistic or comprehensive program needed to serve the multiple goals of development. Do they, by their very nature, take a strongly paternalistic approach to the delivery of microcredits and social services? Do they foster dependency on the part of borrowers rather than either promoting self-reliance and community reliance.[86]

Are NGOs responsible for the diversion of donor resources from inefficient and corrupt governments? This question is central to the growing problems between the state and the NGOs. As Stiles remarks, "NGOs have begun to supplant the State as the primary source of services and credit for tens of millions of Bangladeshis."[87]

The Contrary Example—NGOs' Limited Impact in Pakistan

The conclusion from the available research is that NGOs are relatively weak and far less influential in Pakistan than in Bangladesh. They have had much less impact on social development and, thus, on social progress. According to the Asian Development Bank (ADB), despite a generally positive government attitude (at least toward domestic NGOs), there are few Pakistani NGO success stories in social development.[88] The ADB points out that

---

86   What these social scientists seem to ignore is reality. The alternative in rural Bangladesh is the moneylender. Commercial banks do not provide capital to the poor. That is what the microcredit concept is all about.

87   Ibid., p. 127.

88   Asian Development Bank, *A Study of NGOs—Pakistan* (Manila, ADB, 1999), p. 5.

many of the Pakistani NGOs, even those that have been in operation for forty to fifty years, require continuous support to sustain operations.[89]

Apart from the Family Planning Association of Pakistan (FPAP), "only a handful of other national NGOs involved in the implementation of community-based projects have comparable credentials, coverage, linkages, delivery mechanisms, and documentation systems."[90] The Canadian International Development Agency (CIDA) has estimated in another study that "there are less than 100 effective NGOs in Pakistan."[91]

Probably most NGOs in Pakistan—and certainly the majority of those in its early years —were (and still are) involved in emergency rehabilitation and relief operations. Many of these began operations right after the 1947 partition to meet the vast humanitarian needs of those early days of United Pakistan. Since then, some have evolved into organizations that deliver social services. A smaller number of NGOs in Pakistan began and continue as social service delivery organizations.

Microcredit

Providing microcredit is not limited to NGOs in Pakistan. A number of financial institutions specialize or dabble in microcredit programs but these have a far more ambiguous record than the limited number of NGOs that provide microcredits. One problem often cited by social scientists is that many of the financial institutions seem not to achieve the usual objectives of microcredit by reaching the poorer segments of rural society, and especially women. Lynn Renken, studying microcredit organizations in Punjab (that contains about half of the Pakistani population), argues that, in effect, the microcredit programs of the Pakistani financial institutions serve middle-to-upper-class urban women, and not rural, poor women as their mandates envision. These microcredit programs are clearly not particularly helpful in solving the problems of social development in Pakistan, reaching few of the rural, poor women they are ostensibly aimed at.[92]

---

89   Ibid., p. 5. The ADB is addressing here the enormous difficulties that have confronted the governments of Pakistan in promoting family planning programs and implying that if the governments have such difficulty, it will be even more difficult for NGOs to succeed in promoting such programs.

90   Ibid., p. 5

91   As quoted in ADB document. Ibid., p. 5.

92   Lynn Renken, "Microfinance in Pakistan: Perpetuation of Power or a Viable Avenue for Empowerment?" *Power and Civil Society in Pakistan,* Anita M. Weiss and S. Zulficar Gilani (eds) (Karachi: Oxford University Press, 2001), p. 248.

NGO microcredit programs in Pakistan are a far cry from what we know of such programs in Bangladesh where their equivalents do a far better job. On the other hand, Pakistani NGO micro-credit programs, while not yet in the league of those in Bangladesh, have a much more significant impact than the financial institutions which are engaged in micro finance.

The impact of NGO microcredit programs has been constrained for several reasons. First, there are far fewer of them. Second, they started late and are now only at the early stages of development (about where Bangladesh was in the early 1980s) Third, they have yet to find a formula for general acceptance in the Pakistani environment and have not always had the support of local officials or a local environment which fostered their growth. In the past decade, the mid-levels in the Pakistan government and the local governments have become more receptive to NGO activity (perhaps pushed by the World Bank and other donors).

Renken examined also micro-credit programs of NGOs in Punjab. She found, in comparison to the banking institutions described above, that NGOs are much more flexible and successful "and play a critical role in securing women's access to credit in the Punjab."[93] But she also found that they have not had a major impact.[94]

She concluded that Pakistan has only begun to develop microcredit programs as one means of addressing poverty and providing empowerment to poor, rural women. The problems she found include: 1) Punjabi women "continue to have difficulties securing small loans"; 2) "the majority of women in Pakistan cannot get credit from either NGOs or credit-lending facilities"; 3) "women's access to credit in Punjab greatly depends upon the district in which they live, their proximity to a lending institution, and the institution's lending requirements"; 4) "women who generally benefit from credit in the Punjab are middle-to-upper-class, urban women, with few rural or low-income women being served by the [credit] facilities"; 5) and "only on rare occasion [did] female [applicants] receive a loan without collateral."[95]

Social Service Delivery

There are a few examples of successful and sustained NGO social service delivery programs in Pakistan. Yet even those NGOs that enjoy suc-

---

93   Ibid., p. 269.
94   Ibid., p. 266-7.
95   Ibid., pp. 270-2.

cess with programs delivering social services almost always combine those programs with others involving some sort of "community development" (which most often means political advocacy by another name and are often perceived as a challenge to the government). There seem few, if any, NGOs in Pakistan which concentrate uniquely on social service delivery, as is the case for most NGOs in Bangladesh.

A number of NGOs limit their efforts to various kinds of advocacy. They are the more recent arrivals on the NGO as newcomers to the Pakistani NGO scene. The late Omar Asgar Khan, later a Cabinet Minister in the first Musharraf government, wrote, "as compared to charitable NGOs involved in politically neutral activities, NGOs working in the field of development and advocacy are a more recent phenomenon in Pakistan."[96]

Ironically, Zia ul Huq gets the credit for provoking the growth of such NGOs with the "political repression and human rights violations" which his regime fostered.[97] More specifically, it was primarily the discriminatory Hudood legislation, mentioned above, which the Zia regime promulgated, that led to the formation of many different advocacy NGOs. Many educated women were shocked into political action by this retrogressive act.[98]

The advocacy NGOs in Pakistan now focus on a wide variety of social and legal issues, most of which are fundamentally political in nature. These include organizations that are primarily concerned with legal rights, especially of women and the poor. Other organizations work on broader women's issues, in particular violence against women. Another set of NGOs focuses on human rights; others work mainly on issues pertaining to minorities. There are a few of these advocacy NGOs concerned with children's issues, and others which devote themselves to improving literacy through increasing public awareness.

It is the rapid growth of advocacy NGOs that soured the attitude of the Pakistani government toward NGOs, though this is changing rapidly. The Asian Development Bank (ADB) writes in its NGO report on Pakistan, "a majority of the 'new breed' of NGOs are obsessed with proving the inefficiency and corruption of the government, and with presenting themselves

---

96   Omar Asgar Khan, "Critical Engagements: NGOs and the State," *Power and Civil Society in Pakistan,* p. 276.

97   Ibid., p. 276.

98   Talbot, *Pakistan: A Modern History,* pp. 275-6, gives a good description of the reaction to the Hudood laws.

as the panacea for all development problems. They want to replace rather than work with the government."[99]

In the view of ADB, "much of the alarm of the government about NGOs is recent and a direct result of the activities of the new breed of NGOs that appear less interested in delivering services or implementing development projects than in lobbying and advocacy. Many of these NGOs have sprung up overnight, and many appear to have huge funds and international support at their command, even though they lack a track record. They are often perceived as agents of outsiders with agendas that may be detrimental to Pakistan."[100]

NGOs—A Metaphor for Cultural or Societal Differences?

NGOs are now rooted deeply in Bangladesh culture, though its strong and vibrant civil society is divided on their merits. The attitude of the donors, which is still quite important to Bangladesh, remains highly favorable towards NGOs. The government is unlikely to be able, in the foreseeable future, even with the best intentions, to improve its own service delivery performance. Thus the demand for NGO services will remain robust, and the political party that promises to unfetter NGOs is likely to gain much support. It seems indisputable that, without NGOs, Bangladesh would not have sprinted ahead in social development, especially in family planning, income generation for the poor, literacy, especially for females, and women's development. NGO success often annoys the politicians, but they have brought much benefit to many millions of poor Bangladeshis.

Nonetheless, the general perception of NGOs in Bangladesh is not monochromatic. Though they have generally operated in a permissive and supportive environment and maintained a positive image, they have had to avoid politicization by adopting a policy of rigorous neutrality. This, in addition to intense donor pressure on the government, has provided them the space to deliver the social services that the government fails to provide. Donor funding does not seem to be a problem in Bangladesh. NGOs such as Grameen and BRAC fund themselves from local sources, but maintain their independence and control even when accepting donor funding.[101] One cogent fact:

---

99   ADB, *A Study of NGOs—Pakistan*, p. 18.

100 Ibid., p. 15.

101 We saw above, in the sections which discussed the problems in Bangladesh that spring from the preponderant role of NGOs in the country, that there are concerns about too much donor funding; at present, however, it would not be accurate to conclude that NGOs have been ineffective because of this.

when Grameen, for example, is faulted for only reaching 20 per cent of the, say, 75 million poor in Bangladesh, that means that between 15 and 20 million poor people are benefiting from its microcredit programs. That number seems a very powerful argument in favor of NGO programs.

In Pakistan, the picture is much more complicated. Though NGOs have operated there since independence in 1947, they have concentrated, until recently, on humanitarian relief. The growth of NGOs specializing in social service delivery has been slow, and many have been unable to sustain successful programs, which has helped to increase skepticism about them. The traditional NGOs have been joined in recent years by others which focus their efforts on advocacy—that is, inducing people to demand services or rights—or on promoting policy dialogue. These recent arrivals have, to some extent, soured the atmosphere for NGOs in Pakistan even more because they harden the bureaucracy's attitude and increase its resistance to all NGOs. In addition, some NGOs have proved to be fronts for collecting money for personal enrichment, and this has reduced their wider credibility.

One distinguished academic critic, S. Akbar Zaidi, believes that NGO service delivery is "complicated by the existence of biradaris [clanlike communities of peasant proprietors], heterogeneous communities, *and the poor social position of women* [emphasis mine]."[102] NGO dependence on donor money, according to Zaidi, also helps to undermine NGO acceptability in Pakistan. "[T] heir entire existence," he writes, "depends on donor money, *almost always from abroad*" (emphasis mine).[103] This appears to be a Pakistan-specific problem.[104]

---

102   S. Akbar Zaidi, *The New Development Paradigm: Papers on Institutions, NGOs, and Local Government* (Karachi: Oxford University Press, 1999), p. 194.

103   Ibid., pp. 209-16.

104   Zaidi, for example, cites similar problems in other countries in which NGOs operate as important partners of the government, e.g. Sierra Leone, Gambia, and Sri Lanka. The author, having witnessed NGO operations in several other countries, including most importantly Bangladesh, believes that Zaidi and other critics of NGOs ignore powerful counter arguments based on state failure—which derives from lack of competence or lack of will, or from war or conflict situations, as for example in Sierra Leone.

10

STILL ON THE BRINK AFTER THIRTY-SEVEN YEARS

Two separate, independent countries emerged in December 1971 from the dissolution of United Pakistan. The future for the new Pakistan seemed bright—democracy replaced military government, and economic prospects looked more assured. For Bangladesh, predictions were generally grim— an unruly polity made the democratic beginnings, at best, problematic; and a devastated economy made progress unlikely. Yet, thirty-seven years later both the optimistic predictions for Pakistan and the pessimistic ones for Bangladesh have proven unfounded. Both countries remain works in progress—and the question is, progress toward what?

The Political/Military Rollercoaster—Convergence to Divergence to Uncertainty

Political development in Bangladesh and Pakistan appeared, on the surface, to take an almost identical path between 1972 and 1990. The democracies with which both countries started in 1972 failed miserably after a few years. One factor common to both was poor leadership and poor judgment by their charismatic but badly flawed leaders, Mujib and Bhutto. These failed democracies were replaced by military governments that slowly, under pressure, assumed a civilian façade. Such hybrid arrangements were inherently unsustainable, and were replaced by elected civilian governments. In those years, observers could be forgiven for concluding that one was a pale imitation of the other.

In Bangladesh, Ziaur Rahman started out as an ordinary military strongman in 1975, taking power to "stabilize" the country and keeping it to set the country on the "right" path. But by 1978 the path had switched to one that would get the military out of politics. Ziaur Rahman led the military dispensation, without much notice or articulation, into a civilian façade, then into an elected civilian government in which the military lost predominance. He may simply have been consolidating his own personal power at the expense of both the military and civilian politicians. Whatever the reason, his brief success at subordinating the military to civilian rule was a prominent factor prompting his assassination by a faction of the military which opposed the direction he seemed to be taking.

General Ershad's coup in 1982 seemed the Bangladeshi version of the 1977 military intervention in Pakistan. Its motivation was purely and baldly to wield political power and to benefit from the spoils of wielding that power. Its public rationale was precisely the same as that in Pakistan—civilian politicians have messed up the economy and can't be trusted with national security. In Pakistan, the same argument, that it was "necessary" to stop a spiral of chaos and irresponsible fissiparous political behavior, was used by the military to justify its coups of 1977 and 1999. The explanation evolved into the traditional military rationale that civilian politicians could not be trusted with the national security of Pakistan. It seems more likely that at least some of the military saw the openings that Bhutto's and Sharif's mistakes provided as opportunities to retrieve political power they had lost and regain their control of government policy.

Some elected politicians in Pakistan (not all) have attempted to subordinate the military to civilian governments. Most of the time, these attempts were feckless or simply rhetorical. The best opportunity came in the initial years after separation when the military's image was so tarnished that a civilian administration with democratic vision could have subordinated it institutionally. Z.A. Bhutto and his party failed to do so largely because of their short-term tactical mindset, bent on accumulating power—a mindset that led Bhutto, *inter alia*, to use the army extensively to solve political problems in Balochistan, which only served to strengthen its self-esteem and image.

The only other serious effort to subordinate the military took place in the second Nawaz Sharif government—that of the overwhelming PML majority—and this came apart because of the inept and feckless way it was pursued.[1] More importantly, not only has the Pakistani army declined to

---

[1]   Vali Nasr, "Military Rule, Islamism, and Democracy in Pakistan," *The Middle East Journal*, 58, no. 2, (Spring 2004), p. 200. See Chapter 8. Nasr argues that this was Sharif's political objective in his second term when the large PML majority rescinded the eighth amendment giving the President power to dismiss Prime Ministers and governments, and he arbitrarily dismissed one Chief of Army Staff and tried to dismiss a second to

give up its interest in controlling politics in Pakistan, but over the past six years it has entrenched itself ever more deeply in the nation's economic and social fabric to the point that, as renowned political analyst Hasan-Askari Rizvi has written, "makes it imperative for [the army] to stay involved in policy making and management to protect [its] interests."[2]

The military intervention and rule of Musharraf demonstrates that the Army's rationale, to share power and exert predominant influence, remains intact to this day. As a result, the military has sunk such roots in Pakistan's political structure, and has such formidable power, and experience in governing, that it is able to dominate either in a civilian façade, from the sidelines, or when in direct control. As Rizvi notes, "this ... adversely affects the prospects of autonomous growth of civilian political, economic, and societal processes."[3] The national savior mindset has strengthened in the 1990s, when the elected politicians failed to provide effective governance, but appears to be eroding after eight years of Army rule.

For the last seventeen years, the most important political divergence was in the attitude of the two militaries. In the opening decade, 1972-1982, both militaries, coming from a common tradition and sharing a history of military intervention in United Pakistan, acted from a common view of themselves as the guarantors of national security and unity. The Bangladesh military appeared to have broken out of that mindset—and the vicious political circle such a mindset engenders—in 1990. However, its takeover of the government on January 11, 2007 may signal a return to military-dominated governance, although at this point halfway through its promised interregnum, it still appears a good bet that power will revert to civilian governments by the beginning of 2009. In Pakistan, the Army has retreated

---

find one who would be subservient to him. Many scholars disagree that he had such a clear or well thought-out vision for the country. Certainly, he never articulated any such strategy. (Close contacts of the author suggest that it was not Nawaz Sharif who would have authored such a strategy, but his father who was a powerful influence and at the same time quite pious in the vein of Zia ul Huq.) It can be argued that, even if Sharif's political objectives in his second term were much more self-serving, i.e. the accretion of more and unimpeachable power for him, his family, and his party, the indirect effects of his actions would have begun subordinating the military over time to civilian control. Perhaps there were elements in the military leadership who anticipated this before most politicians did. In any case, we might not have liked the results if Sharif had succeeded, as his strategy seemed to be to entice the Islamic forces, including the Islamists, into his camp by making sharia the law of the land, under the mistaken impression, I presume, that he could control them.

2   Rizvi, Hasan-Askari, "Dimensions of the Military's Role," *Daily Times of Pakistan*, April 11, 2005, accessed on April 11, 2005 at http://www.dailytimes.com.pk./default.asp?

3   Ibid., accessed at same location.

somewhat from direct involvement in politics after the thrashing the government party received in the February 18 2008 election, but whether it is inclined to emulate its Bangladeshi counterpart (i.e. by withdrawing entirely from politics) is unclear. And unlikely.

Economic Convergence and Social Divergence

Both countries have been economic underachievers for most of their separate histories, and in that sense their development profiles are also similar. Each began its independent life in an orgy of statist economic excess, primarily nationalization of most large industrial assets, under widely acclaimed democratic governments. (Bangladesh went much further on this.) In each, this period of statist excess created a serious legacy in both countries, which neither has completely overcome to this day. However, Pakistan under Musharraf has implemented serious reforms that have helped its economy to surge ahead.

Bangladesh has moved far ahead of Pakistan in the rate of improvement of most human development indicators. This is one of the most striking aspects, so far, of our examination of the two countries. Social development continues to lag in Pakistan, yet there is no generally agreed explanation for this important difference. Observers look for an answer mainly in the cultural differences between the two countries, but such partial explanations have not proven satisfactory. In Bangladesh, the simple hypothesis is that greater poverty led to widespread demand for social services, and a permissive attitude toward the NGOs allowed them to meet that demand. Once established, NGOs became part of Bangladesh's socio/economic fabric.

Central to this puzzle is the question of government failure. In Bangladesh, it is the failure of government to implement some of its normal services that has engendered the rise and success of the NGOs. On the other hand, Pakistan has lagged on social development not because of government failure but because of government indifference. In general, what has been missing is a commitment on the part of the political power centers in Pakistan, elected or not elected, to provide resources for serious social development, and a much greater reluctance—or skepticism—about the merits of NGOs on the part of government and society. Now, eight years into the twenty-first century, this outlook is in flux, but success will depend on increasing the revenue base and/or reducing the military share of national expenditure.

The Accelerating Islamization of Pakistan

Islamism, political Islam in its various forms, carries with it a civilizational agenda which calls for the radical transformation of society. The Islamist approach in Pakistan is often referred to as *nizam-i mustafa,* "the system of the Prophet," a return to a more scripturalist approach to life. The scriptualist definition varies, however, with different Islamist organizations. For example, the *nizam-i mustafa* called for by Maulana Abu'l-A'la Maududi (deceased 1979), the founder of Jamat-i-Islami, was that the state should exist "not only to protect Muslim interests but to embody Islamic principles."[4]

The broadest definition in Pakistan of these principles occurred during Zia ul Huq's regime, in a 1980 government document which defined Islamic goals as a better life for more people, *moderate* (emphasis mine) economic growth, and social justice. This included recommendations for such policies as universal education, land redistribution, limits on inherited wealth, and a comprehensive and progressive tax policy.[5] This unlikely social agenda never had a chance of acceptance in Pakistan among any part of the establishment—military, feudal land owners, or industrialists. Instead, the various democratic and military regimes have sought legitimacy through their connection to Islam. The usual Islamic prohibitions and injunctions have been promulgated and alcohol and gambling banned. The mandatory tax (*zakat*) distributed by religious authorities to the poor was implemented. There have also been changes in the judicial system, and the Hudood laws, which sought to launch the process of immuring women, were enacted. Ostracism and persecution of perceived apostate sects such as the Ahmadiyya has made society more intolerant.[6]

Islamist influence has grown steadily in Pakistan since 1972. The process began slowly and almost surreptitiously when Zulfikar Ali Bhutto capitulated on making Islam the state religion of Pakistan in the 1973 Constitution as well as on the requirement that only Muslims hold the offices of President and Prime Minister.[7] Later, when in political trouble and seeking (unsuccessfully) Islamist support, Bhutto gave in again to their demands to close bars, ban alcohol, and make Friday the weekly holiday, and define Ah-

---

4 Metcalf, "Islamic Arguments…," *Islamic Contestations,* p. 240.

5 These are the principles that may have been at the base of the movement for Islamic Socialism which carried Zulfikar Ali Bhutto to power, but which were lost in the wave of nationalization, power accumulation and corruption that characterized his tenure.

6 Metcalf, "Islamic Arguments…," *Islamic Contestations,* p. 241.

7 The Ahmadiyyas were officially declared apostate at the same time.

madiyyas as non-Muslims. Islamization became institutionalized under Zia ul Huq, who embraced it as a way to establish a national identity, and saw in it a useful tool to legitimize his military regime. Much of the Islamization of the society and the juridical process took root during the this period, as he changed the outlook of the government from one in which Islam was, in one way or another, the center of a search for national unity, to one in which Islam became a "program of government action."[8]

With that kind of inspiration in the eleven years of the Zia ul Huq government, Islamism made even father inroads in the political life of the country. During the elected regimes of Benazir Bhutto and Nawaz Sharif, Islamist influence, at best, remained about where it was when Zia ul Huq and the military left office in 1988. If Sharif had remained in office and been successful in passing the 15th amendment he had proposed—to make sharia the law of the land—the influence of the Islamists would have grown enormously. As far as can be surmised, this proposal was the symbol of his strategy to form a center-right coalition that included the Islamic parties so as to undercut the support and the legitimacy of the military as the major political force.[9] In fact, when Musharraf took power in October 1999, one justification often given by some military officers was that the army could not allow the incorporation of sharia into the constitution as the law of the land, as that would have brought the Islamization of the country to a point at which it was irreversible and irreparable. In retrospect, this looks more like a code in which the army was saying that it could not allow the center right coalition of conservative political and Islamic forces, that Nawaz Sharif seemed to be moving toward, to come together. That would have broken its power ultimately, as the military had no popular roots as did the conservative and Islamic parties. An interesting note is that many of the civilian politicians were privately relieved by the military's action and told me that the coup might be justified, in the short run, by the need to stop the march of a constitutional amendment enshrining sharia as the law of the land. In particular, a number of high-level leaders of the PPP mentioned this as one reason why they had hopes that the Musharraf military intervention might not be so bad. It is not clear whether they would have changed their view had they realized that Sharif had more than just Sharia in mind with his proposal.

---

8   Metcalf, "Islamic Arguments…," *Islamic Contestations,* p. 236.

9   Vali Nasr, "Military Rule," *The Middle East Journal,* p. 200.

Those who justified military government on the basis that it could turn back the rising tide of Islamism found, however, that things were not so simple. If Musharraf did not live up to their expectations it is because, in part, of the deep roots Islamists have established in Pakistani society, the legacy primarily of the previous military regime, as well as the sad state of general education in Pakistan, the legacy of all previous regimes.

There is, in fact, some truth in the contention that this inability by a military government to take on the Islamists is the result of the historical weaknesses of Pakistan—the deficient education of the majority of the Pakistani people, the deep Islamic and Islamist roots that have grown in the polity since 1972, and the determination of Islamist leaders to block any retreat in the direction they perceive the country is heading, i.e. a more scriptualist Islamic state. Instead, each time the Musharraf government ventured to push Islamists back by modifying some of their favorite levers of social control, it found that Islamist have the means to push back equally forcefully. Several times, President Musharraf came into conflict with Islamists over these levers, and usually he backed down. This began in 2000, when he proposed changes in the blasphemy law (which is used as much for social retaliation as for religious reasons); at that point, he was in direct charge of the country with no parliamentary body to answer to, but resistance from the Islamists was still too much for him—and the army leadership.

But it is not as simple as that either: political allies that shared his mindset and goal of "enlightened moderation" would have been able to offset and counteract resistance to policies that moved that doctrine forward. The legacy of the Army's traditional repugnance of politicians and political parties, and particularly of mainstream parties that represent the more liberal elements of Pakistani society, is an important factor in judging the validity of the government's rationale for a pusillanimous approach to progress toward "enlightened moderation." This has continued to affect, for example, the government's promise to reform madrassas, which has moved very slowly, if at all. In 2005, the Musharraf government gave way to Islamists again by agreeing to the inclusion of the religion of the bearer in the passport of Pakistani travelers. The President often blamed the National Assembly for continued retreats in the face of Islamist opposition, but the entire government leadership, both civilian and military, despite Musharraf's personal predilections, remains wary of stirring up Islamist opposition.

Only once did Musharraf prevail in his (mostly rhetorical) quest for "enlightened moderation." In late 2006, the Musharraf government sent a bill amending the Hudood laws to the National Assembly. The changes made it easier for a rape victim to bring charges against her assailant and avoid being charged with a crime herself. Getting it through the Assembly proved more difficult than one would think. As would be expected, the Islamist MMA rejected the bill as "anti-Islamic." It was the President's own party, the PML-Q, however, that made things difficult by running from the bill, thinking it would damage them at the polls. (They are generally conservative anyway and do not share Musharraf's moderate social views.) After some back and forth, Musharraf forced the bill through, with the help of the PPP, which had supported it all along.

At the beginning of the military regime, in 1999 and 2000, it was often speculated that there was a core of officers in the army who were Islamist in sentiment, and that Musharraf didn't dare to take them on. After nine years in charge of the Army, he made virtually all its high-level officers into his clones by judicious appointments to key positions, and by easing officers into retirement who may have had some Islamist sympathies. The existence of strong Islamist sentiment in the army command structure is surely not the reason, and likely never was, for the pusillanimous posture *vis-à-vis* Islamist forces that Musharraf often took.

He kept the officer corps happy by following regular promotion schedules—i.e. no officer was promoted beyond what the rules allow—and by ensuring that every retired officer is appointed to a government job. However, the worldview of the officers below flag rank is difficult to discern. Some observers believe that there is significant Islamist sentiment at lower levels of the officer corps which inhibited Musharaff and the senior command in their ability to pursue a bolder anti-Islamist policy. It is hard to know whether piety (and many officers are pious) leads often to hard-line Islamist sentiments, and when such conversion would occur. In 2001, however, at least two of the flag officers were known to be "religious" to the point they became a liability for Musharraf when 9/11 forced him to choose to support the US against the Taliban. The broader question of how deeply Islamism has infiltrated into government and especially the security service circles is very important but little discussed. The intelligence agencies are often thought to be a major part of the problem (though they fall under the military chain of command), because of their longstanding patronage of many jihadi groups. These agencies have often been regarded as semi-autonomous, and it is believed that many of their officers have picked up the Islamist sentiments of their jihadi clients.

Benazir Bhutto's assassination moved this question again to the fore-ground. After the October 18 attempt on her life in Karachi, she claimed to have knowledge of closet Islamists inside government security services that were complicit in the attack. Her party has claimed that similar "fellow travelers" were responsible for the lax security that allowed the assassins to get so close on December 27. Western governments and observers are also troubled by the opacity of this question as they evaluate the potential for Pakistan's 40-50 nuclear weapons to fall into the hands of Islamists who would turn them over to Al Qaeda to fulfill its long-cherished dream of a nuclear attack on the "near" and "far" enemy. It is not the nuclear command and control system that the Pakistan military has established that is the worry; rather it is the danger that this system itself, and thus the weapons that it is supposed to control, could fall into the hands of Islamist agents during an Islamist takeover of the state.

But the ultimate cause of concern, perhaps trumping all the above worries, is the increasing and accelerating "Talibanization" of the Western half of Pakistan. The historical roots of this onslaught go back, of course, to the 1980s jihadi war against the Soviet Union in Afghanistan and are far too complicated and convoluted to recount here. Pakistan adopted the concept of using jihadi groups to fight a proxy war in Kashmir, and trained and nurtured such groups until 9/11, the rapprochment with India, and its "War on Terror" alliance with the US caused a abrupt change in policy and the alleged withdrawal of support and encouragement from most of these groups. They have regrouped in the Tribal areas, especially Waziristan, and are now the spearhead of an internal Taliban movement directed not just at regaining power in Afghanistan, but in supplanting the "apostate" regime in Pakistan with a Salafist Islamist state. It is a case of the monster threatening its creator. Courageous journalists have reported on the growth of these forces, and the frighteningly new aspect that "traditional" Islamist leaders appear to have lost almost all influence with these jihadis. The former's inability to dissuade leaders of the Red Mosque from their confrontational, and ultimately suicidal, policies in the summer 2007 reflect this worrying development. There does not appear to be any effective way of working out politically the approaching confrontation.

The Islamist Attack on Bangladesh

In comparison with Pakistan, Islamism has a weaker foothold and a less influential role in Bangladesh. Islamist parties were on the political fringes in both wings of United Pakistan after independence, and this was particularly true in East Pakistan where they had little support before the war of separation, and even less after. Their support of Pakistan and rejection of Bengali separatism during the war almost destroyed their credibility with the public. In addition, some Islamists such as the leader of the JI, Gholam Azam, were accused of complicity in the savage treatment of Bengalis by the Pakistani army.

In scenarios reminiscent of Pakistan, the Islamist parties in Bangladesh were saved politically by military governments. Both Ziaur Rahman and Ershad reached out to Islamic forces to help secure their legitimacy, and thus Islamist parties had regained their former strength by 1991 when the post-Ershad electoral democracy began. They have remained parties with small electoral bases, able mainly to influence events and policy by joining coalitions with the major parties on specific issues or helping them to form governments after elections. Their political influence has grown because of this rehabilitation and their willingness to form coalitions with the major parties while playing a secondary role. The JI joined with the BNP in 1991 and its influence increased dramatically when it provided the margin of victory in 2001 for the BNP coalition.

Islamism has been growing in strength and influence in Bangladesh society in the past two decades.[10] But there is little empirical evidence of its depth or breadth of support among people in the rural areas. Their advance appears to be as much a symptom of poor governance and disregard for the rule of law as a manifestation of increased religious piety among Bangladeshis. It seems undeniable that the Islamists are capitalising on deficient governance to advance their cause, and using religious structures—compliant mullahs willing to issue decrees which have no basis in law—to create fear and conformity in Bangladesh society, especially in rural areas.

Islamists in Bangladesh come in a wide variety of shapes and sizes. Traditional Sufi schools of thought remain strong, but are losing popular traction to the fundamentalist ones that have sprung up. Operating under the veneer of legitimate political parties are a number of shadowy Islamist groups that function more on the fringes of society and often use violence to enforce their will. They often have informal connections to the political parties.

---

10   Tazeen M. Murshid, "State Nation, and Identity: Ideology and Conflict in Bangladesh," *Region and Partition—Bengal, Punjab, and the Partition of the Subcontinent* (Karachi: Oxford University Press, 1999), pp. 358-69. See also Ali Riaz, *God Willing—The Politics of Islamism in Bangladesh* (Lanham,MD.: Rowman and Littlefield Publishers, Ltd., 2004).

Beginning in the late 1980s, there has been a steady rise in violence against secular elements of Bangladesh society or against individuals, especially women, who are perceived to have violated the social code espoused by strict, scripturalist Islam.[11] Islamists have often been behind these attacks, which are usually the result of *fatwas*, judgements by religious leaders on law and morality. *Fatwas* have increased dramatically in quantity and scope, and have become far more political and virulent. Their use has been perverted over the years as they are increasingly mobilised to target those who hold unpopular opinions or vary in their social behavior from norms defined by the Islamists, or organizations (primarily NGOs that deliver social services to women) that sponsor what are claimed to be "un-Islamic" activities. Women are increasingly harassed as the Islamists successfully narrow the interpretation of how Islam allows them to behave. There is increasing anecdotal evidence that, in rural areas, there is increasing pressure to isolate women within their homes (purdah) and enforce a stricter dress code when they do emerge. NGOs are attacked because of the Islamist claim that they are secular organizations that empower women, through microcredit loans and education, over their husbands, and encourage them to work with men. Such activities are said to "promote atheism." In the last five years, the Islamists have also targeted cultural events that they call "secular," such as movies, concerts, and festivals. Journalists perceived as secular have also been attacked, as well as other civil society organizations.

One little-noticed aspect of growing Islamist influence is the rapid growth of madrassas, especially of those allied to the Deobandis. The growth of madrassas is both cause and effect of the Islamization process. The Bangladeshi scholar, Ali Riaz, has tracked madrassa growth in Bangladesh in some detail. His conclusion is that "the number and influence of all [four types of madrassas found in Bangladesh] have grown remarkably."[12] He believes that several factors have contributed to the rapid "proliferation" of madrassas in Bangladesh: the lack of adequate state investment in education (in other words a supply problem); the shift in domestic politics away from Awami League secularism to the military governments' search for legitimacy through Islam and the search of the two main political parties after 1991 for Islamist

---

11   Ibid. Riaz has documented carefully the increased incidence of violence that appears religiously motivated, as well as the possible connections to political parties.

12   Ali Riaz, "Madrassah Education in Bangladesh: An Overview," paper presented at the Conference on Islamic Trends in Bangladesh, sponsored by the US Department of State and the Carnegie Endowment for International Peace, Washington DC, January 25, 2004.

political allies; the return of millions of Bangladeshi migrant workers from the very conservative Gulf countries, many of whom have been inculcated with a much stricter brand of Islam during their time there (in other words as demand phenomenon); and the growth, with government support, of Islamic NGOs that "place education at the top of their agenda." [13]

As Islamism's influence has grown and its attacks on the "secular" forces of Bangladesh increased, there has been an understandable retreat from the pluralism that has always been a hallmark of Bengali society.[14] Minority groups, perhaps especially Hindus, are suffering increased discrimination, and find it harder to get equal protection from the BNP and AL governments that were transfixed by a desire to stay in office by any means possible, and were often in cahoots with the Islamists politically. The most recent manifestation of radical Islamism (in truth jihad against the "near enemy")[15] was the spate of bombings by the Jamaat ul Mujihadeen Bangladesh (JMB), which received much attention in the Western press. In August of 2005, over 400 bombs were set off, almost simultaneously, throughout Bangladesh. This appeared to be an announcement by the JMB that the group was a factor to be taken seriously in Bangladeshi politics. Its agenda is simple—the complete Islamization of society.[16] It targeted the courts and judges in its round of bombings, claiming that they were following secular law not sharia. After much fumbling and name calling, the BNP government cracked down on the organization, caught a number of its operatives, and executed six of its leaders. But it seems unlikely that this will be the last of such groups to appear (assuming that the JMB is truly on the wane).

The continual flirtation with Islamists by every government since Mujib's has been part of the problem. The perception that civilian and military governments needed them, emboldened and empowered the Islamists, within the context of the prevailing poisonous and violent nature of Bangladeshi politics. The general climate of political terror that prevails in the country spawns religious terror. At times, political terror is also

---

13   Ibid., pp. 4-6.

14   One manifestation of the growing intolerance is the mounting attacks on the Ahmadiyya sect. In 2004, their publications were prohibited, though government ministers have been quoted that this was a mistake. See "Bangladesh," *The Economist,* June 16, 2005.

15   See page 4 of the introduction for a definition of jihadism.

16   Zayadul Ahsan, "Profiles Show Them Interlinked," *The Daily Star,* August 28, 2005, *The Daily Star* Wed. edition, vol.5, no. 447, accessed on March 21, 2006 at www.thedailystar.net/2005/08/28/d5082801022.htm.

religious terror, as it is highly likely that the thuggish elements of all parties will retain their links to religious terrorists until politics is truly transformed.

Ali Riaz believes that Bangladeshi Islamist forces use religion mainly to gain political power.

Their activism is more to serve political-economic interests than to attain religious objectives. They draw on Islamic referants—terms, symbols, and events taken from Islamic tradition—in order to articulate a distinct political agenda. To them Islam is more a political blueprint than a faith, and the Islamic discourse is, to a large extent, a political discourse in religious garb…which is understood as a form of instrumentalizion of Islam by individuals, groups, and organizations that pursue political objectives and which provide political response to today's societal challenges by imagining a future, the foundations of which rest on reappropriated, reinvented concepts borrowed from the Islamic tradition.[17]

While Islamists have not fared so well in elections, the growth of their influence and ability to target and intimidate the secular and/or non-religious forces is reason enough to be concerned about the future of whatever form of democracy emerges from the present dispensation. That they increasingly set the tone of public discourse is worrisome; that a fragmented civil society has not yet mounted an effective response is more so. If the major political parties in the future system can resist the Islamists' electoral blandishments, and if the zero-sum-game character of political culture and the use of violence and intimidation as a political weapon can be eliminated from Bangladeshi politics, the Islamists' challenge will be overcome.

It is easy to conclude that, like a thorn in the foot, Islamism is an unnatural addition to the Bangladeshi polity that can be easily removed when governments become more efficient and effective. In general, this is a valid metaphor. Islamism is after all a movement that sees all virtue largely in a distant past, and in the book from that long-ago period that contains God's word. Yet, while it would be an exaggeration to say that Islamism is the threat in Bangladesh that it is in Pakistan, it has made dangerous inroads. The outcome of the Islamist effort to capture Bangladesh society depends greatly on that of the current experiment to build an effective democracy.

---

17   Ali Riaz, *God Willing*, p. 14. As quoted from Richard Hrair Dekmajian, "The Anatomy of Islamic Revivalism: Legitimacy, Crisis, Ethnic Conflict and the Search for Islamic Alternatives," *Middle East Journal*, 34, no. 1 (Winter 1980): pp. 1-12; and "Islamic Revival in the Middle East and North Africa," *Current History* (April 1980): pp. 169-74.

Bangladesh—Is the Past Prologue; or Is the Present a Blip on an Upward Trajectory?

Primarily through rapid social development, Bangladesh has escaped the "basket case" label it was unflatteringly bestowed soon after it separated from United Pakistan. Despite a falling birth rate, it has a young population in which, comparatively speaking, education is widespread, if not deep. This provides the basis of a productive labor force that can enable its dynamic private export-oriented industrial sector to remain competitive in the global economy, and its strong economic growth and development will continue. Under the surface of political disorder, many observers believe that these underlying, and often invisible, strengths could propel Bangladesh toward a "take-off" into the ranks of middle income countries. The main missing ingredients are political stability and good governance.

Yet the image of the country is one of imminent failure. In part, this is the result of the rapid accretion of Islamist influence in a society that is poorly governed and vulnerable to the excesses of selfish and opportunistic politics. Also the image of imminent failure results from the perception of instability and ungovernability—all this too the outgrowth of a failed political culture and a failed political class. Thus, we see from another angle the high stakes involved in the current attempt by an unelected military/civilian government to remake Bangladesh's political culture and build a modular democracy on a stronger institutional foundation. Traditional Bengali tolerance and diversity, as well as the attachment to constitutionalism and democracy, are being tested again, and the country's future is up for grabs. Timing is everything in such experiments. If politics is turned back to the civilian politicians before solid foundations are established, the country could revert to the bad old ways of the recent period of electoral democracy, 1991-2007. Equally dangerous and scary is the alarming possibility that the unelected military/civilian government could enjoy wielding power too much and stay too long, which could return politics to the worst old days of 1982-1990, when political and economic stagnation and human rights abuses characterized a government dominated by a corrupted military.

Before early January 2007, the Bangladesh Army showed no signs of wanting to intervene in politics. When it did so, on the 11th of that month, the immediate reason was to spare the country from looming civil strife and extensive bloodshed. The reckless, winner-takes-all strategy of both major party leaders appeared to leave little room for any other action. Though the intervention was welcomed by the public, it was, at first, a stealth intervention, maintaining a civilian façade in running the administration, and insisting that the Army was only "assisting" the caretaker government. Like the Musharraf intervention in Pakistan in 1999, the Bangladesh Army and its civilian cohort appeared to have taken power without a predetermined agenda, only some vague notion that reform was necessary. It took weeks for the government to indicate a series of objectives and a timetable, and these have continued to be modified, seemingly on the latest whim of temporary leaders. What this military/civilian dispensation had to decide was which model to emulate, either the Turkish form of military intervention, with a more limited agenda and time frame, or the Pakistani one that usually involves a more ambitious agenda and extended time frame.

While the military and civilian leaders of this interim government have so far been careful to avoid the word "Turkish," that appears to be the model they are following. Eighteen months after the coup of January 11, 2007, there is nothing in their rhetoric or behavior to suggest an agenda goes beyond fixing what can be fixed in a limited time frame before returning full power to elected civilians at the end of 2008. The limited, short-term agenda would concentrate on repair of the electoral machinery, i.e. the makeup of the election commission, the badly flawed voters list, and the procedures for selecting the Caretaker Government. To build the foundations of a stronger democratic culture, the Caretaker Government would also have to establish the framework for such institutions as a stronger and independent judiciary, a strict accountability mechanism, and an independent public service commission. If it is to cede power to civilians on the timeframe it has set out, the Caretaker Government would have to turn over to the elected governments and to parliaments these infant institutions to be nurtured and strengthened.

Army political interventions in South Asia, and elsewhere, have a history of going bad. Though the Caretaker Government's weak economic performance in the past six months has muted the positive public reaction that greeted the January 11 intervention, there is always the danger that the Army's agenda could become more ambitious, and its intentions to return power to the civilians attenuated. But if it follows that well-worn path of other extended military interventions, the welcome mat will soon begin to fray, both domestically and internationally. History also shows that such regimes usually need to become progressively more oppressive to remain in power as well as to reach out for legitimacy to Islamist elements poised for the opportunity to be politically rehabilitated.

It seems likely that there are growing tensions within the military/civilian government, not just between the military and civilian side, but within the military and among the civilians of the Caretaker Government. The primary split will be between those officers and CG advisors who wish to limit "mission creep" and keep the intervention to less ambitious goals, and those who believe that, now in power, the mission must be to carry out a thoroughgoing reform—perhaps even a revolution—before relinquishing it.

It is too soon to declare the Bangladesh experiment in building indigenous modular democracy either a success or a failure. The head of the CG has promised that elections will be held before the end of 2008. As we know from several earlier chapters, this is the kind of promise that is often honored in the breach by other unelected governments. But these kinds of promises are broken mainly by those unelected governments that came to power for self-serving reasons, with or without a reform agenda. We have seen regimes of that nature take power in Bangladesh in 1982 and in Pakistan in 1977. There are no visible signs yet that this intervention or its agenda are self-serving. So the question is: will it be willing and able to restrain and circumscribe its ambition and tenure in ways that give the necessary reform some chance of success? Will it actually return full power to elected civilian politicians in a two-year time frame? Or will that power be qualified and diluted as it was in Pakistan in 2002 when Musharraf and his military government returned only the façade of power to Pakistani civilians? Will Bangladeshi reform pass the Musharraf test?

Pakistan—the Praetorian State in Extremis?

In Pakistan, a myopic political class and its leadership, both of which lack a national vision, have failed to overcome the country's historical contradictions and institutional deficiencies. The legacy of the long string of Faustian bargains with Islamists, especially those of Zia ul Huq, the feudal rigidities which continue to constrict society, as well as fissiparous regional and ethnic tendencies have erected barriers that diverted and distorted a healthy political evolution. The result is political stasis. The state stumbles along, unable so far, despite the Army's occasional tactical retreats from direct power, to subordinate the military to elected civilian politicians. Now threatened by Islamism it is, in the view of many outsiders, tilting towards crisis and failure. Ironically, military rule for nineteen of its thirty-six years has probably contributed to the sense (and fear) of "sustainable failure."[18] Yet Pakistan is not a failed state, not while the military remains a coherent institution. But it is a country of failed politics with a failed political class.

The February 18 election has ended the Musharraf-led hybrid military/civilian dispensation, but civilian politicians appear at the time of writing still to be searching for a viable and effective combination to replace it. Pervez Musharraf remains a somewhat shadowy feature on the political landscape because he is still President, but the character, makeup, and outlook of what will follow him remaims very much open to question. Moreover the range of possible scenarios presently imaginable is wide and troubling.

Until mid-2007, it seemed clear (at least to the author) that the Pakistani military would have a permanent role in the country's politics and that its many civilian supporters concurred that it should continue to control the country's political destiny. The military has had such a role since 1977 (and enjoyed that role in United Pakistan from 1958-71), either directly in charge of the government, or in a hybrid military/civilian setup, or exercising veto power over the decisions of elected governments from behind a democratic facade.

It would surprise most observers if the Army ceded full power to civilians without a fight. Yet, at the present time, a return to direct military rule seems unlikely. The Army is widely unpopular after eight years of steadily deteriorating governance and likely to want to influence politics from behind the scenes, as it did from 1988 to 1999. Despite the predictions of many observers (including the author), the Army largely refrained from interfering in the February 18 election. Unsurprisingly, without the expected level of rigging, the "King's Party," the PMLQ, ran third, behind the PPP, and behind the PMLN in Punjab. Whether this signals that the Army is rethinking its domination of Pakistani politics or is simply lowering its profile till the mess it and its leader created has dimmed in the public memory are questions that the civilian politicians who now control the government must wrestle with.

The most important question in any scenario is whether the Army retains its deeply ingrained view that its interests are congruous with Pakistan's national interest and that civilians cannot be trusted to govern. If the

---

18   A term borrowed from Stephen Cohen, *The Idea of Pakistan* (The Brookings Institution, Washington, 2004). In counting the years of military rule, I have included those of what I call hybrid government—three under Zia ul Huq and five so far under Pervez Musharraf. This is an arbitrary and subjective definition which some would quarrel with.

Army's mindset changes in such a fundamental manner, a concomitant change would occur in its attitude toward India and it would no longer use the perceived threat from the East to justify its continual involvement in politics. The India-centric policy is increasingly counterproductive both in terms of security and political/economic strategy.

The danger to national security comes primarily from the West, not the East, and from inside the country. The increasing militancy of jihadi extremists threatens the coherence of the state. The jihadi/Taliban nexus has become more pervasive and is able, through fear and intimidation, to control larger parts of Pakistani territory. In other words, the writ of the state is progressively attenuating, even disappearing, in ever widening tracts of the country. The insidious creep of Islamism threatens to transform society retrogressively into one in which intolerance and discrimination are dominant characteristics. A Talibanized or Islamicized Pakistan would run counter to the increasingly globalized economy of the future and would lead to a slow but inevitable economic downslide and the pauperization of its people.

The rest of the world is already ill at ease with the fact that Pakistan, while challenged by the Islamists, has an arsenal of nuclear weapons. These were developed only as a deterrence to India, but are seen now as vulnerable to an Islamist takeover of the country, or to the presumed presence of Islamist sympathizers in the Army and Command structure.

The lamentable lack of progress in social development continues to be one of the factors that enable the Islamists to gain further credibility. It is given low priority by the Army leadership, which continues to milk the bulk of state-generated resources, and by most civilian politicians and the political classes. The public education system is near collapse while the madrassa network produces a mostly scripturalist-oriented clergy which feeds the Islamist cause. Moreover the increasing fissiparousness that results from the mindless insistence on central control of all matters from Islamabad constantly weakens national unity.

The idea of an apolitical Army that protects national interests as defined by elected civilian governments has seemed almost an "impossible dream" in contemporary Pakistan. In the short- and medium-term, policy makers in the West have grown accustomed to the idea that depolitization of the Pakistani Army is a long-range goal. Musharraf's blunders in 2007 may have opened an opportunity to transform the Army's mindset. In fact, his leadership in normalizing the relationship with India has started that process.

Pakistan will remain central to success in the "War on Terror," but the country itself has become one of the main targets of the terrorists and is vulnerable to progressive encroachment by radical Islamism. President Musharraf often seemed tentative about the "War on Terror" on his own soil, perhaps because of constraints imposed by his Army colleagues and supporters. His seemingly half-hearted attempt to deploy the Army to reestablish the writ of the state in the Tribal Areas came to naught when it appeared the Army pressured him to find another way to stop Taliban incursions into Afghanistan. If such ambiguity persists under the elected civilian dispensation now in charge, Pakistan may become, before the "War on Terror" ends, part of the terrorist problem instead of part of the solution.

11

EPILOGUE

The first ten chapters of this book offer readers a history and analysis of the evolution of Bangladesh and Pakistan from their beginnings as separate countries in January 1972 through the end of January 2008. In the subsequent six months, events in both countries have moved swiftly, in unpredictable directions, and much has changed, at least on the surface. This epilogue gives a brief overview of the dramatic events in both countries between February and July 2008. It is a story that begins with great hope of a welcome political sea change and ends in ambiguity about the future direction of both Bangladesh and Pakistan.

Their situations remain unsettled as this book goes to press. There is little evidence yet that anything fundamental in the politics of either country has changed. In the meantime, both continue to drift. The newly elected civilian government in Pakistan has so far been no more effective than the preceding Musharraf regime in dealing with its three main problems: the erosion of state authority and control in the tribal or settled areas west of the Indus River, terrorist attacks that continue throughout most of Pakistan, and the sharp economic decline that is the result of increased world energy and food prices Nor was it able to resolve what has become a political problem—whether and how to restore the Supreme Court judges that Musharraf had sacked.

In Bangladesh the news is better, but mixed. On the one hand the military/civilian interim government, though distracted by global inflationary forces, appears determined to return power to an elected civilian government at the end of 2008. On the other hand it has abandoned an important element of its ambitious reform program, which would have cleansed the nation's political culture. Thus when the civilians take over they may return to the poisonous politics of 1991-2007.

247

The Musharraf Era Peters Out—Pakistan's Troubles Only Multiply

The February 18 2008 election, in which voters rejected Musharraf and his party, the PMLQ, as well as the Islamist parties, appeared to be akin to a revolution in the political mindset of Pakistan. In the space of a day, eight years of military and military/civilian hybrid government were overturned. Suddenly civilians were in charge of Pakistan's destiny, and the Army at that moment looked to be in retreat from politics. Idealists imagined a thoroughgoing political revolution, a popular reaction to the head-in-the-sand governance of the last eight years (and perhaps to the assassination of Benazir Bhutto); cynics wondered if the change was genuine, and whether the public verdict that the military stay out of politics would last beyond the first major crisis.

The anti-Musharraf opposition had broken through because the widely expected rigging in favor of the "King's Party," the PMLQ, did not occur. The new Army Chief, General Kayani, honored his pledge that the Army would remain neutral. It seems doubtful if this minimalist approach signaled a change of heart on the part of the military; more likely it reflected the top brass's concern that the institution had become very unpopular, in part reflecting the almost total erosion of support for Musharraf.

In a fairly honest election, the PPP, now run by Ali Asif Zardari, the widower of the slain Benazir Bhutto, and the PMLN of the politically reinvented Nawaz Sharif, swept to victory. Zardari's PPP won 86 seats in the National Assembly, about 32 percent of the popular vote, and demonstrated that it remains a national party, though a fading one, by winning seats in all four provinces.[1] Once again, the core of its strength came from rural Sindh where it took nearly half (30 of 61) of the seats and rural Southern Punjab where it won 43, a number that might have been greater had Benazir Bhutto been at its helm. While Balochistan and the NWFP are not particularly fertile ground for the PPP, it won 4 of 14 seats in the former and 9 of 35 in the latter.[2]

---

[1] The Center for Research and Security Studies (CRSS), a Pakistani think-tank, points out that the PPP's voter base is mainly rural and illiterate, a shrinking segment of Pakistani society, while that of the PML is mainly urban and literate, one that is growing. From a paper sent by e-mail to the author on July 13, 2008 with the title "Reviewing the PPP and PML in Pakistani Politics." Available on the CRSS website http://www.crss.pk

[2] The numbers in this paragraph and the rest of this section come from election statistics issued by the Election Commission accessed on July 30, 2008 at http://psephos.adam-carr.net/countries/p/pakistan/pakistan.txt

Many observers were surprised by the strong showing of the PMLN, which won about 24 percent of the vote and 67 seats in the National Assembly—almost all from Punjab. It failed to win any seats in Sindh and Balochistan, but gained four in NWFP. Nawaz Sharif had returned to Pakistan at the end of November, on the heels of Benazir Bhutto's October return (see Chapter 8). Sharif immediately lashed his party's election campaign to one issue: the restoration of the Supreme Court judges dismissed by Musharraf during the emergency he had declared in early November. Sharif's only real objective, at least in the shortrun, was to see Musharraf off from the Presidency.

The PMLQ received the third largest number of votes, about 16 percent of the total, and won 43 seats in the National Assembly. Like the PPP, it won seats in all four provinces, and staked its claim as the only other national party. A number of voters it had attracted in the 2002 election appear to have returned to the mother ship, the PMLN, with the return of its leader from exile and, perhaps, after the assassination of Benazir Bhutto.

While receiving less attention, the voters' almost-total rejection of the Islamist alliance, the MMA, was an important outcome of the election. After the October 2002 election it had controlled the NWFP government and, in a coalition, shared control of the Balochistan government. These provinces had been governed so poorly that the alliance retained only 6 National Assembly seats (4 from NWFP and 2 from Balochistan) on February 18, in contrast to the 53 it had won in October 2002 (29 in NWFP, 6 in Balochistan, 3 in Punjab, and 7 in Sindh). In addition, voters throughout Pakistan expressed their dismay at the rising incidence of suicide bombings by turning against the MMA.

Coalition Politics Painted Over a Partisan Mindset

Hope surged early in the new political era as the PPP and PMLN, after a few weeks of talks, agreed in March to join a coalition government that would be backed by an absolute majority of the National Assembly. Many reasoned that such a coalition would finally address the many serious problems the country faces. Almost immediately, however, the cracks began to show. It soon became clear that the two main parties in the coalition did not share the same agenda—in fact, on the issue of restoring the dismissed Supreme Court judges, it seemed as if their objectives were contradictory.

On this issue, PMLN leader, Nawaz Sharif, has been uncompromising all along. Restoration of these judges (and, as a sub-text, the removal by one means or another of Musharraf) has been the PMLN's sole agenda. Asif Zardari and most of the PPP, on the other hand, have been much more nuanced, wavering as to the timing and the extent of a judicial restoration. Observers speculated that Zardari probably did not want the Chief Justice back in his chair as that would open the way for suits to be brought to the court that challenged the National Reconciliation Order (NRO) under which the Musharraf government undertook not to press criminal charges against Zardari and Benazir Bhutto. As described in Chapter 8, the NRO allowed them to return to Pakistan in October 2007 and participate in politics.

The coalition government began to unravel almost before it was up and running when, in April, Sharif abruptly withdrew his party's ministers from cabinet. The PMLN said it would remain in alliance with the PPP, support the government but not participate in it, a maneuver designed to put pressure on Zardari to reinstate all the dismissed judges. Since then, there have been ongoing talks mainly on how many and which judges to restore as well as the constitutional and political questions that might be involved in unseating President Musharraf. There are various opinions as to whether this would involve a constitutional amendment, judicial action, legislative action, or some combination of those. In late July, Sharif increased the pressure by implicitly threatening to end the PPP/PMLN alliance and take his party into the opposition.

Ulimately the two parties averted a split over restoring the judges by agreeing to impeach Musharraf through the National Assembly and Senate (in a sense, skipping over the middlemen, the judges who were supposed to do the job for them when restored).[3] Whether they have the two-thirds majority of either house is not clear, and the timing and tactics of the impeachment do not seem to have been worked out fully. Perhaps the most interesting aspect of this development is whether the suddenly re-forged ties of the PPP-PMLN alliance/coalition—Sharif even sent his party's ministers back into the cabinet—are genuine or not. Are the parties reacting to public opinion that is favorable to the coalition, or is this just another way for Nawaz Sharif to accomplish his only observable political objective: getting rid of Musharraf by any means possible?

---

[3] The principled objection to this idea is being made by Aitzaz Ahsan, who was Benazir Bhutto's number two in the PPP and became the driving force in the lawyers movement: that by impeaching President Musharraf the National Assembly implicitly validates his election as president in October 2007, which Ahsan and many others claim was illegal and unconstitutional. Perhaps one question is whether the lawyers will turn against the coalition government as a result of this effort at compromise.

Meantime, the Taliban/Extremist Challenge Deepens

While the judges issue (and now perhaps the impeachment) hold the attention of the leadership of both parties, other important—perhaps more important—issues have lacked the attention they deserve. Their neglect is eroding the credibility and popular support of the newly elected government. This is certainly true of the continued encroachment of the Taliban and its extremist allies in the west of the country, and the related terrorist strikes in much of Pakistan. The feeble response of the Musharraf government to militant encroachment was described in Chapter 8. Though many observers had thought an elected government would have a more coherent and forceful policy, this has not so far been the case. In fact, the response of the current government has been equally confused and unsuccessful, and it seems almost as much in denial about the issue as was the military/civilian hybrid it displaced.

Till recently there has been no discernible effort on the part of the new government to try to convince the public that the constant encroachment of militants is, in fact, an existential challenge to the state of Pakistan. The PPP Prime Minister, Youssef Raza Gilani, has begun lately to assert that the nation's sovereignty is threatened by the militants, and some observers suspect that the extremists' indiscriminate suicide bombings are beginning to make the public more receptive to that line of thought. Nonetheless, there remains a widespread belief among the public, which the political establishment and the proliferating media have exacerbated, that this is an American war not a Pakistani one. Some media outlets and politicians even go so far as to assert that Pakistan will no longer be challenged by the Taliban and its extremist allies (i.e. the war on terror will go away) when the judges are restored.

Unfortunately, the harder line that Gilani is now articulating is not shared by all members of the government, and clearly not by the PPP's current partner. The PMLN has maintained an ambiguous position on whether to launch an aggressive crackdown against the militants. Nawaz Sharif's history of courting the Islamist parties is enough to raise suspicion that he sees political benefit for his party in such ambiguity.

And, as also explained in Chapter 8, the Army seems in two minds on the issue. In part this may stem from its losses in encounters with the well-armed militants in the Tribal Areas and Swat. In part, it comes from the belief (one shared by many Pakistani civilians) in sections of the armed forces that ultimately the West will abandon the fight in Afghanistan and that therefore Pakistan needs the Taliban to protect its vital strategic interests on its Western border. Since the mid-1990s the ISI has had links to the Taliban in Afghanistan and provided assistance to them before 9/11 in their war against the Northern Alliance, perceived as an ally of India. There is a growing belief among many governments, including that in Washington, that ISI/Taliban links have been maintained since 9/11 and that these are aiding the latter in its attacks on US and NATO forces in Afghanistan.

The truth, and extent, of these allegations may never be known, but they are roiling the US-Pakistan relationship which has been based since 9/11 on joint action to combat terrorism in the region. Such a bifurcated policy on the part of the Army (does one hand know what the other is doing?) could explain why it is so inconsistent in its attitude toward the internal struggle against militancy in Pakistan: one week it seems to want to follow a very un-military pusillanimous approach and rely on "peace deals" to keep the militants at bay; the next week it proposes further military operations in the tribal areas, in Swat, or elsewhere. Strangely enough, it appears that the Army has been the main instigator of the so-called "peace deals" with the Taliban that have been, for the most part, such spectacular failures.

The international and domestic aspects of this struggle against the Taliban have come together in ways that may have surprised Pakistanis and will provide a severe test for the elected civilian government, both domestically and in its relations with its Western allies and regional neighbors, Afghanistan and India. The Taliban that constantly challenges the writ of the state in Pakistan is closely related, if not identical, to the Taliban that fights the West and seeks to take power in Afghanistan (same overall leaders, same links to Al Qaeda and other Pakistani jihadi groups, same agenda). The distinction that many Pakistanis have made in recent years between "good" Taliban and "bad" Taliban (perhaps a euphemism for "our" and "their" Taliban) just doesn't work any longer, if it ever did. Pakistan will no longer be able to maintain a dual policy, whether conscious or unconscious, and keep its alliances intact and its attenuated writ from being overrun.

"It's the Economy, Stupid"

In the meantime, the Pakistan economy has weakened significantly, hit hard by the global escalation of energy and food prices, as well as the fall in domestic and foreign investment that is linked to a decline in confidence about both the domestic political situation and uncertainties about the government's anti-terrorist policies. Though the poverty statistics are unreliable and sparse, it is likely that a number of Pakistanis have fallen back under the "poverty line" after climbing out in the middle years of the Musharraf dispensation. Energy shortages disrupt everyday life, and the constant and increasing "load-shedding" cause daily black- or brown-outs that reduce industrial output as well as making life for the poor even more miserable. The rising price of food staples has exacerbated the misery.

One would think that the PPP, its traditional slogan of "*roti, kapra, makaan*" (bread, clothing, housing) designed to identify it with the have-nots of Pakistan, would have directed far more energy to alleviating the burdens on the poor caused by the economic deterioration. However, the new government's policy approach has been feeble and sporadic. Ultimately, the economy may be the primary cause of this government losing popular support; it could prompt both the establishment and ordinary Pakistanis to look elsewhere for leadership.

Exit Musharraf, Enter Zardari: What Has Democracy Dealt?

Literally the last words written in this book are that the Musharraf era of military government ended in a whimper on August 18, 2008, when, under great and growing threat of impeachment, he resigned as President. The third era of democratically elected civilian government began formally on September 6, with the selection by the National and Provincial Assemblies of Asif Ali Zardari to be President of Pakistan. It is not a propitious time to take that job: the economy is in a freefall; extremists of various stripes and ideologies continue to encroach on the writ of the state and to conduct suicide bomb attacks throughout its territory; demands mount from its U.S. and NATO allies to push back against extremism with more force and single-mindedness and to stop the unhindered flow of Taliban fighters back and forth the across the Afghan border. The alternative, at least in the long run, is to face increased US incursions and bombings along that border.

Zardari's freedom of action on these critical problems will be circumscribed by an ambiguous relationship with an inscrutable army as well as political threats on his domestic political flank. As soon as Musharraf had gone, the grand PPP/PMLN coalition came apart over the issue of whether and how to reinstate the judges that Musharraf dismissed. Nawaz Sharif and his party are trying to consolidate control of Punjab from where they can wait for the right time to pounce. But Zardari's more serious challenge will be to forge a relationship of cooperation and trust with the army, one that will allow his and subsequent democratic governments to deal with the toxic legacies left by military regimes. The key is whether the army's mindset will evolve toward a role that accepts civilian sovereignty.

Bangladesh—Plus Ça Change, Plus C'est La Même Chose?

A somewhat sadder but wiser caretaker government has had to retreat from two of the most heralded reforms in its initial agenda, and the sea change in Bangladesh politics that these promised now seems more remote. Nonetheless, it is very likely that the military/civilian interim government will honor its pledge to return political power to civilians by the end of 2008. This, in itself, will be a great step forward in South Asia, the Muslim World, and the Third World. Only in Turkey, another Muslim country, has the military kept its word and restored power to civilians within the promised time frame.[4]

The interim government's ambitious plan to reform and democratize the political parties has foundered in the choppy shallows of Bangladesh politics. Its even more ambitious program to extirpate corruption in politics also ran aground — in the deep waters of the Bangladesh judicial system. From the outset both of these objectives appeared somewhat difficult to achieve. To reform the political parties required sidelining the two party leaders, Sheikh Hasina and Begum Khaleda Zia. The hold that both have over their parties, however, prevented any reform movement developing inside either organisation that would have weakened the ladies' power and led to a more democratic structure based more on merit and less on patronage. The interim government tried many inducements on both the party faithful and the two leaders, finally putting them both in jail on corruption charges that probably would have been difficult to prove in court.

Nor was it a surprise that the massive anti-corruption drive had to be rethought. The author visited the Chairman of the newly set-up Anti-Corruption Commission in June 2007. The latter admitted to an enormous gap between aspirations and tools in the Commission—it had no computers, few well-trained investigators, and only freshly qualified lawyers to face the enormous resources that the accused would be able to bring to bear in the Bangladeshi courts. Some of the more notorious among the corrupt have been convicted on corruption or related charges, though even these cases may ultimately be lost on appeal. Many others await trial, and a few of

---

4   It is not clear that the Mauritania Military should be listed with that of Turkey as having returned power to civilians in two years as the Army took over again on August 6, 2008 after having returned power a year earlier.

those are out on bail, including Sheikh Hasina. It appears that Begum Zia will also be allowed bail very soon.

The interim government took office in January 2007 with a great deal of public support and momentum. But perhaps because the decision to intervene was made very quickly as the political situation fell apart almost overnight and the threat of serious violence escalated, the Army had not put a lot of thought into a plan for reform. Early ideas were, I suspect, too wide-ranging and comprehensive as neither the Army nor its civilian appointees had considered carefully enough the trade off between deep and wrenching reform and the length of time it requires. Their early plans made it seem as if the Army might be tempted by a longer-term "Pakistani option," rather than the shorter-term "Turkish option." There were some Army officers who advocated a longer intervention during which deep structural reform could be accomplished, but the Army leadership, at least to the author, seemed determined always to limit the duration of its indirect governance to two years.

The serious economic problems that beset the new government in the early months set it back and distracted it from the political reform agenda it was trying to formulate. Two factors were important. First, global prices of food and energy rose swiftly during 2007, and Bangladesh could not escape the consequences. For half of the Bangladeshi population, who live at or under the poverty line, these increases hit hard and became the center of their attention. After some confusion and procrastination, the government acted wisely to protect the most vulnerable section of the population. The second factor, one of those negative unforeseen consequences that flow from positive acts, was that domestic investment dried up as a lack of confidence stemming from global economic changes was exacerbated by political uncertainty among the investing class prompted by the interim government's sweeping anti-corruption agenda. As investment fell, so did economic activity, unemployment rose, and the poor suffered a second blow.

The Game of Chicken Begins

The interim government is not without leverage and creative energy, however, and has significant success to its credit in the contest that seems to be developing between it and the political parties. It has, among other achievements, cleaned up the more technical aspects of the political process. The voters list has been purged of all the extra names it contained in January 2007. That very flawed list was a major reason why the opposition boycotted the election scheduled for January 18, 2007, and set in motion the military takeover and installation of the civilian technocrat caretaker government. About 80 million voters have been registered and documented, and each has been issued with a photo ID card for easy and quick identification. This was a remarkable technical achievement in itself and highlighted the efficiency of the Election Commission appointed by the caretaker government, one of its first acts after taking power.

The new list and IDs will be tested in municipal elections in the four major cities in August 2008. Although the government intended these to be non-partisan (a favorite idea of South Asian militaries, it seems), the Bangladesh High Court, at the last minute, ruled out the complete prohibition of partisan involvement. These elections will test the ability of the Commission to conduct elections in what is still a tense situation, and it will give the politicians the chance to flex their partisan political muscles.

The interim government wants to conduct elections in the fall in a majority of the over 460 upazilas. Though it talked of making these elections non-partisan also, the court decision puts that in considerable doubt. These elections, which may well be partisan in nature, will be held a month or two in advance of the national polls planned for late December 2008. Here is where the high stakes politics begins: the parties are threatening to boycott these elections unless the government gives in to their demands. The first is that the state of emergency be rescinded. The parties argue that a free and fair partisan election cannot be held if the stringent emergency rules, such as the ban on large outdoor public meetings, are still in place. They have a point, and this may be an area of compromise. They are demanding also that the incarcerated party leaders be released on bail, as Sheikh Hasina has been. As mentioned, the government is now negotiating with Begum Zia on conditions for her release on bail, the sticking point being her insistence that her two sons be released with her. The release of her son, Tariq, will be a costly concession by the government as it may undermine its anti-corruption program. It would appear that the Begum will have to agree to some very stringent conditions to achieve this.

A more dangerous and risky (for both sides) contest has just begun over the fate of the many former leaders who have been arrested for corruption. The increasingly pragmatic interim government has concluded that it is both politically and judicially impossible to convict most of these scofflaws before it leaves office. It has instead devised an innovative (almost ingenious, if it works) way to handle the issue—on which its prestige is certainly riding as much as is the fate of the many accused.

It is in this context that the possible involvement of other countries becomes an acute issue, and suspicion falls especially on Pakistan, though also on India. Rumors that the ubiquitous ISI has been working hard to get some of its local favorites out of jail have been circulating for months, and they may finally be succeeding. There is some concern that the will of the interim government is weakening as it nears the end of its promised tenure. It may prove unable to resist the subtle pressure on it from other countries that perceive they have a stake in how the Bangladesh experiment works out. It also has to contend with public pressure, exacerbated by political parties and vested interests who want to put the program on the defensive, and from human rights organizations and spokespersons concerned about the massive arrests that have occurred.

If there is such outside involvement, it may become more discernible as the government seeks to cut through the corruption thicket in a way that preserves the thrust of its anti-corruption program and challenges those who want it to fail. A government ordinance, called the Voluntary Disclosure of Information Ordinance, passed in May 2008 and amended in late July, has led to the creation of a Truth and Accountability Commission (TAC). Three senior and highly respected commissioners have been named to judge its cases. It is chaired by a former High Court judge and includes a former comptroller and auditor general and a retired Major General. For five months, the TAC will be empowered to hear cases submitted to it by the Anti-Corruption Commission after consultation with those formally accused of corruption. It will involve those who have been accused admitting their culpability to the commission and repaying their ill-gotten gains to the government. In recognition of their admission and repayment, the accused would not be tried in the courts, but would have to forego political activity for five years.[5]

One critical question is whether party leaders are likely to abide by this when power is restored to civilians at the end of 2008. If those accused of corruption believe that Sheikh Hasina and/or Begum Zia are determined to return to the corrupt political culture of the period 1991-2007, then they may well gamble that the cases against them will be dropped after the general election now planned for late December 2008. But if their party doesn't win, they run the risk that the winning party will use judicial indictment to punish opposition party leaders and supporters, so as to weaken them for future elections. Losing a gamble on being absolved by one's political cronies

---

5   See "Truth Commission Rolls into Action Sunday," *The Daily Star,* of August 1, 2008. Access at http://www.thedaily star.net/story.php?nid=48414.

would mean jail for many of these accused; that or spending much of their resources, whether ill-gotten or not, on lawyers to defend them. It would be logical that many would find the TAC option more appealing. But logic is a thin reed to grasp in Bangladesh politics.

Conclusion—The Tipping-Points Between Real Democracy and More of the Same in Bangladesh and Pakistan Are Yet to Be Reached

The future direction of politics remains cloudy in both Bangladesh and Pakistan. Perhaps there is more hope that a real, sustainable democratic culture can develop in Bangladesh, but old habits die hard. Much will depend on the deals the interim government has reached with the two party leaders as to their behavior when power is restored to civilians, and whether these leaders have any intention of carrying out such agreements (if there are any). Nor is it clear that the party leaders have any understanding of what is needed, or indeed if they have any desire to move Bangladeshi politics forward to a better, more democratic era in which governance can concentrate on increasing the resources available to the hard-pressed Bangladeshi people. The historical record does not augur well that things will change for the better.

In Pakistan the situation is, unfortunately, bleaker. Unlike Bangladesh, the Pakistani state is under attack by militant Islamists who seek to impose their social agenda on the country and, it can be surmised, link up with terrorist groups in the region to continue the jihad against other Muslim states they consider "apostate" as well as against the West. (While occasional inflammatory press reports appear about this danger in Bangladesh, it does not seem very acute at present.) This failure to rein in Islamist militants has slowly corroded Pakistan's ties with its Western allies who increasingly believe that the ISI is among those aiding the Taliban in Afghanistan.

This complicated and closely interrelated set of serious problems seems to have stymied the newly elected government, which has focussed instead on restoring the judges that were sacked by Musharraf. It has issued contradictory pronouncements almost every other week on its anti-terrorist strategy, and it has ignored the serious economic weaknesses that beset the country. If the impeachment of Musharraf is not successful (or even if it is), there is no assurance that the PPP-PMLN alliance can hold together. The two are not natural allies. If Nawaz Sharif's party goes into opposition, the PPP will have no alternative but to manufacture a governing coalition from among the smaller parties, or with the remnants of the PMLQ — not a pretty prospect from any point of view.

A highly unstable coalition at the center in Islamabad, and a powerful PMLN riding high, if not in actual control, in Punjab is a volatile mixture that probably cannot stand the test of time. There have been similar situations in Pakistan's past, and they did not prove stable. Another election may be called, but one wonders whether it would be definitive, or, as in the 1990s, if it would merely usher in a series of elections in which weak and divided governments come to power but cannot make difficult decisions, in part because the politicians always put their interests to the fore.

WORKS CONSULTED

Books

Afzal, M. Rafique, *Pakistan—History and Politics, 1947-1971*, Karachi: Oxford University Press, 2001.

Ahsan, Aitzaz, *The Indus Saga and the Making of Pakistan*, Karachi: Oxford University Press, 1997.

Amin, Ruhal, *Development Strategies and Socio-Demographic Impact of NGOs: Evidence Fromn Rural Bangladesh*, Dhaka: University Press Ltd., 1997.

Arif, General K.M., *Khaki Shadows 1947-1997*, Karachi: Oxford University Press, 2001.

———, *Working With Zia, Pakistan's Power Politics 1977-1988*, Karachi:Oxford University Press, 1995.

Baxter, Craig, *Bangladesh—From a Nation to a State*, Boulder: Westview Press, 1997.

Burki, Shahid Javed, *Pakistan, Fifty Years of Nationhood*, Boulder, Westview Press, 1991.

Chen, Martha Alter, *A Quiet Revolution—Women in Transition in Rural Bangladesh*, Dhaka: BRAC Prokashana, 1986.

Chisti, Lt. General Faiz Ali, *Betrayals of Another Kind—Islam, Democracy, and the Army in Pakistan*, London: Asia Publishing House, 1989.

Cohen, Stephen, *The Idea of Pakistan*, Washington: The Brookings Institution, 2004.

———, *The Pakistan Army*, Oxford: Oxford University Press, 1998.

de Bary, William Theodore, *Sources of Indian Tradition, Volume One*, New York: Columbia University Press, 1958.

De Soto, Hernando, *The Other Path: the Invisible Revolution in the Third World*, New York: Harper & Row, 1989.

Eaton, Richard M., *The Rise of Islam and the Bengal Frontier: 1204-1760*, Berkeley: University of California Press, 1993.

Ewing, Katherine, *The Pir or Sufi Saint in Pakistani Islam*, University of Chicago: Ph.D disertation, 1980.

Gerges, Fawaz A., *The Far Enemy, Why Jihad Went Global*, New York: Cambridge University Press, 2005.

Haqqani, Hussain, *Pakistan—Between Mosque and Military*, Washington: Carnegie Endowment for International Peace, 2005.

Hussain, J., *A History of the Peoples of Pakistan Towards Independence*, Karachi: Oxford University Press, 1997.

Islam, Mahmudul, *Constitutional Law in Bangladesh*, Dhaka: Bangladesh Institute of Law and International Affairs, 1995.

Islam, N., *Development Planning in Bangladesh: A Case Study in Political Economy*, London: Hurst and Company, 1977.

Jalal, Ayesha, *The Sole Spokesman: Jinnah, The Muslim League, and the Demand for Pakistan*, New Delhi: Cambridge University Press, 1994.

Jacques, Katherine, *Bangladesh, India, and Pakistan—International Relations and Regional Tensions in South Asia*, New York: St. Martin's Press, 2000.

James, Lawrence, *The Raj—The Making and Unmaking of British India*, London: Little, Brown and Company, 1997.

Karelkar, Hirenmay, *Bangladesh: The New Afghanistan?*, New Delhi: Sage Publications, 2005.

Keay, John, *India, A History*, New York: Grove Press, 2000.

Kochanek, Stanley, *Patron-Client Politics and Business in Bangladesh*, New Delhi: Sage Publications India, Pvt. Ltd., 1993.

Newberg, Paula, *Judging the State: Courts and Constitutional Politics in Pakistan*, Cambridge: Cambridge University Press, 1995.

Qureshi, Ishtiaq Hussain, *The Muslim Community of the Indo-Pakistan Subcontinent (610-1947)*, Karachi: Ma'aref Ltd., 1977.

Rashid, Harun Ur, *Foreign Relations of Bangladesh*, Varanasi: Rishi Publications, 2001.

Riaz, Ali, *God Willing—The Politics of Islamism in Bnagladesh*, Lanham: Rowman & Littlefield Publishers, Inc., 2004.

Rizvi, Hasan-Askari, *Military, State, and Society in Pakistan*, London: MacMillan Press Ltd., 2000.

Sen, A. K., *Poverty and Famines: An Essay on Entitlements and Deprivation*, Oxford: Clarendon Press, 1981.

Siddiqi, Brigadier Abdul Rahman, *East Pakistan—The Endgame: An Onlooker's Journjal, 1969-1971*, Karachi:Oxford University Press, 2004.

Sobhan, Rehman, *Bangladesh-India Relations: Pertspectives from Civil Society Dialogues*, ed. Rehman Sobhan, Dhaka: Dhaka University Press, 2002.

Stiles, Kendall W., *Civil Society by Design: Donor, NGOs, and the Intermestic Development Circle in Bangladesh*, New York: Praeger, 2002.

Talbot, Ian, *Pakistan—A Modern History*, New York: St. Martin's Press, 1998.

Tharpar, Romila, *A History of India, Volume One*, London: Pelican Books, 1966.

Wolpert, Stanley, *Jinnah of Pakistan*, New York: Oxford University Press, 1984.

———, *Zulfi Bhutto of Pakistan*, New York: Oxford University Press, 1993.

Zaidi, S. Akbar, *The New Development Paradigm—Papers on Institutions, NGOs, and Local Government*, Karachi: Oxford University Press, 1999.

Ziring, Lawrence, *Bangladesh—From Mujib to Ershad, An Interrpretive Study*, Karachi: Oxford University Press, 1992.

———, *Pakistan in the Twentieth Century—A Political History*, Karachi: Oxford University Press, 1997.

Articles

Ali, Sayed Mahmud, "The Demise of Zia," *The Zia Episode in Bangladesh Politics*, ed. by Habib Zafarullah, Denver, Academic Books, International Academic Publishers, Ltd., 2000.

Amin, Sajeda, Basu, Alaka and Malwade, Alaka, "Conditioning Factors for Fertility Decline in Bengal: History, Language Identity, and Openness to Innovation," *Population and Development Review*, vol. 26, no. 4, December 2000.

Amnesty International, "Mass Arrests in Bangladesh's Operation Clean Heart," *The Wire: Amnesty International's Monthly Magazine, Heart*, December 2002.

Caasterline, J. B. and Montgomery, M. R, "Social Networks and the Difusion of Fertility Control," *Policy Research Division Working Paper no. 119*, New York: Population Council, 1998.

Chowdhury, Mahfuzul, Hakim Mohammed A., and Zafarullah, Habib, "Politics and Government: The Search for Legitimacy," *The Zia Episode in Bangladesh Politics*, ed. Habib Zafarullah, Denver: International Academic Publishers, Ltd., 2000.

Chowdhury, Anis and Hossain, Achtar, "Fiscal Policy," *Policy Issues in Bangladesh*, New Delhi: South Asia Publishers PVT, Ltd., 1984.

———, "Monetary Policy," *Policy Issues in Bangladesh*, New Delhi: South Asia Publishers PVT Ltd., 1984.

Eaton, Richard M., "The Political and Religious Authority of the Shrine of Baba Farid," *Essays on Islam and Indian History*, New Delhi: Oxford University Press, 2002.

———, "Who Are the Bengal Muslims?" *Essays on Islam and Indian History*, New Delhi: Oxford University Press, 2002.

Ewing, Katherine, "The Politics of Sufism: Redefining the Saints of Pakistan," *Journal of Asian Studies*, vol. 42, no. 2, 1983.

Fazlur, Rahman, "Some Islamic Issues in the Ayub Khan Era" *Muslim Studies Sub-Committee Occasional Paper Series*, Chicago: University of Chicago, 1972.

Hakim, M.A., and Huque, A.S., "Constitutional Amendments in Bangladesh," *Regional Studies*, vol. 12, no. 2, 1994.

Hardy, P., "Explanations of Conversion To Islam in South Asia: A Preliminary Survey of the Literature," *Conversions to Islam*, New York: Holmes & Meier Publishers, Inc., 1979.

Haroon, Habib, "A Year of Troubles," *Frontline*, no.21, October 2002.

Hashmi, Taj-ul-Islam, "Peasant Nationalism and the Politics of Partition: The Class Communal Symbiosis in East Bengal 1940-1947, *Region & Partition—Bengal, Punjab, and ther Partition of the Subcontinent*, ed. Ian Talbot and Gurharpal Singh, Karachi: Oxford University Press, 1999.

Hossain, Achtar, "The Economy Towards Stabilization," *The Zia Episode in Bangladesh Politics*, ed. Habib Zafarullah, Denver: Academic Books, International Academic Publishers Ltd., 2000.

Iqbal, Javed, "The Judiciary and Constitutional Crises in Pakistan," *Pakistan: Founders' Aspirations and Today's Realities*, Karachi: Oxford University Press, 2001.

Jaffrelot, Christophe, "Nationalism Without a Nation: Pakistan Searching for Its Identity," *Pakistan—Nationalism Without a Nation*, ed. Christophe Jaffrelot, London: Zed Books Ltd., 2002.

Khan, A. R., "Bangladesh: Economic Policies Since Independence," *South Asian Review*, vol. 8, no. 1, 1974.

Khan, Omar Asgar, "Critical Engagemments: NGOs and the State," *Power and Civil Society in Pakistan*, ed. Anita M. Weiss and S. Zulficar Gilani, Karachi: Oxford University Press, 2001.

Looney, Robert E., "Pakistan's Economy: Achievements, Progress, Constraints, and Prospects," *Pakistan: Founders' Aspirations and Today's Realities*, ed. Hafiz Malik, Karachi: Oxford University Press, 2001.

Loshkin, M. and Sawada. Y., "Household Schooling Decisions in Rural Pakistan," *Policy Research Working Paper 2541*, Washington: World Bank, February 2001.

Mauss, M. "La Nation" (1920), *Ouvre*, Tome 3, Paris: Minuit, 1969.

Metcalf, Barbara, "The Case of Pakistan," Islamic Contestations, Karachi: Oxford University Press, 2004.

Murshid, Tazeen M., "State, Nation and Identity: Ideology and Conflict in Bangladesh," *Region and Partition—Bengal, Punjab, and the Partition of the Subcontinent*, Karachi: Oxford University Press, 1999.

Nasr, S.V.R., 'Islam, the State, and the Rise of Sectarian Militancy in Pakistan," *Pakistan—Nationalism Without a Nation*, ed. Christophe Jaffrelot, London: Zed Books Ltd., 2002.

———, "Military Rule, Islamism, and Democracy in Pakistan," *The Middle East Journal*, vol. 58, no. 2 (Spring 2004).

Qadir, Shaukat, "An Analysis of the Kargil Conflict 1999," *RUSI Journal*, April, 2002.

Racine, Jean-Luc, "Living With India," *A History of Pakistan and Its Origins*, London: Wimbledon Publishing Company, 2002.

———, "Pakistan and the India Syndrome: Between Kashmir and the Nuclear Predicament," *Pakistan—Nationalism Without a Nation*, London: Zed Books Ltd., 2002.

Rahman, Sheikh Hafizur, "Convention of Consultation with Chief Justice Should Be Maintained," *The Daily Star,* Dhaka: April 13, 2003.

Renken, Lynn, "Microfinance in Pakistan: Perpetuation of Power of a Viable Avenue for Empowerment," *Power and Civil Society in Pakistan*, ed. Anita M. Weiss and S. Zulficar Gilani, Karachi: Oxford University Press, 2001.

Richter, William, "The Political Dynamics of Islamic Resurgence in Pakistan," *Asian Survey*, vol. 19, no. 6, 1979.

Singh, Gurharpal, "The Partition of Indiain a Comparitive Perspective: A Long-Term View," Region & Partition—Bengal, Punjab, and the Partition of the Subcontinent, ed. Ian Talbot and Gurharpal Singh, Karachi: Oxford University Press, 1999.

Talbot, Ian, "The Punjabization of Pakistan: Myth or Reality," *Pakistan—Nationalism Without a Nation*, ed. Christophe Jaffrelot, London: Zed Books Ltd., 2002.

Weinbaum, Marvin, "Pakistan: Misplaced Priorities, Missed Opportunities, *India & Pakistan—The First Fifty Years*, Cambridge and Washington: Cambridge University Press and Woodrow Wilson Center Press, 1999.

Wright, Denis, "The Rise of Zia: From Soldier to Politician," *The Zia Episode in Bangladesh Politics*, ed. Habib Zafarullah, Denver: Academic Books, International Academic Publishers, Ltd., 2000.

Zafarullah, Habib, "The Legacy of Zia," *The Zia Episode in Bangladesh Politics*, Denver: Academic Books, International Acedemic Publishers, Ltd., 2000.

Other Publications

Ahmed, Khaled, "Second Opinion," *Daily Times of Pakistan*, February 9, 2006.

Ahmed, Sadiq, *Explaining Pakistan's High Growth Performance Over the Past Two Decades: Can It Be Sustained*, World Bank Policy Research Working Paper, Washington: IBRD, 1994.

Ahmed, Sadiq and Sattar, Zaidi, *Trade Liberalization, Growth, and Poverty Reduction—the Case of Bangladesh*, Washington: World Bank, May, 2004.

Amnesty International, "Bangladesh: Urgent Need For Legal and Other Reforms to Protect Human Rights," May 16, 2003.

———, *Pakistan—Women in Pakistan Disadvantaged and Denied Their Rights*, 1995.

Andrabi, Tahir, Das, Jishnu, Khwaja, Asim Ijaz and Zajonc, Tristan, *Religious School Enrollment in Pakistan, WPS3521*, Washington: World Bank, February 1, 2005.

Asia Resource Centre for Microfinance (ACRM), *Pakistan Country Profile*, ACRM, Nay 2004.

Asian Development Bank (ADB), *A Study of NGOs—Pakistan*, Manila: ADB, 1999.

———, *Judicial Independence Overview and Country-level Summaries—Bangladesh 2003*, Manila, ADB, 2003.

———, *Judicial Independence Overview—Pakistan*, Manila, ACB, 2003.

Azhar, Saeed, Hussain, Zahid and Solomon, Jay, "As Growth Returns to Pakistan, Hopes Rise on Terror Front," *Wall Street Journal*, November 9, 2004.

Baden, Sally, Green, Cathy, Goetz, Anne Marie, and Guhathkurta, Megna, *Background Report on Gender Issues in Bangladesh*, Sussex: Institute for Development Studies, University of Sussex, BRIDGE report no. 26, 1994.

Cartwright, Jennifer, Khandker, Shahidur R. and Pitt, Mark M., *Does Micro-Credit Empower Women?—Evidence from Bangladesh*, Washington: World Bank, 2003.

Cheema, Faisal, *Macroeconomic Stability of Pakistan: the Role of the IMF and World Bank (1997-2003)*, ACDIS Occasional Paper, Champaign-Urbana: University of Illinois, 2004.

Council on Foreign Relations, *Microfinance in Pakistan: A Silver Bullet for Development*, New York: CFR, 2004.

Deolaikar, Anil B., *Attaining the Millenium Development Goals in Bangladesh*, Washington: World Bank, 2005.

Dugger, Celia, "Debate Stirs Over Tiny Loans for World's Poorest," *New York Times*, April 20, 2004.

Editorial, "India-Afghan Action in Balochistan," *Daily Times of Pakistan*, February 8, 2006.

————, "Government Should Let the PPP Remove 'hudood' (sic)," *Daily Times of Pakistan*, February 9, 2006.

European Union Election Observation Mission To Pakistan, *Final Report of EU Observation Mission to Pakistan*, Brussels: EU, 2002.

Fatima, Mahnaz, ""Smugness About the Economy," *Dawn*, February 6, 2006.

Grare, Frederic, *Pakistan: The Resurgence of Baluch Nationalism*, Washington: Carnegie Endowment for International Peace, Carnegie Papers, no. 65.

Heitzman, James and Worden, Robert, ed. *Bangladesh, A Country Study*, Washington: Library of Congress, 1988.

Human Rights Watch, *Crime or Custom? Violence Against Women in Pakistan*, HRW, August 1999.

Human Rights Watch, *The Jurisdiction Dilemma*, HRW, 2005.

IMF/World Bank, *Joint Staff Assessment of Poverty Reduction Strategy Paper— Pakistan*, Washington: IBRD, February 12, 2004.

International Crisis Group (ICG), *Understanding Islamism, Middle Eas/North Africa Report No. 37*, ICG, March 2005.

————, *Building Judicial Independence in Pakistan*, November 9, 2004.

International Monetary Fund, *Government Finance Statistics—Yearbook, 2004*, Washington: IMF, 2004.

————, *International Financial Statistics—Bangladesh*, Washington: IMF, 1991.

————, *International Financial Statistics—Pakistan*, Washington: IMF, 1979.

————, *Pakistan: Staff Report for the 2004 Article IV Consultation, Ninth Annual Review Under the Three Year Arrangement Under the Poverty Reduction and Growth Facility, and Request for Waiver of Performance Criteria*, Washington: IMF, 2004.

Iqbal, Zafar and Lorie, Henri, *Pakistan's Macroeconomic Adjustments and Resumption of Growth*, IMF Working Paper, Washington: IMF, 2005.

Mahbub ul Haq Development Centre, *Human Development in South Asia: The Crisis of Governance*, Karachi: Oxford University Press, 1999.

Marcus, Rachel M., *Violdnce Against Women in Bangladesh, Pakistan, Egypt, Sudan, Senegal, and Yemen*, Sussex: Institute for Development Studies, University of Sussex, BRIDGE report no 10, 1993.

Mir, Amir, "Balochistan: Dire Prophecies," *South Asia Intelligence Review*, vol. 4, no. 30, February 6, 2006.

Mollah, Anwar Hossain, *Separation of Judiciary and Judicial Independence in Bangladesh*, New York, United Nations, 2004.

Rizvi, Hasan-Askari, "Dimensions of the Military's Role," *Daily Times of Pakistan*, April 5, 2005.

————, "Major Obstacles to Enlightened Moderation," *Daily Times of Pakistan*, April 24, 2005.

————, "The Federal Budget and Human Security," *Daily Times of Pakistan*, June 13, 2005.

Saeed, Rana Riaz, *The Controversial Hudood Ordinance 1979*, Pakistan: Development Advocates & Lobbyists, December 2004.

Shahid, S. A., "Monetary Policy: Filling the Gaps," *Dawn*, February 6, 2006.

The Economist, "Bangladesh," June 16, 2005.

The Daily Star, "AL Makes JS Comeback," June 15, 2004.

The Daily Star," 2794 Killed in Nine Months," September 30, 2003, accessed in October 2004 at http://www.thedailystar.net .

Transparency International: The Coalition Against Corruption, "Corruption Perceptions Index, 2003, *Transparency International*, London: October 7, 2003.

Transparency International Bangladesh, "Corruption in Bangladesh: A Household Survey, 2002, Executive Summary, *Transparency International*

World Bank, *Bangladesh Development Policy Review*, Washington: IBRD, December 14, 2003.

World Bank, *Bangladesh Growth and Export Competitiveness*, Washington: IBRD, May 4, 2005.

————, *Bangladesh PSRP Forum Economic Update—Recent Developments and Future Prospects*, Washington: IBRD, November 2005.

————, *Implementation Completion Report (IDA-35170) on a Credit in the Amount of SDR 239.5 Million (US 300 Million Equivalent) To the Government of Pakistan for a Banking Sector Restructuring and Privatization Project*, Washington: IBRD, 2005.

————, *Pakistan—Country Gender Assessment, Bridging the Gender Gap: Opportunities and Challenges*, Washington: IBRD, October 2005.

————, *Pakistan Development Policy Review—A New Dawn?*, Washington: IBRD, April 3, 2002.

————, *Pakistan Public Expenditure Management—Strategic Issues and Reform Agenda*, Washington: IBRD, January 28, 2004.

————, *Taming the Leviathan: Reforming Governance in Bangladesh*, Washington: IBRD, 2005.

————, *World Development Indicators*, Washington: IBRD, 2004.

World Bank and International Development Agency, *Joint Assessment of the Poverty Reduction Strategy Paper—Pakistan*, Washington: IBRD, February 12 2004.

Zaman, Habida, *Violence Against Women in Bangladesh: Issues and Responses*, Women's Studies International Forum, vol. 22, issue 1 1999.

Online only

Countries of the World website, Bangladesh 2005, *Bangaldesh Judiciary*, http://www.geographic.com , accessed in December 2005.

Unpublished

Datta, S. K., "The Recent Plight of Minorities in Bangladesh: A Post-Election Perspective," paper presented to an international seminar organized by the Centre for Research in Indo-Bangladesh Relations, in Kolkata, India on January 28 2002.

Kamal, Ahmed, *NGOs and Civil Society*, paper presented the meeting of the European Commission/NGO Dialogue Project, in Dhaka, Bangladesh on March 1, 1999.

Khan, Mushtaq, *9/11, Pakistan's Economy & the IMF*, Public presentation at the Woodrow Wilson Center for International Scholars, January 10, 2006.

Riaz, Ali, "Madrassah Education in Bangladesh: An Overview," paper presented at the conference on growing Islamism in Bangladesh, sponsored by the US Department of State and the Carnegie Endowment for International Peace, Washington DC, January 25, 2005.

INDEX

Chittagong Hill Tracts 105, 124
Chowdhury, A.Q.M. Badruddoza
129, 130
Chowdhury, Abul Muhammed Ahsanuddin 96, 100
Chowdhury, Chief Justice Iftekar
183, 186
Christians 87
Civil Service of Pakistan 47, 147
Clinton, President Bill 3, 4, 157-8
Commonwealth 44, 121
Congress/Congress Party 18-19, 171
constitution, Bangladesh 32, 41, 53,
98, 104-5, 112, 127
constitution, Pakistan 39-40, 80, 90-
2, 144, 151, 166, 175-6, 177,
187, 231-2
contraception 201-3, 208
corruption in Bangladesh 65, 67, 101,
105, 128, 132, 254-5, 256-7
corruption in Pakistan 5, 139, 142,
198
crime in Bangladesh 35, 126, 127,
206-7
crime in Pakistan 142, 146-7, 212-13

debt, Pakistan 85, 137, 138, 139,
200
Deobandi school 83, 85, 237
Desai, Morarji 66
Dhaka 1, 2-3, 18, 57-8, 103-4, 107,
120, 125, 128

economy, Bangladesh 8, 69, 95, 128,
189-95, 255
economy, Pakistan 85, 137-9, 161,
195-201, 207
education, Bangladesh 203
education, Pakistan 86, 185, 208-11,
233, 237-8

elections, Bangladesh: *1973* 37; *1979*
60; *1981* 63-4; *1986* 102; *1991*
109-11; *1996* 122-3; *2001* 125
elections, Pakistan: *1977* 49; *1985* 90;
2002 94, 172-3, 176; *2008* 7, 94,
248-9
Ershad, President Hussein Muham-
mad 1-3, 62-5, 68, 95-106, 110,
112-13, 118, 125, 228

Fakhruddin Ahmed 132
famine 110, 191-2, 202
Faraka Barrage 56-7
FATA, *see* Frontier and Tribal Areas
Federal Security Force (Pakistan) 40
floods 37, 104, 122
Frontier and Tribal Areas (FATA)
159, 174, 178, 184, 235, 245,
251, 252

Gandhi, Indira 45-6, 57
Gandhi, Rajiv 93
Ganges 13, 56-7
Geneva Agreement on Afghanistan
88-9
Gilani, Youssef Raza 251
Grameen Bank 205, 215-16, 225
Gujral, I.K. 153
Gulf states 136, 238

Hasina, Sheikh 2, 63, 99, 101-2, 105,
130, 131, 132, 254-7
health problems, health services,
Bangladesh 204-5
health problems, health services, Pakistan 211-12
Hindus 11, 17, 18, 23, 66, 87, 120,
156, 238
Hossein, Kamal 63, 130
Hudood Ordinances/Laws 84, 181-2,
213, 231, 234